CREEPING FAILURE

CREEPING FAILURE

HOW WE BROKE THE INTERNET AND WHAT WE CAN DO TO FIX IT

JEFFREY HUNKER

McCLELLAND & STEWART

Library and Archives Canada Cataloguing in Publication

Hunker, Jeffrey Allen
Creeping failure : how we broke the Internet and what we can do to fix it /
Jeffrey Hunker.

Library of Congress Control Number : 2010921959

ISBN 978-0-7710-4148-8

1. Computer crimes. 2. Internet. 3. Computer crimes – Prevention. 4. Internet – Security measures. I. Title.

HV6773.H864 2009   364.16'8   C2009-905035-8

We acknowledge the financial support of the Government of Canada through the Book Publishing Industry Development Program and that of the Government of Ontario through the Ontario Media Development Corporation's Ontario Book Initiative. We further acknowledge the support of the Canada Council for the Arts and the Ontario Arts Council for our publishing program.

Typeset in Adobe Garamond
Printed and bound in the United States of America

McClelland & Stewart Ltd.
75 Sherbourne Street
Toronto, Ontario
M5A 2P9
www.mcclelland.com

1   2   3   4   5   14 13   12   11   10

To Monica, with love

CONTENTS

INTRODUCTION

YOUR CITY, MY CITY, NO MAN'S LAND

Do you live in a big city? Imagine that you do. It is dynamic and flourishing, the very model of a great metropolis. Its population has been growing, it's an excellent place to start a business, and there is no end of exciting things to do and learn. Just a casual stroll down the street will take you past shops full of exotic goods, myriad newsstands and bookstores, and open-air cafés where you can meet fascinating people from around the world.

The chief drawback to living in this big city is a bizarre security problem. Crime has been growing along with the population – all sorts of crime, from break-ins and burglaries, to fraud and extortion in the business district, to citizens being stalked and harassed. There are police, of sorts, but they are not effective. Few people even know who they are or where to find them, perhaps because there are also few laws, and it is not clear which police have jurisdiction over what in which places. So the honest inhabitants have taken to investing in window bars, alarm systems, guards, and guns. Some have created gated communities. But these steps do not help much because the buildings in the city are of a peculiar construction. Some parts are quite solid while other parts – indistinguishable from the rest – have walls made of cardboard.

1

Every so often a cardboard section is discovered and replaced, patched over with free plaster from the building contractors. (There are even special services that search for these weak spots to correct them.) Unfortunately, criminals often find the weak spots first. The builders are constantly on talk shows voicing their concern about the cardboard walls, and outlining aggressive steps to reduce and repair them, but the situation doesn't seem to be improving. And since the police are of little use, many crimes are not reported, which only makes policing and preventing crime more challenging.

Things keep getting worse. Almost everyone has been a victim at least once, and though only a few have suffered severe loss or injury, no one feels comfortable now. People are afraid to let their children go out to play. There's a lot of troubled murmuring – how can the city's vitality persist under such conditions? – and some experts are warning that with security so weak, it's only a matter of time until a true disaster strikes.

This little story is of course a parable about the Internet. More than a simple analogy, it is a useful framework for starting to think about the issue of cyber security, because the Internet is not merely *like* a city.

The Internet *is* a city.

People once called it the information highway, but in fact the Internet contains an immense tangle of streets, highways, and interchanges that have been built over the years. All along these thoroughfares it has homes and businesses, playgrounds and theatres. It has addresses (one or more are yours). You don't live in this city in the strictest physical sense, but you spend a lot of time in it – and whether your Internet abode is a humble home address or a corporate complex, you own property that is part of the city, and you pay rents and fees.

As with any city, commerce is external as well as internal. Goods and services flow across the borders between the Internet and the rest of the world, and crime and trouble flow across too. This city is not the kind that Las Vegas claims to be: what's done on the Internet doesn't stay on the Internet. It can follow you anywhere.

HOW WE GOT TO WHERE WE ARE

To understand why security has become such a problem, we need to look back at the Internet's beginnings. It originated in the late 1960s as a network for use by a select group of scientists and government people in the U.S. – to continue the analogy, more resembling a "commune" than a city. This precursor to the Internet was called the ARPANet, and because its founder was the Defense Department's Advanced Research Projects Agency (DARPA), the main security issue at that time was concern about physical attack from outside. The system was designed to keep working even if a bomb or natural disaster were to take out some of its "nodes." The ARPANet started with only three nodes (or sites, as we might call them today) and settled in at around twenty-four, all known to each other. Many of the users at a given site even knew people at other sites personally, from working on the same kinds of research, and this network linking their computers gave them a new way to communicate and collaborate at a distance.

None of these pioneers gave much thought to the kinds of threats that plague the Internet today: threats against other users by malicious hackers working within the boundaries. Like any commune, the early Internet was a community of trust. Who would do such things? And if anyone did, wouldn't that person quickly be noticed and dealt with?

But as the Internet grew, it was opened to the public. A series of events in the 1980s and early 90s – including the invention of the World Wide Web technologies – made it habitable and usable by people who were neither scientists nor computing experts. The little commune transformed into a great city. And what we now have is equivalent, in many ways, to the burgeoning cities of the early Industrial Revolution in the 1800s. The Net is teeming with energy, but it is also rife with forms of mischief, danger, and filth previously unimagined – and lacking both the technical infrastructure and the administrative and policy structures that might keep these problems under control.

It is often said that no one really owns the Internet, which is true. The very term is short for *internetwork* and refers to methods of interlinking different electronic networks (and the computers attached to them) so that a common mode of communication is possible. The result is thus a network of networks. Some parts are more crucial than others and many parties own different parts, but no one owns the whole. The truth is that no one really governs it either.

A patchwork of communal-style bodies, with origins in the ARPANet commune days, handles some tasks. For example, ICANN (the Internet Corporation for Assigned Names and Numbers, established in its present form in 1998) oversees the assigning of domain names (so that cmu.edu means only Carnegie Mellon University and not Central Michigan University, and that the extension .ml is used for Mali while .mw is used for Malawi). The IETF (Internet Engineering Task Force, 1986) proposes technical standards for the design and use of Internet features. There are various national and international entities that look after other concerns: for instance, most countries have laws and agencies that try to censor some forms of Internet content – be it child pornography (as in most democracies) or any content the government doesn't like (as in China) – while the UN's Internet Governance Forum bills itself as a vehicle for "multi-stakeholder policy dialogue" on governance issues generally. Citizens' groups emerge to work for various causes: the Electronic Frontier Foundation (freedom of expression and other rights), the SavetheInternet.com Coalition ("net neutrality," or equality of access to Internet services), and many more. We will return to this issue again, but it is important to understand that the Internet is not only used by many different kinds of organizations (e.g., universities, small companies) but also attracts the special interests of many.

As for security, it is the province of a vast and confusing welter of entities. Within any given country, the responsibility for different aspects of Internet security may be divided (not always very clearly) among various police, military, and intelligence agencies, plus special units such as the CERTs (Computer Emergency Readiness Teams) – of which there are more than two hundred worldwide, some of them arms of national governments (like the US-CERT) and some not.

There are also private groups for Internet security, one example being the financial industry's FS-ISAC (Financial Services Information Sharing and Analysis Center). Groups of this kind try to address urgent threats for the benefit of their members – not unlike Ben Franklin's private fire company in early Philadelphia, which responded to the fires of members only.

Yet despite these efforts the Internet is much like the London that Dickens described in his novels: vibrant, bustling, but without much of the social apparatus and the laws that we take for granted today, from integrated public safety departments to good water and sewage systems. The cardboard walls (known as "vulnerabilities") exist, in part, because we have no building codes: software can still be engineered with practices that were perhaps good enough for the rustic early days of computing but are not for today's high-traffic urban use. Spam, one of the banes of the Internet, is often compared to junk mail, but it is really far worse. It is more like uncollected garbage. Underfoot everywhere, it carries diseases – viruses and worms – that can spread and infect us all, but we have no equivalent of a public health or sanitation department to deal with them. As well, few laws govern Internet access and use specifically. There are laws relating to conventional crime (theft and fraud, for example) that apply to the Internet, but catching and prosecuting criminals becomes more complicated there.

These problems all point to the greatest lack of all: we have, as yet, no coherent set of policies for dealing with any of this. We have instead a muddle of policies, which amounts to a policy of no-policy, based largely on the naive belief that a combination of market forces and new technologies can somehow adequately police the streets and keep the rats under control. As if private posses could maintain order in a great city; as if putting six-guns in everyone's hands could tame the Wild West.

I know. I was one of the architects of this policy of no-policy. In Washington in the late 1990s – when it was becoming clear that measures well beyond those of the early days would be needed for cyber security – I was the founding director of CIAO, the U.S. Critical

Infrastructure Assurance Office. I then moved to the White House and onto the National Security Council staff, as Senior Director for Critical Infrastructure, with the brief to create and implement the first national strategy for cyber security. In prime position to do something, I helped lead the U.S. (and with it, many other countries) down the non-path to our current predicament. And now, with the benefit of hindsight, I am writing this book to rectify that mistake.

I am neither a Washington insider nor an armchair academic. The common focus of the degrees I've earned is how to best solve complex problems that require melding technology, the incentives of business, and the public interest. Most of my career has been in the private sector. I've moved machinery around on factory floors and restructured major technology companies. My public service started as advisor to the late Ron Brown, whom I consider the greatest Commerce Secretary the U.S. has had. I'd like to think I share his view that a country is strongest when it works to unite the interests of business with those of the nation.

The true stories I will tell you, along with the opinions shaped by my ongoing work in cyber security, also have a common theme: the Internet (and our other communication networks) are not nearly as secure as they could be and need to be, and the main reason is not the lack of technical tools. What we have here is policy failure.

WHY POLICY MATTERS

There are many books on cyber security. Most of the good ones are practical how-to books, full of tips for home personal computer users or information technology (IT) administrators. They contain sound advice that most of us heed, most of the time. But meanwhile the threats keep evolving, so that in the best cases our efforts produce a draw, and at worst the attackers gain on the defenders. Over time no one could call this a win.

You probably know the feeling of being on the losing side. Perhaps, like me, you've had a computer so infected by malware that you had to wipe the hard drive and start over. Perhaps you've experienced worse, such as hearing the chilling news, from a security auditor, that copies of your company's most sensitive files have somehow been sent to computers in locations where you don't have offices. Perhaps, even if you have avoided taking a big hit, the security measures you use have themselves taken a toll: for example, spam filters are very good at blocking out important e-mails.

By 2005-06, some people on the front lines of cyber security were suspecting there might be a fundamental flaw in the battle plan. The signs they were losing the battle could be seen in Web postings of the time. A Canadian security consultant, Noam Eppel, posted a widely read article chronicling what he called "The Complete, Unquestionable, and Total Failure of Information Security." To which another writer, the Internet entrepreneur Phil Becker, replied on his own ZDNet blog:

> [W]hile the author clearly sees the failures of current approaches, the only thing he really knows to say about how to improve things is that we should do more of the same, but work harder, do it better, and innovate more. Folks, this is what things look like when a failed paradigm meets its match . . . [We need to] adopt new ways of modeling and understanding the problem . . .

What exactly is the nature of the "failed paradigm" Becker is referring to? And what might that tell us about how to approach the problem differently? I would answer as follows.

The paradigm that has failed relies too heavily on many discrete individuals and entities doing their best to deal with the parts of the problem that concern them. Cyber security isn't the kind of problem that can be addressed well by that approach – just as the stench and filth in the streets of London centuries ago couldn't be addressed well by ladies and gentlemen holding scented handkerchiefs to their noses while they tiptoed around puddles and tried to dodge slop buckets being emptied from windows above.

In fact, many modern-day public issues are like cyber security in that they, too, are not very amenable to the let's-all-do-our-part approach. If you want to do your part to fight climate change, there are plenty of steps you can take. You can use energy-efficient light bulbs and other green products. You can ride a bike to work, generally avoid wasteful consumption, and more. But even if all of us do some of these things and some do all, individual action won't be enough to stop climate change.

Likewise, if you are a parent unhappy with the education system, you can watchdog your own children's education diligently. You can confer with the teachers and be sure the children do their homework. You can enroll them in special programs outside the school to "enhance" their learning (just as you might buy special software or hire a consultant to enhance your cyber security), or move the kids to a different school entirely (just as you might switch from Windows to Mac or Linux). But if the whole education system has fundamental shortcomings, they won't be remedied by such steps.

Cyber security, climate change, and subpar education systems all belong to a family of social problems that have two other traits in common.

- They are cases of creeping failure. Such cases are not marked by catastrophic failure stemming from a glaring mistake or grand miscalculation. Rather, they are more like festering disorders that we either can't cure or have neglected to cure. Without a cure, things resist improvement or gradually get worse, and since an urgent crisis has not occurred (at least not yet), it is hard to muster the political and social will to make deep-seated changes. Creeping failure seems to be growing more prevalent in today's societies, and the cyber-security issue can serve as a prime case study.

- They are connected to innovations we have made. Indeed, they're sometimes seen as unwanted side effects of progress.

Before the Internet, we didn't have to worry about Internet security. Before industrialization, humans weren't changing the earth's climate significantly. Until fairly modern times, universal classroom education wasn't even seen as a societal need in most places. (And education critics in some countries argue that the basic systems and structures developed long ago are obsolete, leaving their societies with schools that are relics of the industrial age.)

In each of these areas, we find old institutions and ways of doing things no longer adequate to the new world we've created. Each is an example of what Einstein meant when he said, "The problems we have cannot be solved at the same level of thinking that created them." And we can't deal with these new realities simply by counting on individuals to step up and do their parts. Problems of this nature tend to call for new kinds of institutions, and for new kinds of *collective* action, organized and driven on a large scale. In other words, they call for new kinds of public policies.

Public policies are courses of action, including formal and informal steps, decided upon and carried out by governments and their constituents. The cyber-security policies I helped to craft – the ones that set the tone for the failed paradigm – specified a very limited role for government itself. They *intentionally* relied on market forces and private initiative to produce most of the solutions needed. And there was a good reason for taking this tack, aside from blind faith in the power of the market. People want cyberspace to be free and open; we don't want anyone to control it.

But governments can do many things to improve a situation short of imposing autocratic rule. Tools in the public-policy toolkit, besides a sledgehammer, include, to name just a few: incentives and disincentives, selective regulation or deregulation, and the creation of special entities for special tasks. All these tools come in many forms and their use is common. For example, they can be used to stimulate the economy (or to cool it down when it overheats), to manage the use of land and resources, to protect the environment, and to improve public health. In each case the goal is to maintain a healthy balance, often by keeping various interests and forces from running amok.

In cyber security, the failure isn't the use of the wrong tools. It is that too few of the tools have been used at all. The balance has been lost and the problems grow worse. Without catastrophic failure, they continue to creep up on us. It is time to find ways of wresting the balance back.

CHAPTER 1

WASHINGTON, WE HAVE A PROBLEM

Although it wasn't so long ago, the autumn of 1999 belongs to an era now past. Today, cyber security is a serious issue that touches nearly everyone personally; in those days, it was still seen mostly as a nuisance issue. Today, there are armies of specialists charged with taking it seriously; in those days, there were few. Then, some of us were housed in a place now called the Eisenhower Executive Office Building. But even in those old days, its name was "Old."

The Old Executive Office Building, or OEOB, was built in Washington, D.C., in the 1870s. One of the few surviving examples of Second Empire architecture in the U.S., it looks like an ornate layer cake with a mansard roof. It stands a few feet away from the West Wing of the more classical White House, and shares with the White House both the black iron fence surrounding the White House Complex and the strict security that greets any visitor who, passing the brass cannon on the grounds (captured from the Manila arsenal by Admiral Dewey in the Spanish American War), enters its lobby.

My office in November 1999 was OEOB 302. One Colonel Oliver North had been a previous occupant. North was notorious for taking policy into his own hands during the Iran-Contra affair of the 1980s, and when I moved into this office I found he'd also taken architecture into his own hands, destroying the magnificent twenty-foot ceilings to install a warren of desks in a loft. However, he couldn't take away the view. On one particularly beautiful day that fall, my view of the Washington Monument, and in the distance the Jefferson Memorial and the planes landing at National Airport, never looked better.

I was Senior Director for Critical Infrastructure Protection on the staff of the National Security Council. On this November 1999 afternoon I was talking with a visitor from Pittsburgh: Rich Pethia, head of the federal government's Computer Emergency Readiness Team/Coordination Center (CERT/CC) based at Carnegie Mellon University, which was and still is the closest thing the United States has to a headquarters for Internet security.[1] That made Rich Pethia the closest thing to the country's chief cyber-inspector.[2]

"You might be interested in a small workshop that we've just had," Rich told me. "It's about a set of new attack tools we've spotted on the Internet." It's not a figure of speech to say my ears perked up. One of the tools, he went on, was a software program that went by the name *Stacheldraht* – German for "barbed wire." The program could launch against a Web site a "distributed denial-of-service attack." A major attack of this type could shut off all traffic to and from the site, as if a barbed-wire fence had been thrown around the perimeter.

The basic means of working such mischief was (and is) fairly simple. Web sites respond to incoming signals. When you enter a Web address in your browser, you send a signal requesting that site to display a page view, and as you click through the site you may ask it to perform transactions: download a file, sell you a book, play a video. However, even big Web sites can't process an unlimited volume of traffic at the same time. They can be overloaded. When this overloading is done intentionally, by someone (through some program) flooding a site with signals that induce it to use up its resources doing useless tasks, you have what is called a denial-of-service attack: legitimate users can't be served. Depending on the effectiveness of the attack, results may range from a mere slowing of the site to a system-crashing takedown for hours or days.

Many hackers had tried the trick before.[3] However, Pethia and his crew were now seeing ever-more-powerful forms of the insidious variation just mentioned: the *distributed* denial-of-service (DDOS) attack. Instead of attacking a site directly from their own computers, some hackers had figured out how to have armies of "zombie" computers do their bidding. As Internet use grew, millions of poorly protected machines, many of them home PCs (personal computers), were coming online. It wasn't hard to find, say, a few thousand – and then to implant upon them small, automated program modules called bots (short for "robots"). The owners of the PCs would never know they were harbouring these bots, and each machine could be made to send signals to any Web site that the botmaster might target. This gave the dark side thousands of points from which to launch an attack.

DDOS attacks remain very difficult to defend. When a Web site is bombarded by signals from all over the Internet, with various tricks thrown in to hide the many sources of attack, filtering out the bad stuff becomes a tall order. And there is little that systems administrators can do in terms of prevention. As with many challenges in computer security, preventing a DDOS attack requires making everyone else on the Internet secure from intrusion. This still remains impossible to achieve.

The first DDOS attacks had been noticed in the summer of 1998. They were primitive and fairly small-scale attempts, not serious enough to merit much concern. But by the fall of 1999, sophisticated master tools like *Stacheldraht* had appeared and victims were starting to feel the effects. One attack had brought down a crucial Web server at the University of Minnesota, knocking related systems at the school out of kilter as well. Recovery to normal Web service had taken several days.[4]

Worse, Pethia told me, new attack tools were evolving. His CERT/CC team had seen evidence of scary advances as recently as October, while planning the workshop. Some tools were being put into easy-to-use form and then passed around, almost like packaged commercial software, so that even inexpert hackers (called "script kiddies" for their lack of skill in writing code) could dream of being DDOS commandoes. Meanwhile, CERT/CC was labouring to put together a public report on its findings. What could be said that might be useful, other than warning the world to brace for major DDOS incidents?

To me this was bad news at a bad time. In November 1999, like most people working with computer security and network reliability, I was busy preparing for the Y2K event. There, of course, we were dealing with a software problem that was self-inflicted. In the past, to save memory space in computers, a lot of code had been written with date fields that registered the year in two digits: 76 for 1976, and so on. Important functions in many programs were tied to the tracking of the current date, and yet for a long while, few of us worried about whether those functions might get boggled when the calendar seemed to flip backward from 99 to 00. We assumed our programs would be obsolete and out of use by then. Thus, as the late 90s ticked away, we all became caught up in a massive act of penance for this sin of omission: trying to track down and patch countless programs that were still in everyday use, often for critical work such as managing power grids and air traffic.

Some argued that Y2K fears were overblown – *The Economist* published a cover cartoon of a tiny Y2K "bug" grinning under a magnifying glass that made him look monstrous. But no one was certain what could occur, and none in my circle cared to take chances. My position had put me in the midst of coordinating Y2K efforts in the U.S. In the last weeks before 00 hour there were myriad lists to be gone over once more, and the conversation with Rich Pethia started a new list forming in my mind. It was a list of reasons why some people might find the Y2K moment a perfect moment to launch waves of DDOS attacks.

Following my meeting with Rick, I briefed my colleagues and then the National Security Advisor, Sandy Berger. We pulled together a team of experts from government and industry to confront this new threat. As December 31 drew near, we worked around the clock, learning a great deal about DDOS tools but failing to come up with an effective defence. (In hindsight this is not surprising, given that only partial and imperfect defences have been developed in all the years since.)

Fortunately, there were no major attacks or serious Y2K glitches of any kind come the new millennium.[5] Exhausted, I fell asleep before midnight on New Year's Eve. By then we knew that computer systems across Europe had survived the turnover from 1999 to 2000 without crashing or letting planes fall from the sky. I awoke to a world of blessed normality on January 1.

The calm before the storm lasted not quite six weeks. On February 8, 2000, the public Web site of Yahoo! was taken down by a DDOS attack. The next few days brought similar attacks against Amazon, Buy.com, CNN, eBay, Datek, E*Trade, Excite@Home, America Online, and others. Whoever was doing it couldn't be traced. Although the service disruptions were for hours, not days or weeks, the attacks set off ripple effects that magnified their impact. The targeted companies saw their stock prices drop; collectively they lost billions in market valuation. A media frenzy ensued. Moreover, the dotcom boom was then in full swing (though it would end soon), and the targeted firms were all among the darlings of the new economy. The fact that they had somehow turned up on a hit list – and had been shown to be vulnerable to a new menace – was unsettling.

That's why, less than ten days later, I found myself sitting behind President Clinton in the Cabinet Room of the White House.

THE PLAN

Few people get the opportunity to examine the back of the President's head for a couple of hours. Bill Clinton has a full head of hair, silvered, with a nice swirl in it. The Cabinet Room, with chairs marked for every Cabinet member (they get to buy them upon leaving office), opens out onto the Rose Garden and sits next to the Oval Office. As the President remarked, "The room is smaller than it looks on television,"[6] and on that day it was quite full.

The occasion was a meeting with industry and civic leaders to announce joint actions for strengthening Internet and network security. Present were top executives from information-technology companies – Microsoft, IBM, Cisco, and others – plus experts from security firms, research universities, and civil liberties groups. President Clinton had brought his Chief of Staff, John Podesta; Attorney General Janet Reno; Commerce Secretary Bill Daley; and his Science Advisor, Neal Lane; also there were National Security Advisor Sandy Berger and the National Coordinator for Security, Infrastructure Protection, and Counter-Terrorism, Dick Clarke.

I had organized the meeting. It was the first time – and to date the only time – that the U.S. President and many of his Cabinet met with industry and academia because the Internet was shown to be insecure. We were using the power of the White House as a bully pulpit to declare a high-level, widespread commitment to improving cyber security.

Practical steps had not been ignored, either. We had made sure an actual groundwork for policy was in place before taking our seats in the Cabinet Room that day. The Administration's "National Plan for Information Systems Protection, Version 1.0" (a.k.a. "the Plan") had been put into draft form and released just a month before. It was the first-ever such policy statement. Having had a key hand in crafting it, I was proud of it.

The plan had been written in consultation with those now gathered around the table, so I was confident of their agreement. Essentially, the plan called for the federal government to take a seed-and-support role through actions such as funding research and setting good examples through its own practice. It would largely refrain from regulating, or intervening in, the private sector on cyber security. In return, the private sector would come together to do the lion's share of the work needed.

Along with research funds, government steps announced by President Clinton included new programs for education in cyber security and for protection of the government's own computers. A new Institute for Information Infrastructure Protection would be formed (the I3P, which I later served as vice-chair. The purpose of this consortium of universities, government labs, and nonprofits would be to identify and study problems in cyber security that were outside of the direct mission of any existing agency – in other words, to plug gaps in the R&D portfolio). Also, the government's Cabinet officers were to meet with members of the business community.

Individually, business leaders pledged to work to make each firm's products more secure. Collectively, they would create an industry mechanism to share information on cyber attacks in order to better respond to them. Nearly forty leading IT companies and most major industry associations signed the agreement.

The course was set and publicly declared. The government would fund, facilitate and educate, and become a model for others to emulate, but it would neither regulate nor dictate. For its part, the private sector would collaborate, marshalling its problem-solvers for the challenges that now loomed.

It was a policy in keeping with the market-driven, deregulating spirit of the times, and one whose basic wisdom seemed to be affirmed by recent events. Government and industry had just worked together well along similar lines to address the Y2K issue. The IT industries were booming and innovating brilliantly. The U.S. government had turned its own huge budget deficit into a surplus and seemed to have perfected the art of deftly nudging a free-market economy ever upward. Surely the emerging threats in cyber security could be conquered – or at least brought under control – before long.

Through the first decade of the 2000s, these policies have been carried forward in the United States with almost no real changes. Approaches in other countries have differed a bit in the organizational details, but except for countries like Singapore and China, most countries in the Organisation for Economic Co-operation and Development (OECD) have followed the non-regulatory government-business partnership model blazed by the U.S. In both Canada and the European Union, policies are less explicit than in the U.S. In Canada, various government departments and agencies, including the RCMP, deal with cyber crime, and there is also an integrated partnership between international, federal, and provincial law enforcement agencies.[7] And the EU has moved to strengthen its countries' cyber-policing systems (which are just one aspect of cyber security, by the way) – forging ties between police and the private sector, creating a common alert platform for coordinating with Europol, and allowing more latitude for cross-border searches (whereby investigators in one country can pry remotely into computers in others, searching for evidence).[8] Still, there are no national differences in cyber-security policy that are anything like the differences in, say, health care policy between the U.S. and Canada or Europe. Although the Internet is worldwide and not governed by any single entity, the U.S. has long been the de facto leader in matters related to the Net, so that what is done in the U.S. largely shapes what's done elsewhere.

The question is: Has it worked?

THE SHORT ANSWER, THE REAL STORY

The short answer is no. Many would say the *obvious* answer is no. The record for "biggest data theft in history" keeps being broken. Business and government computers are frequently hacked into, making it ever more likely that your personal information has been stolen at least once. Your own computer may be hacked into use as part of a botnet, a malicious hacking network. The odds of this may still be less than fifty-fifty, but the estimates have kept rising, with various sources saying that anywhere from one of every ten to one of every four PCs harbours a bot.[9] If you are Estonian, you saw your entire country crippled by massive waves of DDOS attacks in 2007. If you live anywhere else and work in national security, you know that your country could be the next target of cyber war or cyber terror and you can think of scenarios in which the effects would be far more serious than they were in Estonia.

Leading periodicals are handing in their verdicts – "Internet security is broken" (*New York Times*),[10] "Just Another Oxymoron: Internet Security" (*PC World*).[11] This is not hysteria. This and following chapters will revisit some major incidents and trends on the cyber-security front since the first plan was launched. I hope that by inviting you behind the scenes you will see the real story that has led so many of us to conclude that the cyber-security system is, indeed, broken.

ARE WE DOING THE BEST WE CAN?

The question of whether policies have worked is tricky, as another question lurks behind it. How does a society decide if policies are "working"? Ideally goals and metrics are clearly defined. For example, "Our goal is to reduce drunk driving by 25 per cent over the next five years, as measured by police reports. To achieve this, we will . . ." Our policies for cyber security do not provide such clarity, however. They tend to set "process" goals – create this new organization, fund that program. Or they are hortatory: We hereby exhort and encourage others to do something. "Output" or "performance" metrics are mostly lacking, and those that exist are fuzzy. For example, a key goal of U.S. policy has been to "minimize disruptions" to critical infrastructure (including the Internet and other not-so-public networks).

Just asking the question about "working" reveals one of the key underlying problems in Internet security. It is hard to set specific goals or even measure progress when statistics and data-gathering are spotty. For tracking physical crime there are excellent records such as the Uniform Crime Reports in the U.S., but for cyber crime we have a hodgepodge of data ranging from the reliable to the dubious, plagued by gaps and under- or over-reporting. What evidence we do have is mostly bad news. It shows marked increases in both the frequency and the scale of many kinds of cyber incidents since 2000, along with a rapid growth of new kinds. DDOS extortion – pay us or we'll shut down your Web site – was once unheard of but now is rampant, say law officers in England and elsewhere. Spam and phishing attacks have gone from unheard of to nearly uncountable.

But noting that cyber crime has "gone up" is just one metric and a rather simplistic one at that. There are two more tests we ought to apply, two further questions that any keen observer would ask.

First: Isn't it possible that the cyber-security people are doing the best they can, against a very tough and fast-growing variety of threats?

Not surprisingly, this line of thinking is often promoted by software firms and other firms in the IT industries, which have a natural interest in persuading customers that they're doing everything they can. At one press event, when Microsoft's security chief was badgered about vulnerabilities in the software, he came back with a sly twist on the old what-if-Microsoft-made-cars jokes: How well do you think your car would hold up if it was attacked every fifteen minutes?

Still, it is well worth exploring whether business and government are in fact doing "the best that they can." In public policy, when the results are disappointing, one must always look at the effort side of the equation – to ask if appropriate strategies are in place and are being carried out properly; to ask if all reasonable options have been tried. So are we doing the best that we can in cyber security?

The answer appears to be "not by a long shot."

Having pledged to become a model of good security practice after that White House meeting in 2000, the U.S. government set internal standards. It also began issuing a Federal Computer Security Report Card, giving "grades" to its major branches – not for actual security outcomes but just for implementing good practice and adhering to the standards. Some two dozen departments and agencies have been graded yearly. In 2008 the Report Card gave grades of D or lower to ten of these, including the Department of Defense (D minus), Treasury (F), and the Nuclear Regulatory Commission (F).

Some experts say the government's approach was flawed from the start – that in cyber security, it doesn't work well to prescribe common, do-it-this-way procedures for organizations with different IT systems and different functions. Still, the grades are not good.

Nor does the private sector seem to have done better. IT vendors, the firms that make the software and hardware we all buy, have uneven records at making their products less vulnerable to intrusion. Software companies are often slow to issue patches for vulnerabilities once they are found; it's sometimes months later.

Internet service providers (ISPs), the companies that link users to the Internet, have been criticized for not deploying security features that are within their purview. In a survey in 2008, the chief security engineers at major ISPs worldwide reported progress in some respects, but expressed pessimism and frustration overall. According to Arbor Networks, the private firm that did the survey, more than half of these engineers "believe serious security threats will increase . . . while their security groups make do with 'fewer resources, less management support and increased workload.'"[12]

In another 2008 survey, many end-user firms – big companies using the Internet – were found to have boards of directors that gave little or no thought or oversight to information security. This survey was done by the CyLab research centre at Carnegie Mellon. The researchers spoke of their concern at finding large numbers of board members who, in their view, still "don't get it," who still don't seem to grasp the importance of cyber security.[13]

Across the public and private sectors there are countless stories of security improvements that could have been made, should have been made, but that were left undone or poorly done. One is the story of the so-called SCADA systems that control electric power grids and other vital infrastructure such as chemical plants, oil refineries, and pipelines. SCADA stands for "supervisory control and data acquisition," and it is frightening how easy it is to hack into many of these systems. A U.S. government security review of the control systems at TVA, America's largest public power company, resulted in a searing indictment of the network security systems, or lack thereof.[14]

When SCADA systems fail, the consequences can be significant. In August 2003, an alarm processor in the control system of an Ohio-based electric utility failed, so that control room operators were not adequately alerted to critical changes to the electrical grid. Then the regional electric grid management system failed, compounding the problem. With these two systems compromised, when several key transmission lines in northern Ohio "tripped" from contact with trees, it was enough to set off a cascading failure of electric power across eight states and a Canadian province.

SCADA software comes from firms like Siemens that are not active in the personal computing market, and until recently industrial plants using SCADA have felt themselves free of security threats.[15] But as industrial processes such as pipelines have connected to the Internet, these systems have become fully open to cyber intrusions. So far only accidental SCADA failures have occurred, but the vulnerabilities are there.

Another story about a missed opportunity in security is that of Internet Protocol version 6, or IPv6, a "new" set of technical standards meant to change some of the digital rules for transmitting data over the Internet. Among other benefits, if all software and hardware were set up to follow these standards, it would help make the Internet more secure. The trouble is, though the IPv6 standards are actually not new – they were written and duly promulgated by the Internet Engineering Task Force in 1998 – a sweep of Internet traffic in 2008 showed that hardly anyone was using them.[16] With there being no one to orchestrate a mass conversion (the IETF has neither the power nor the ability), it just didn't happen. Thus for ten years IPv6 remained little more than an urban legend, discussed fondly and poked at skeptically, like tales of a superhero who might someday come along to help save Gotham.

One can find many areas like these where we are doing far from our best. In nearly all of them, it's clear that what are needed are new public policies or policy changes – to manage the adoption of new core technologies and protocols for the Internet; to truly protect critical infrastructure rather than counting on staying lucky. Recent history shows that adopting new technologies for networks is not inherently impossible: the Canada and the U.S. have both shifted from analogue to digital TV transmissions. Mobile telephones worldwide have migrated toward 3G and 4G cellular technologies. The poor adoption of new Internet technologies is a failure of policy.

And in cyber security, just as in economics, we need policies that can correct for market failures in the private sector. After years of relying largely on private initiative and market forces to address security, it is apparent that the market alone just does not respond well. I work with many security experts from the private sector, brilliant people who work long and hard. They are also aware of the complex perversities of the security marketplace. Markets alone may drive companies to push to increase revenues or to rush a breakthrough product to market, but they will not necessarily drive companies to do their utmost in security. Public policies must provide the carrots and sticks that will balance market forces.

BUT IS IT GOOD ENOUGH?

So we haven't been doing "the best that we can." But we are left with the next question: Is what we are doing, perhaps, "good enough"?

Although that too is a fuzzy standard (and highly subjective), it is the ultimate test of any policy, the one that can lead to political regimes being toppled or not. Are the results good enough to satisfy people, good enough to keep society functioning at a level we'd like, good enough to be, well, acceptable?

Some would argue that in cyber security, yes, the results *are* good enough. After all, despite alarming increases in cyber crime, the cyber city has been ticking merrily along. Despite rumours of imminent disaster, the sky hasn't fallen. For many of us, the main issue is not securing the Internet but getting more of it. We can't stand to be away from cyberhome; we want to access the Internet from our cellphones and a growing array of other mobile devices; we want to transform Africa with one laptop per child so the children can be on the Internet. Yes, one can find room for improvement in security, but isn't it obviously good enough?

Unfortunately, there is evidence that the name of this tune is "Fiddling While Rome Burns" – so much evidence that it's hard to know where to start.

In the realm of security, be it the physical kind or the cyber kind, we actually have a pretty fair definition of "good enough." The security consultant Noam Eppel used it in the article I mentioned earlier, which argued that cyber security has broken down utterly. He said that people should feel able to "conduct 'normal and common' activities" without being victimized, so long as they take reasonable and not-too-onerous precautions.

Eppel gave a parked-car example. If you park on a public street in daytime and lock your car, with no valuables left visible, the risk of a break-in should be very small. But if someone does break in, it's probably because you are in a bad neighbourhood where the security is not up to par and, though the locals may have grown used to toughing it out, this is a place where the prospects are not good.

Is the Internet a place where we feel able to "conduct 'normal and common' activities" without being victimized? Hardly. We hesitate to click on a link or open a file, knowing that we could be opening the door to strangers. We've learned that even if it looks like a friend at the door, it could be a bad guy in disguise.

And the precautions we are advised to take are extremely oner-ous. If you are diligent about security on your home PC, you may spend so much time surfing the Web to learn about the latest worms and viruses that you feel like a hypochondriac browsing WebMD for symptoms. If you want the best possible protection, you will be spending even more time (and now money) shopping for and installing arcane items such as anti-spyware software, server certificates, and secure FTP clients. (What, you don't have those last two? Or even know what they are?)

For administrators of big networks with hundreds or thousands of computers, such work is vastly multiplied. And still we aren't secure. Even the gated communities are not safe. I've lived in one of the best – while writing this book, I was on the faculty at Carnegie Mellon, behind the cyber firewalls at one of the most technically savvy universities in the world. Yet while I was working on this very chapter, I asked another professor to join me for coffee and he declined because "my computer has been completely taken over by something, and I can't use it. I need to get this sorted out."

Sorting it out can be tough when you can't trust anyone. At the university I received a courteous but firm e-mail from the security staff, asking me to please do a series of tasks on my office com-puter to assure that it was guarded against the latest round of threats. I almost did. It was a perfectly official-looking e-mail like others I had seen, but at the risk of seeming paranoid I placed a couple of phone calls instead. The security staff had sent no such e-mail; it was a phishing attack.

Things have gotten to the point where many experts wouldn't think of engaging in some "normal and common activities." At a conference of cyber-security experts I decided to ask the attendees if they used online banking. While some thought it was fine to do so, about one-third said they did not and would not. Another third said they did, or would, but only while taking extra security measures far beyond the ken of lay Internet users.

Things have gotten to the point where normal and common activities are being disrupted or, in some cases, prevented from happening at all. In late 2008 and early 2009, the Conficker worm raced across the Internet. The potential for damage was so great that government systems in France and hospital systems in England were shut down to clean out the worm, even though it had not yet done any harm. And after it was learned that the Conficker worm could not only propagate over the Internet but also ride on the USB flash drives that people like to use for moving files from one computer to another, some big institutions (including the U.S. Department of Defense) took drastic steps: they banned USB drives in their offices and sealed up the USB ports on computers with cement.

Paranoia? Perhaps, but paranoia is one of the inevitable results of security that's not good enough. Two security researchers, Klaus Kursawe of Switzerland and Stefan Katzenbeisser of Germany, co-authored a paper whose title aptly described what the security situation has come to even in the eyes of dispassionate experts – "Computing Under Occupation."

If in early 2009 you had gone to Professor Katzenbeisser's Web page at the Technische Universität Darmstadt, thinking of contacting him for further information, you would have found this notice (in English) under his e-mail address:

> Due to the large amount of spam I use rigorous anti-spam filtering. If you suspect that your mail does not reach me, please contact me by phone or fax.

Why not use Morse code and send a telegram? Delivery is said to be reliable.

CSIS (the Center for Strategic and International Studies in the U.S.) is a think tank devoted to subjects it considers of great consequence, such as nuclear proliferation. In December 2008, aiming to catch the eye of then President-elect Barack Obama, CSIS released a report titled "Securing Cyberspace for the 44th Presidency." It said that "inadequate cyber security and loss of information has inflicted unacceptable damage to U.S. national and economic security."[17]

Inadequate, unacceptable. Notable breaches of U.S. security have ranged from the Titan Rain cyber-espionage attacks (see Chapter 5) to incidents in which U.S. businesses and trade delegations have gone overseas to find that the negotiators across the table from them somehow seemed to know all their key negotiating points, and what the Americans would settle for. They'd been hacked.

Nor are damages limited to the U.S. At the 2009 World Economic Forum in Davos, Switzerland, the cyber-security firm McAfee presented a survey and rough estimate of the global costs of cyber insecurity. It was a shocking one trillion dollars per year. Granted, that estimate could be off by a few hundred billion either way. But it counted *only* the costs incurred by business firms, and only from a certain type of cyber incident, data breaches leading to the loss or compromise of valuable information. If the number is anywhere close to correct, it would represent a stunning burden on firms operating in the world's already-troubled economies. Is that acceptable? Good enough?

Or look at a series of events around the history-making times of Barack Obama's election and inauguration.

• November 4, 2008: Mr. Obama wins the election, becoming the first American whose run to the Presidency touched off a mass epidemic of phishing scams. E-mails with startling messages have been flooding the Internet for months; now the tide is rising higher yet. The teaser lines range from "Obama Sex Scandal!" to "Amazing Speech!" and each e-mail has a link to a fake Web site such as greatobamaonline.com. The Web sites look very convincing; some use actual campaign graphics. A visitor who clicks to get the real news gets a malicious download – perhaps a keystroke-logger that will record every password the victim uses on the Internet, so others can get in to see what's worth stealing. Of course, not everyone takes the bait. But still these complex schemes have all the earmarks of professional, well-planned criminal operations.*

- December 9, 2008: "Patch Tuesday." On the second Tuesday of every month, big software firms such as Microsoft and Oracle release patches to fix recently found security flaws in their products. IT administrators at companies and non-profits around the world brace for Patch Tuesday. They may be sent dozens of patches, for various software programs, all to be installed on thousands of PCs under their care. On this Tuesday, several critical patches are for the Internet Explorer program. Installing doesn't help. Within days, hackers are exploiting or working around the patches.

- January 20, 2009: Barack Obama is inaugurated. A firm called Heartland Payment Systems is criticized for trying to bury its own bad news by announcing it on that day. Heartland – one of the world's largest online processors of credit- and debit-card transactions – admits that hackers have broken into its system and stolen an estimated one hundred million customer card-numbers, breaking the existing record for cyber theft of personal financial data.

    If you have ever used a card to pay for a restaurant meal or buy a gift, your number might have been part of that haul. Heartland's niche is clearing payments for restaurants, bars, and small retailers: the clerk swipes the card through the machine, the data goes up into the system, someone swipes

---

* You may also enjoy a footnote. In this election Sarah Palin, the losing candidate for Vice-President, won a consolation prize. Phishing counts showed that phishy e-mails themed to Ms. Palin outnumbered those themed to the less colourful Joe Biden, Obama's VP. The ratio was about five to four.

the data. *What's done on the Internet doesn't stay on the Internet* – the trouble can follow you anywhere.

• March 1, 2009: This day's data-breach news story concerns the special military helicopter used to carry President Obama on short trips. Copies of the blueprints and other sensitive data for this aircraft have been stolen, a security audit has shown. The files were stored on a computer at a defence contractor's office. Apparently, someone at the office downloaded a file-sharing program to receive and send free music over the Internet, which allowed everything else on the person's hard drive to be inadvertently "shared" as well. The audit found that hackers in Iran and other countries came window-shopping via the Net, and helped themselves to the details of Mr. Obama's high-security helicopter.[18]

THE END OF AN ERA

We have come a long way – in the wrong direction – since the days in early February of 2000, when a then-unprecedented wave of DDOS attacks prompted a White House meeting and the announcement of the first National Plan for cyber security.

The perpetrators of those attacks turned out to be just one person: a fifteen-year-old boy in the suburbs of Montreal. Michael Calce, who went by the online name Mafiaboy, wasn't really Mafia, or even a computer prodigy. He was just a software-literate teenager, a script kiddie, who got his hands on some of the easy-to-use automated attack tools that had started to circulate. It appears that he brought down Web sites across North America mainly to see if he could do it and then brag about it online.

Which he did. Bragging was not as risky as it might seem because the news coverage of the attacks meant that all sorts of people were likely to claim credit, giving investigators a maze of false leads. But then Mafiaboy bragged about hitting the Dell, Inc. Web site, which had indeed been one of his targets but not one publicly reported in the news accounts, and he was traced and caught.

Mafiaboy was a historic figure in more ways than one. When so many Web sites went down in February 2000, we thought we were seeing the start of a grim new era in cyber attacks, and this was certainly true in terms of the scale and scope of the attacks. But really these attacks were farewell salvos. Like the climax of a fireworks display, they signalled the end of an era, for Mafiaboy was part of the last great wave of "mischief hackers." His attacks were among the last significant cyber exploits done for thrills, for bragging rights. Since 2000, the teenaged vandals have been replaced by real *mafiosi*.

The nature of the adversary has changed profoundly and the world's cyber-security policies – its laws and regulations – have not kept up.

CHAPTER 2

INTO THE UNDERWORLD

"In one sense," said the magazine article, the entity in question "does not exist. It has no legal identity; it is not registered as a company; its senior figures are anonymous, known only by their nicknames. Its web sites are registered at anonymous addresses with dummy e-mails. It does not advertise for customers. Those who want to use its services contact it via internet messaging services and pay with anonymous electronic cash. But the menace it poses certainly exists . . ."

The article appeared in *The Economist* in August of 2007. The subject was RBN, the Russian Business Network, said to be one of the largest cyber-crime organizations in the world. RBN was believed to be based in St. Petersburg, Russia, but its location or locations and other aspects of its being may have been shifted since then, perhaps as evasive moves. Further investigations through 2008 and '09 – by security firms, news reporters, private investigators, and others – found evidence that RBN was linked, in a sort of global supply chain, to other outfits worldwide. Some of these appeared to be quasi-legitimate Internet companies in places like Concord, California – where, on a given morning, their "employees" might be sitting in Silicon Valley traffic jams, or in coffee houses, next to unsuspecting employees of major IT-industry firms such as Google and Hewlett-Packard.

The global supply chains exist to provide software and services to still more criminal groups, which in turn use them to hack into computers at banks and defence agencies – or into the computer that's sitting in your office or family room right now.

If you have read about such things while browsing the Web, you may have been inspired to buy the most up-to-date protection for your home PC. Perhaps you bought a software product like Advanced XP Defender, touted as giving you "a powerful mix of Anti-Malware, Anti-Virus, Anti-Trojan, Anti-Backdoor, Anti-Worm and Anti-PornoDial in one program." All you had to do was enter a credit- or debit-card number and download the software. If you did, too bad.

Advanced XP Defender turned out to be a rogue program, one that delivered the same bad stuff it was supposed to prevent – while taking your money, along with your card number. In fact, by early 2009, the Web was abuzz with ads for new programs designed to remove Advanced XP Defender from your hard drive. To get one of these, all you had to do was enter a card number and download the program . . .

It's hard to know who is who in this world. Seldom are actual human beings named publicly as perpetrators, because seldom can law officers get the kind of evidence and cooperation that can lead to an actual indictment. In this chapter, I will be quoting often from sources who wish to remain anonymous themselves.

The cyber underworld was a world that barely existed when I began working in cyber security in Washington in the 1990s. Over the next few years I witnessed an evolution that took us far from the early days of cyber crime as a sometimes, and mostly small-time, thing.

THE ORIGINS OF HACKING

"Hacking" – the act of getting into an electronic system to do something the owner doesn't want you to do – had its hazy origins in the time before the public Internet. An early form, in the late 1960s and into the 1970s, was phone phreaking. This involved tricking the recently automated telephone systems into letting you make free long-distance calls. One seminal phone phreak was a young American named Joe Engressia, a.k.a. Joybubbles, a.k.a. the Whistler. Blind from birth but gifted with perfect pitch, Engressia learned how to whistle into a telephone mouthpiece the beep tones that would signal the system to put a call through.

Young geeks started building electronic devices called blue boxes to do the same trick, and more. Photographs from the 1970s show a long-haired Bill Gates proudly holding a blue box, and the German computer activist Wau Holland busily using one. A blue box built by Stephen Wozniak is now enshrined in the Computer History Museum in Silicon Valley.

What drove such bright young men to engage in such behaviour? They typically cited three reasons. First, they were driven by the nameless urge that has always driven young people to pull elaborate pranks and to try to top one another's pranks. Second, as the phone phreakers claimed when they were caught, they wanted to "explore the system" – which was true. Access to state-of-the-art research systems was scarce in those days. By pranking your way through the phone network, or the budding computer networks of that time, you could learn things you couldn't learn any other way. And third, you could get free phone calls.

The hacking scene began to change markedly in the 1980s. For one thing, the range of possible targets and possible activities expanded. Whereas the phone network had been a single-purpose network – designed and used for telephone service – the computer age was now coming into full bloom. More computers were being used to store ever more kinds of information, and control all kinds of tasks. And while personal computers were still a novelty in the early 1980s, some big mainframe computers *were* being connected to public networks. Namely, to public telephone networks.

This trend was especially strong in Europe. Systems like France's Minitel, started in 1982, offered many features of the modern-day Internet. Since most users didn't have PCs, the standard access device was a so-called dumb terminal, with a keyboard and a video screen. But if you had a terminal, a new world awaited. Over the phone lines you could "call up" various computers to make train or airline reservations, buy mail-order goods, or post messages on proto-chat boards.

In Germany the BTX system allowed limited forms of online banking. Members of the Chaos Computer Club, a geek collective, were unhappy with the BTX system, which they judged to be clunky and insecure. So in 1984, they proved the point by hacking into the computers of a bank in Hamburg and transferring a total of 134,000 Deutschmarks to the Club's own account – keeping each transfer within the permitted maximum of 9.99 Deutschmarks. The Club then publicly returned the money, in one of the first major acts of "showcasing" vulnerability in a computer network.

Also in 1984, a book was published that painted the darker possibilities, William Gibson's science fiction novel *Neuromancer*. Interestingly, Gibson wrote the book on a manual typewriter; he has said he was not very interested in computers but in how people behaved around them.[1] The central character of the dystopian novel is Case, a "jacker" involved with shadowy gangs that hire him to jack into the vast realms of data and intelligence residing in "cyberspace" (the origin of that word).

By the early 1990s, life had begun imitating art. Cyberspace was now a reality. Government-sponsored computer networks in the U.S. had been fully opened to the public in 1988, and linked up with other networks to create an entire parallel cyber universe, the Internet.

Some of the early criminal ventures on the Internet looked not so much like gangland hits but more like buddy movies gone wrong. In one case, two Russian hackers were invited to fly to Seattle for a job interview. The young men had been pulling a variety of online exploits through the late 1990s, sometimes making substantial sums, and now it seemed they had caught the attention of a shadowy U.S. security firm that wanted to employ them full-time, perhaps for some not-quite-legal business tasks. At the interview they described their work history in detail. Asked to demonstrate their skills at a computer, they complied. Armed FBI agents then closed the jaws of the sting, arresting them.[2]

Greater sophistication was coming, fuelled in part by two technical advances since the 1980s. One was the development of viruses. In the old days, hacking had to be done personally, in real time – by a phreaker with a blue box or by an outlaw at a keyboard, like Case the jacker, maniacally tapping out commands to try and induce some faraway computer to give up its secrets. But now a lot of the work could be automated. Once you found a vulnerability in a system (or better yet, a typical vulnerability existing in many systems), you could write a software program to exploit it. Sent over the Internet, the program could replicate and propagate itself.

That automated quality was important because of the other advance, the growth of personal computing. No longer did a big hit have to be a frontal strike against a big target, in the style of a bank robbery or a jewel heist. Now there was money to be made by hacking into, or through, myriad little targets. The era of mass production in cyber crime was just around the corner.

THE SHIFT FROM GEEKS TO GANGSTERS: MUDGE'S VIEW

I first met Peiter Zatko, alias Mudge, in a dirty warehouse loft in Watertown, Massachusetts, in 1998. At the time, Mudge was everyone's idea of a young hacker with long, unkempt hair, holding down a day job while hacking beyond the fringe off-hours. He and a half dozen others were the founding members of a now-legendary hacker group called the L0pht. As Mudge explained later, "We decided to kind of poke fun at the 'hacker elite speak' (e.g. c001, r4d, 0nw3d, etc.) and changed the 'o' (oh) to a 0 (zero). We incorporated as LHI Technologies, which stood for 'L0pht Heavy Industries.' I always wanted to run a company that had 'heavy industries' in its name – sounds like we make rail-cars and trans-atlantic cable-pullers :)"

The L0pht viewed themselves as "grey hats," not really bad guys (in black hats) but not heroes (in white hats) either. They would break into systems to identify vulnerabilities, and then share that knowledge, sometimes with anyone who would listen (including criminals), but sometimes to earn an income by working with the system vendors to fix the vulnerabilities.[3]

However they described themselves, their "offices" were a geek's dream. The L0pht were experts in dumpster diving, a polite term for going through other people's garbage to find carelessly discarded private data that would help hackers break into a computer system. By such means they had also, in the course of time, acquired variously the parts of a Cray supercomputer (a large national lab was not far away); a very tall radio antenna mounted on the roof; and up-and-running systems of nearly every computer available – and probably some that weren't.

They certainly seemed to know how to do things. Mudge subsequently went on to testify before Congress that he could "take down" the Internet in thirty minutes, perhaps a dubious claim, perhaps not. At any rate, he and the L0pht reflected the face of computer crime then. Hacking was the activity of individuals or small groups, mostly young men, and only a fraction of it in the 1990s had anything to do with making money.

As Mudge explains it, "We were into exposing security problems, and making people aware of them. At the time, there weren't security organizations in companies like Microsoft or Intel, and no responsible mechanisms for handling security vulnerabilities. The software vendors only cared if their customers were complaining, and at that time few customers had any awareness of the problem. So sometimes we had to beat them up in the media."

For example, in 1996 a prominent security solutions vendor had a major vulnerability in its newly released product. The company refused to fix it, even after conversations with the L0pht. So Mudge published a set of papers, "in Canada, to confuse the trail," exposing the vulnerability publicly. "We weren't really concerned about who knew about the vulnerability, even if that meant the black hats. Our focus was on getting the vulnerabilities fixed."

Making a name for oneself in this fashion was a hacker motivation.[4] For Mudge, that attitude changed after he developed L0phtCrack, a popular hacking program. L0phtCrack could be used by bad guys to discover Microsoft Windows passwords or it could be purchased by good guys to test the strength of their passwords. Mudge quit his day job. He migrated to the white-hat side, advising system owners on how to protect against malicious hacking; he commanded thousands of dollars for speaking and consulting fees. But there were many who went the other way.

THE ESTABLISHMENT REACTS

In the 1990s, the occurrence of real cyber crime, along with the awareness of Internet connectivity and our reliance on networked systems, had made clear to government and corporate managers that a problem was emerging. These networked computer systems, many of them crucial to national security or to the global economy, had vulnerabilities that could be exploited – perhaps with dire consequences.

In 1994, President Clinton created the President's Commission on Critical Information Protection (PCCIP)[5] in order to examine new threats to the nation's infrastructure. (Reportedly, Clinton became concerned about new, post–Cold War security threats after a late-night reading of *The Hot Zone,* a nonfiction book by Richard Preston about an accidental near release of the deadly Ebola virus from an animal test lab.) By the mid-1990s, the private sector was starting to act – Intel now had its own security development group – and in 1996 the foundation piece of U.S. cyber-crime law, the Computer Fraud and Abuse Act,[6] was substantially revised.

Other nations were taking similar steps. A framework for international cooperation, the Council of Europe's Convention on Cybercrime, was authored in 2001 and signed by most Western nations, including Canada and the U.S. In the interest of privacy and security, the European Union developed a variety of oversight organizations as well as rules for its members – such as laws governing how personal data stored in large computer systems is to be handled. Over time, cyber-security initiatives were mounted by groups from the OECD and the Group of Eight (G-8) to the United Nations. It would seem that well-integrated global efforts were taking shape nicely, but this was not quite the case.

Within the U.S., for instance, the Department of Justice, the FBI, and the Secret Service (not always working on the most harmonious of terms) each built cyber-crime units. In 1997 the PCCIP had concluded that, yes indeed, the nation was growing ever more dependent on vulnerable infrastructures, including the Internet. Unlike most Presidential commissions, the PCCIP report led to immediate action, including an order – Presidential Decision Directive (PDD) 63 – that made cyber security a national priority and put mechanisms into place to begin coordinating federal and private sector efforts. That work culminated in the first National Plan, which I helped to write and now wish had been different.

Meanwhile, the motives for cyber attacks had started changing as people noticed the money to be made. In 2000, the security expert Avi Rubin, then of AT&T Labs, noted: "The only thing missing until now is the incentive to hack. Now, there's plenty of incentive, it's easier than ever, there's not enough talent out there to combat it, and companies are more interested in being on the Internet than being secure on the Internet."[7]

Or as Mudge puts it: "Hacking for bragging rights ended because knowledge about vulnerabilities and how to exploit them became intellectual property that was valuable."

IT'S LIKE PROHIBITION

Between 2001 and 2004, the world of hacking changed utterly. Mudge eventually went to the "good" side where, instead of showcasing vulnerabilities he found, he wanted to "sell the solution to the customer." He helped to start one security consulting firm, then went on to work for BBN Technologies, another security firm. He had his hair cut; he wore suits; he got married.

Others found careers in a line of business where a different vision of the cyber marketplace was emerging. Looking back from the perspective of the mid-2000s, Mudge noted:

If you had approached organized crime ten years ago about using computers to steal credit cards on the Internet, they'd say "What is the Internet?" There wasn't any sort of system for selling secrets, or stolen data, or knowledge about new vulnerabilities. If I had a vulnerability there was no market to sell it to back then. Now there is. Sure, it's always been the case that when someone broke into a remote site they could get valuable information. People used to steal credit card data then too. But it was like phone phreaking – small time stuff. Those thefts weren't really the primary focus of organized crime back then. Now, they realize how easy it is to commit these crimes.

One source told me he noticed a key inflection period: "In the summer of '04 everything went quiet. Everyone of the 'pay attention to my hack' orientation had been courted by the criminal groups." It did not remain quiet. Another source compared the next period, the one we are still in, to the time in the U.S. when liquor was illegal and bootleggers and racketeers flourished: "Now it's like Prohibition. Crime is rampant, and law enforcement makes an effort, but it's not having an impact."

Actually the cyber-crime situation is worse than Prohibition, because it is global, and because of how the economics of cyber crime play out.

SO YOU WANT TO BE A MILLIONAIRE?

In cyber crime, the payoffs are compelling and the risk is low. Consider the lowly spam. In its most benign form spam is just electronic junk mail, but, because it is electronic, a spam solicitation costs three hundredths of one per cent that of regular junk mail.[8] Spam also often carries with it links to other malware that collects information on you or loads unwanted software onto your computer – anything from pop-up ads to programs that take complete, if silent, control of your computer. All of these activities, from selling Viagra to providing the conduit for malware, earn the spammer money, because the acts are valuable to somebody.

Moreover, catching and prosecuting spammers is difficult. Even attempting to regulate them is difficult; the CAN-SPAM Act in the

U.S. is a dismal failure.[9] It requires there to be clear notification that the message is spam, along with a valid opt-out provision for the recipient, requirements easily evaded by most spammers. CAN-SPAM was passed in 2003 and it was not till June 2007 that the first conviction occurred under the Act – by which time Earthlink, the Internet service provider most affected by this particular spam scam (a phishing scheme), had spent about one million dollars to detect and combat it.

Most cyber crime involves multiple players with differing roles. Do you want to extort money from a U.K. betting parlour just a few days before a big match? Botnets – networks of computers, already loaded with illicit software without their owners' knowledge – are ready to rent for a DDOS attack. Do you want to break into an otherwise well-protected system? Zero-day vulnerabilities – ways of breaking in that have just been discovered – are for sale. Do you need specialized software to commit a crime? Someone will build it for you, and someone else will run it for you, for a price.

At every stage, there are attractive opportunities for those with enterprising minds. As one source explained to me, "Kids who build botnets do it to rent them to crime groups who in turn use them for spamming, or to collect credit-card information. The going rate is between five and ten cents per bot, per hour – maybe twenty-five cents for a daily rate, or for five hours. Twenty thousand or more bots rented at a single time is a pretty good return considering that some kid spent an evening writing the code."

A successful identify theft can net over $160,000.[10] Cyber-extortion demands range from $10,000 to several million.[11] Any information that's otherwise difficult to get – ranging from e-mail addresses of potential buyers of some company's product, to national security secrets – has value on the black market. Zero-day vulnerabilities bring what the highest bidder will offer; they have auction markets. One auction, for a vulnerability in Microsoft Excel, was shut down by eBay – where a daring hacker/auctioneer was conducting it.[12]

But the eBay auction was an anomaly. The real chat rooms and markets of the cyber underworld are hidden. Sometimes they float, being hosted on a series of compromised servers. Others rely on systems outside the normal IRC (Internet Relay Chat) channels. All require an invitation to participate, but as one source said, "if you've made anything of a name for yourself in hacking, you'll be approached by organized crime."

In 2009, the U.S. journalist Jim Giles gained access to an illicit chat room. He reported watching a stream of messages such as "I got fresh hacked U.K. cvv2's" – a cvv2 being a credit-card number complete with expiration date, billing address, and security code – or "Selling USA Fulls Cvv2 Info + SSN MMN DOB," which you can probably decipher. This is the credit-card info plus the holder's Social Security number, mother's maiden name, and date of birth. "Criminals can use these details to apply for [new] credit cards, take out loans or set up bank accounts to launder money," Giles explained. He noted that one researcher, tracking chat-room trading for seven months, witnessed transactions totalling $93 million.[13]

This is not the underworld of Tony Soprano – local, with a mostly known and fixed set of participants. Like the Internet, the cyber underworld reflects a new global model. It is made up of shifting groups or coalitions that form or dissolve depending on the opportunity of the moment, and in this world, information on where to find the right sites to make deals travels largely through word of mouth.[14]

One complex web of markets and outsourced tasks was highlighted on *Dateline NBC* in July 2007. The division of labour and specialization of function would have made Adam Smith proud. Credit cards (reportedly with the cooperation of a credit-card issuer) were offered on a site specializing in their sale. The cards were snapped up by various parties, then within hours used to make major purchases, which were in turn shipped to domestic (U.S.) addresses. The recipients appeared to be pathetically duped individuals, forwarding the goods on to foreign addresses at the behest of a love interest "established" – you guessed it – over the Internet. These poor individuals (and in many cases they really were poor) sometimes even paid for the overseas shipping. The goods, mostly consumer electronics, were then sold overseas. The scheme, like many others, was masterminded in Nigeria.

The Nigerian economy is thought to benefit greatly from cyber crime. In fact, Nigeria has very strict laws against all forms of cyber crime – security experts refer to scams coming out of Nigeria as "419 cases"[15] in reference to that section of the country's legal code. But just as there are narco-states that, whatever their protestations, earn a significant part of their foreign exchange through drugs, so too are there cyber rogue states. Nigeria stands out as such a state but it does not stand alone.

The complexities and the division of labour can get very interesting when it comes to national security secrets. The so-called Titan Rain attacks of 2003–2004 are still ranked among the most serious acts of cyber espionage. For over a year, intruders systematically siphoned files from defence-related computers across the U.S. The work appeared to be done by expert hackers whose operations were traced to Guangdong province in China. Two possible culprits, not mutually exclusive, stood out. The Chinese government of course vehemently denied carrying out the intrusions. Alternatively, at least one civilian security expert, Ira Winkler, theorized that the Titan Rain attacks may have been perpetrated by traditional Chinese gangs known as triads – which broadens the possibilities, as the triads could then have sought to maximize their profits from the stolen files. They could have peddled the information, variously, to intelligence agencies in China or elsewhere; to firms and enterprises wishing to copy U.S. technology for the purpose of competing in global markets; or to other criminals. Other security experts[16] have supported the assessment that criminal gangs were behind the attacks.

Said one: "Now [the cyber underworld] is much more sophisticated. It's gone very commercial. There are software companies that specialize in building bots, or other criminal software. It's just like the economy for building and marketing children's games." Attackers and attack-technique developers have diversified into highly specialized roles, even with a service culture that provides hotlines.[17]

In this parallel world, jobs are contracted out much as they are in the legitimate over-world. "You [potential cyber criminal] can submit a request for bids on a job – 'who has a 10K system of botnets?'

They'll [another entity on a trusted chat room] run it for you." And, just as in the real-world underworld: "Larger organizations are willing to have little kids do their dirty work for them. They're very sophisticated, and hire 'mules.' If the kids get caught, then it's not much of a crime, and there's not much risk of that."

In identity theft, cyber thieves don't necessarily use the stolen data directly, as a physical thief might do after taking your wallet and trying to use the credit cards. Often the stolen data is used to apply for, or generate, new cards or purchasing agreements – perhaps in the name of some "synthetic" person. Data for this purpose can come from any number of perpetrators and be used by any number of others. It all begins to look eerily like the bundling and rebundling of toxic securities, with one difference: here, the racket doesn't blow up in everyone's faces because the goods have been discovered to be worthless.

More ominous yet, cyber attacks don't have to come from the outside. A company or government agency can put up state-of-the-art defences to shield its networks and servers from attack via the Internet; it can use fancy password and authentication schemes to keep unauthorized users from logging into laptops and PCs. But if the attacker is an employee or a contractor, he's already "inside the perimeter."

Insider threats are probably more misunderstood than any other form of cyber attack. In no small part this is because organizations do not willingly disclose the incidents. Yet surveys of security managers consistently rank insider threats as one of the top one or two cyber threats to their organizations.[18] Almost all of the insider cases that show up in the public record (studying them is one of my specialties) are cases of disgruntled or greedy individuals taking revenge upon, or exploiting, their employers' systems.[19] These represent just the tip of the iceberg. Other kinds of insider cases make it into the public record only rarely, such as the case of the California cybersecurity consultant who moonlighted as a botmaster and trader in stolen data on the basis of access to his clients' systems.[20] Or they are suggested by tidbits like the conversation I had with a source who coolly remarked, hypothetically I am sure, that *of course* the best virus writers would be ones who have day jobs at anti-virus companies.

None of this is new human behaviour. Insiders, double and triple agents, and racketeers of every stripe abounded long before cyberspace existed. What cyberspace offers is unprecedented *leverage* for doing wrong.

CYBER LEVERAGE: THE HACKER'S FRIEND

Almost any form of misbehaviour that humans are capable of can be practised over, or aided by, the Internet. The very scope of the Internet and the many private networks connected to it allow perpetrators to extend the reach of their crime. Why pick pockets one by one when you can pick millions at once? Why should pranksters be content with stirring up trouble locally when they can attempt pranks on a global scale, and why should tomorrow's terrorists limit themselves to attacking a power plant or military base physically when they might wreak equal – or additional – havoc by sitting at a PC somewhere and hacking into control systems?

The whole economics of the situation are tilted in favour of the bad guys. Cyber networks give malefactors a new form of leverage, a means of getting more bang for their buck, while for the rest of us the hazards and the costs increase. We still have to protect ourselves physically but now we have to protect our virtual exposures as well. And protecting our virtual exposures can be devilishly hard because there are so many of them, giving intruders many possible avenues in. They may have to find only one, if it leads to where they want to go.

The solution is not to declare a "war on cyber crime." Someone once said that bad metaphor makes bad policy. Declaring war on anything other than an actual, identifiable military opponent is usually bad metaphor, carrying the wrong connotations and possibly leading to the wrong actions. We would not want to impose the equivalent of martial law on the Internet.

But the cyber-security situation does look like a classic case of asymmetric warfare. The criminals and hackers have gotten the leverage, not by overwhelming force, but by infiltration and by the nature of the playing field. The situation is truly insidious because cyber leverage so often works to the average user's benefit – put your needs or wares out on the Internet and watch the magic. It makes us unwilling to give up this benefit and consequently makes us all extremely vulnerable.

The road ahead will take us through a rocky terrain. As we navigate our way, we will have to sort and sift through the obstacles in our path. We need to look at the breadth of the problem before us. We need to find unused abilities and points of leverage where we can pry, pry away. That is the trick to turning things around.

And we must take inventory of the tricks being thrown at us, to see why they are so effective.

CHAPTER 3

MODES OF ATTACK

In the 1983 movie *WarGames,* Matthew Broderick plays a teenage hacker who breaks into the Pentagon's computers and unwittingly almost causes a nuclear war. Even today that role defines the popular conception of both hacker and cyber attack – the young geek sitting at his computer cleverly overcoming the defences of his chosen computer target.

Today, attacks of that sort are only a small part of the cyber threat. If we're to look at the breadth of the problem, we need to understand the variety of different attacks being used.

THE NUMBERS

To start, it helps to appreciate the sheer number and frequency of attacks taking place today. As was said in Chapter 1, getting consistent data about cyber-security problems is a problem in itself. However, there are some numbers that tell an interesting tale. One way to try to gauge the overall trend in frequency of cyber attacks is to look at the numbers of incidents each year that are serious enough to be reported to the CERTs, the Computer Emergency Readiness (or Response) Teams in various countries. For the US-CERT, the oldest one, here are the incident counts from 1997 onward.

INCIDENTS REPORTED TO US-CERT

1997:	2,134
1998:	3,734
1999:	9,859
2000:	21,756
2001:	52,658
2002:	82,094
2003:	137,529

The CERT stopped releasing overall figures after 2003, explaining on its Web site that "attacks against Internet-connected systems have become so commonplace that counts of the number of incidents reported provide little information with regard to assessing the scope and impact of attacks."

Still, these numbers need some examination. For one thing, from 1997 to 2003, the Internet grew. Couldn't that drive up the number of incidents, just as a growth in auto traffic might be expected to increase auto accidents? To try to control for growth in Internet traffic I ran a simple calculation. I divided the incident counts by the number of Web site hosts in operation each year. That ratio also grew, from 132 incidents per 100,000 Internet hosts in 1997, to 801 in 2003. By that rough relative-to-size measure, US-CERT incidents had an increase of over 600 per cent.

Nor is it likely that incident counts went up because people grew more diligent about reporting. The U.S. Government Accountability Office (GAO) found that during 2005–2006, *under*-reporting to CERT was rampant at federal agencies. One agency, mercifully not named by the GAO, had over 800 incidents that were either the subject of internal reports or actually involved calling in law-enforcement help. Not one was reported to CERT.[1] Private firms also have strong disincentives for reporting. Many hesitate to say much about cyber incidents for the same reason they do not like to publicize internal crimes such as employee fraud and embezzlement: it doesn't inspire confidence among the customers and stockholders.

Other numbers and trend lines from cyber security are no better. Spam, not measured and barely existent in 2000, is accounting for 90 per cent of all e-mail traffic today.[2] When a major spamming group called the McColo Corporation was closed down in 2008, spam volume dropped so dramatically that Internet users could notice it without seeing statistics. The holiday was short. In a few months, spam volume was back to the usual.

But above all, the CERT people were right to say that just counting "incidents" no longer tells us much. To begin with, while a spam e-mail or the planting of a bot on someone's computer is a small "incident," they come in millions. Little incidents are interlinked with other incidents and they can build and grow in weird tangles. The spam you respond to may trigger the virus that plants the bot. The bot becomes part of a botnet, now used for large misdeeds. A large misdeed may be a single strike or series of strikes at one target (such as a DDOS attack) – or it may be a large, ongoing campaign of diffuse digital pickpocketing.

Or just as lots of little attacks can be used to set up a big one, the converse also happens. A single big strike can set up many little ones – the prime example being a corporate data breach that reaps information on thousands or millions of individuals who can then be attacked in turn.[3]

ATTACKS IN THE AGE OF MASS PRODUCTION

In short, the days are gone when one could simply say, "Oh, that was an incident" or "That was an attack." The reality is a crawling, ever-shifting infestation of incidents and attacks that defy counting.

This infestation is the product of the cyber underworld described in the last chapter. Just as the mass media inundate us in an interminable "surround" of commercial messages, we now have a mass-production underworld that immerses us in an ongoing surround of cyber attacks.

We might also complain that commercialism in the mass media is so pervasive that it's hard to separate "the show" or "the story" from "the advertisements." Entire television programs, movies, and magazines are conceived from the start as marketing vehicles; they advertise their own sponsors and generate their own spinoff products. So it is, too, in the realm of cyber attack. Not only do the attacks defy counting, they defy classifying. Even if your computer has been infected with something very specific – making it very specifically *your* problem – it is wrong to think that it is *only* your problem. What you have, in effect, is a product placement within a feature movie that has prequels and sequels playing everywhere.

It is thus difficult to classify distinct modes or types of cyber attack. Chillingly, it can also be difficult even to speak of distinct motives (for instance, to separate cyber "crime" from cyber "war," "terror," and "espionage") – or, at the other end of the spectrum, to separate cyber "crime" from mere "annoyance." Just about any single *type* of attack can be used for any or all of these purposes, at various times. And in some cases, a single attack (or attacker) can have multiple purposes at the same time.

So it's no surprise that rarely is there a good parsing of the range of threats currently active. We're going to attempt one, although the descriptions can only be snapshots, samplings of what is out there today. What may develop tomorrow is impossible to predict.

With those caveats, there are five general types of threats:

1. Targeted penetrations and data breaches
2. Viruses, worms, and bots
3. DDOS attacks
4. Spam, phishing, and spear phishing
5. Insider threats

Chapter 5 will look specifically at cyber threats as they pertain to issues of national security – espionage, war, and terror. In this chapter we are concerned primarily with "crime."

Of course, as a European Commission report says, "There is no agreed definition of cyber crime." Our concern in what follows regards "crimes unique to electronic networks, i.e. attacks against information systems, denial of service and hacking."[4]

TARGETED PENETRATIONS AND DATA BREACHES

The original type of cyber attack that caused the most concern in the early days was an attack focused on a big target or set of targets: hackers breaking into a corporate system, or into defence computers, usually to steal the data inside, but sometimes to steal money or services. This category of threat is still very much with us, and the incidents keep getting bigger and scarier.

In October 2008, Express Scripts, the biggest pharmacy-benefits management company in Canada and the U.S., was the target of extortion by hackers who threatened to disclose a major security breach. In the extortion letter, the hackers claimed to have gotten their hands on the personal details of millions of the company's customers and enclosed samples as proof. The seventy-five patient records in the samples included names, addresses, Social Security numbers, dates of birth, and prescription information – more than enough for identity-theft attacks on the individuals. The company offered a one-million-dollar (U.S.) reward for information leading to the arrest and conviction of the perpetrators.[5]

Interestingly, though at the time of this writing the perpetrators have not yet been caught, one may gather from their letter that they were not experienced cyber criminals. Hard-core criminals probably wouldn't have bothered to blackmail the company; they would be familiar with the underground data-trading markets, where the stolen data could be sold easily, and with less risk.[6]

The 2006–2008 attacks on the Princeton, N.J., payment processor Heartland Payment Systems compromised over 130 million credit- and debit-card accounts,[7] making it the largest data breach of its type ever reported. Heartland, which processes payments for more than 250,000 retail and dining businesses, most of them small, began receiving fraudulent activity reports late in 2008 from MasterCard and Visa on cards that had been used at merchants in the Heartland system. It wasn't until January 2009 that investigators uncovered a piece of malicious software planted on Heartland's network, which recorded data as it was being sent for processing. The stolen data included names, card numbers, and expiration dates – all of the information encoded in the magnetic strips on the backs of the cards. The theft had been going on from late 2006 to early 2008, but it was another eight months after the discovery of the malware before the perpetrators were identified, in August 2009. (Interestingly, the chief hacker had once worked with federal investigators to identify former conspirators in the cyber underworld. There were also two unnamed Russian hackers in the indictment.)[8]

The Heartland disclosure capped a year of similar breaches reported at other major U.S. card processors, including RBS Worldpay and Hannaford Brothers Co. And even before these attacks were disclosed, in early 2007, TJX Companies Inc., the parent of retailers Marshalls and T.J. Maxx, reported it had experienced a number of breaches over a three-year period. The data for ninety-four million customer accounts had fallen into the hands of cyber criminals through these breaches. According to court documents, Visa alone incurred fraud losses of between sixty-eight and eighty-three million dollars. Of the eleven people eventually charged in U.S. courts, only three were U.S. citizens; the others were from Eastern Europe and China.

What may be most worrying about the TJX case is the company's subsequent record. More than eighteen months after the breaches, TJX fired an employee after he left posts in an online forum that made disturbing claims about security practices at the store where he worked (such as that he could log onto the company's servers using blank passwords).[9] And Canada's privacy commissioner criticized the company for collecting too much data and using inadequate means of protecting it.

Also in 2007, Monster.com (after waiting five days to tell its users) reported a security breach that resulted in the theft of confidential information from some 1.3 million job seekers.[10] Hackers broke into the online recruitment site's password-protected resumé library using credentials that Monster Worldwide said were stolen from its clients. They launched the attack using two servers at a Web-hosting company in Ukraine and a group of personal computers that the hackers controlled after infecting them with a malicious software program known as Infostealer.Monstres.

While the main motive for targeted intrusion is profit, nation-states have a strong interest as well, for espionage and intelligence. Regardless of the motive, however, this type of attack usually requires some patience and skill. Big, important systems tend to be heavily protected. One ex-hacker told me how he liked to proceed:

> You've got to realize that almost all software is just a modification of some previous software. So the first thing I do is try to find out everything I can about the system that I want to break into – its hardware, software, what they're using it for, who uses the system – everything. Once I have an idea of what the software is, and when it was installed, I have a pretty good notion of what the most likely vulnerabilities are going to be. You see, if you do this long enough, you can identify individually which programmers wrote the code, and what types of errors typically show up in their work. And then I start to poke around the edges of the system. Sure, there are generic lists of the top vulnerabilities like the one that SANS [a major non-profit security organization] puts out, but to be really sophisticated I want to know the unique weaknesses in the system I'm attacking. And generally if you know your stuff that's not too hard to figure out. If I can, I'll try to social-engineer my way into the organization to learn even more; it's amazing what people will tell you over the phone if you've got a halfway plausible reason for asking.[11]

You may begin to see why expert hackers can often go on to second careers as consultants in the cyber-security industry. Although highly tailored attacks against single systems have not gone away, whole other genres of threats have grown up.

VIRUSES, WORMS, AND BOTS

Viruses and worms are programs that can replicate themselves, travelling from one computer to another and "infecting" each by settling in to conduct unwanted operations. Usually the programs travel over the Internet and/or private networks, although many early viruses in the 1980s propagated among personal computers by riding on floppy disks.

There are technical differences between viruses and worms, but unless you are a techie they don't really matter. A worm or virus has two parts – one determines how and how quickly it spreads; the second contains the "payload." Early worms and viruses were designed to spread quickly, without much of a payload. The problems they caused were due mainly to their lemming-like proliferation; they could overwhelm computers and networks literally by eating up the systems' capacity.

The first worm of any consequence was written in 1988 by Robert Tappan Morris, then a Cornell University graduate student, who said he wanted to launch a program that would harmlessly travel around the Internet (at that point just recently opened to use by the public). Morris claimed his worm was merely an exploratory device, meant to find out how many computers were connected. If that's true, the research project backfired: once implanted on any computer, the "Morris Worm" began to replicate out of control. It knocked out about 10 per cent of the sixty thousand computers then attached to the Internet. The experiment did have a useful outcome, prompting the U.S. Air Force to establish the first Computer Emergency Response Team (this was the CERT at Carnegie Mellon). Robert Morris was fined and sentenced to perform community service; he is now a professor at MIT.[12]

For years, most worms and viruses seemed to be designed either for prank-playing or for outright cyber-vandalism. They corrupted or deleted files stored on computers; they poisoned application programs to make them run incorrectly. That was damage enough, but in the late 1990s a more potent use made its appearance. Some hackers began putting a new kind of program module into the payload. This was the bot, short for robot (the term is also used for a computer infected by one). Once delivered, a bot could do more than just swing into action automatically.

A bot could be communicated with over the Internet – commanded to do certain things at certain times, reprogrammed to do somewhat different things at other times, and so forth. Better yet (from the hackers' point of view), viruses and worms could now sow *networks* of bots – botnets – across many computers. All of the bots in the botnet could then respond, in concert, to the instructions of a "botmaster," which could be an actual human or, more likely, a command program on a server controlled by the human. The possibilities fanned out from there.

Not all bots and botnets are malicious. In fact, the largest botnets extant today are believed to be those used for distributed scientific computing. PC users worldwide volunteer to have bots implanted, which allow research scientists to parcel out very complex computing tasks to their machines: the tasks are run with processing capacity that the PCs aren't using at a given time. Perhaps the best known scientific botnet is the SETI@home network, SETI being the Search for ExtraTerrestrial Intelligence. As of 2009, more than 2.2 million computers worldwide were helping to analyze radio waves from deep space picked up by a radio telescope. The idea is to find patterns that might indicate the waves were consciously generated.[13] While SETI@home continues to sift for these, other science botnets are being used to solve biomedical or pure-math problems.

Malicious botnets, unfortunately, are finding wide use as well. While many are used to send spam and for DDOS attacks, others are made up of spybots that log your keystrokes or spy in other ways, to steal data. And some bots plant things on your computer such as Trojan horses, backdoors, and rootkits – all of which, as their names suggest, can "open the doors" to allow future intrusions. The permutations are endless, for while it is rare to see a bad botnet as big as the scientific ones, there are vastly more of them. Some experts think that the fifty-fifty mark has already been passed – which would mean better-than-even odds that your computer is part of a bad botnet – and some think that nearly all home PCs (as distinct from office PCs) now harbour bad bots.

Bad bots are increasingly ingenious. Some are nearly impossible to find, let alone remove, and some fight back. Security researchers trying to monitor bad botnets have reported being lashed out at, their computers stung by ad hoc DDOS attacks or other kinds of defensive barrages.

"Malware," short for malicious software, refers to worms and viruses as well as the bots and other payloads they can deliver. Malware can arrive on your computer in any number of ways – from clicking on the wrong Web site, to installing corrupted software, to. being the victim of a specialized attack against your individual machine.

Botnets are often named for the worms or viruses that created them, and a list of those in operation as of early 2009 comprised a gruesomely colourful roster of names. There was the Storm botnet, created by the Storm Worm and widely considered one of the most ingenious spam botnets; Srizbi, once considered the most massive spam botnet with an estimated 450,000 infected computers; Bobax, a botnet that once rivalled Srizbi in size and longevity, if not also in sophistication; Rustock, a sophisticated botnet using rootkit techniques to hide; Pushdo (a.k.a. Cutwai); Xarvester, noted for sending lots of junk e-mail for weight loss drugs, stock investment scams, and debt settlement offers; and Donbot. There is also the Conficker (a.k.a. Downadup) worm, which in 2008–2009 rapidly infected millions of computers worldwide, and was thought to be building perhaps the largest botnet of any kind thus far.

Botnets often are divvied up and rented out to many spammers, who send a variety of spam for many purposes, including solicitations for pharmaceuticals, replica watches, and online casinos, plus phishing scams and malicious software. Some botmasters operate multiple variations at once.

Jonathan Kenneth Schiefer of Los Angeles, a.k.a. Acidstorm, is one perpetrator whose true identity is known publicly because he was convicted in a U.S. federal court in 2009. He headed a criminal enterprise that infected some 250,000 PCs worldwide. The victims' machines had spyware put on them that sniffed out passwords for their online banking accounts. That information was then used to make fraudulent purchases and withdrawals from the accounts. Adding insult to injury, many victims' machines were also loaded with pop-up adware. The ads were for legitimate businesses – they were placed by a Dutch advertising agency, Simpel Internet, which showed it did not know Schiefer was using such means to put its ads in front of customers' eyes. Schiefer collected nineteen thousand dollars in commissions from Simpel, which the court ordered him to repay.

While building his Acidstorm botnet, Schiefer held a day job at a legitimate American firm, 3G Communications, which also didn't know about his criminal activity: Schiefer worked in information security at 3G. Botmasters and virus-spreaders like to diversify their revenue streams, just as any business manager does, except that they're happy to create a mix of revenue streams from both sides of the legality fence.

For you, the Internet user, there are two disheartening notes. One is that these criminals will try to take your money any which way they can. This fact puts a burden of constant watchfulness on you, because you are likely to be taken in at any turn – whether it's in the course of a legitimate real-world business transaction that pulls you into the sphere of deceit, or in the course of a click-on-the-link in cyberspace that downloads a virus, with a bot, onto your hard drive.

The second disheartening note is that the protection you are buying may not provide quite the protection you think. Even if you buy legitimate anti-virus software – not one of the rogue packages that actually infect your computer – there are experts who say the genuine brand-name products are close to worthless. They might not say so for attribution, naturally, since many of them consult to the firms that make the brand-name products. But listen while my anonymous source explains why he thinks they're worthless.

He starts by noting that most anti-virus programs rely on detecting the digital "signatures" of known viruses. The signature includes the encryption key that the virus writer uses to disguise his malware. The encryption key keeps changing – in fact, most virus writers use very simple keys, instead of the super-hard-to-crack kind, so they can change them just by writing a few lines of code.

And that's fine with the virus writer, says my expert source, because it will still take the anti-virus folks around ten days to catch up – to detect and catalogue the new signature, and to tune the blocking software and retest it to be sure the update won't cause problems for the user. More days may pass before many users actually install the update. This gives the criminal plenty of time to wreak havoc – to pump out the altered virus, to get it onto people's computers and actually reap returns. Then the whole cycle begins again: change the virus, make hay while the anti-virus folks respond.

My source concludes: "This situation serves everyone's interest except for the user. The virus people can keep up their botnets just by taking a few minutes every so often to change the encryption key, while the anti-virus people can brag to their customers about how many updates they're providing."[14]

DDOS: A TOOL FOR EXTORTION AND CYBER WAR

Distributed denial-of-service attacks are simple, very painful to the organization targeted, and hard to stop. Consequently, they are the perfect instruments to extort money – the extorter is unknown and hard to trace, yet can credibly promise to (at least electronically) break both of your legs if you don't pay up. No one has a reason to make these disgraceful incidents public. Hence it should be no surprise that the CERT data report no DDOS attacks in many month-long periods – while a major consultant can say that "every week there are at least a dozen major DDOS attacks underway."[15] For some of the same reasons, DDOS attacks are a favourite in emergent cyber wars as well.

One expert describes a DDOS attack as the equivalent of someone who doesn't like you ordering thousands of pizzas to be delivered to your house.[16] Although no long-term damage is done, you are totally preoccupied for the evening with wrangling pizzas, instead of whatever else you had planned. In the Internet world, DDOS attacks are the result of thousands of zombie computers all sending messages to a single address; the flood essentially shuts down the target address, severing connectivity to the Internet.

There are no good data on the number or consequences of DDOS attacks, only anecdotes, but they suggest that DDOS extortions are common and successful. Over time the size of the attacks has increased, both in terms of how many zombie computers are employed in launching an attack and in the quantity of flooding packets (parcels of digital data). The largest known DDOS attack flood (measured in gigabits per second) has grown from 0.4 in 2001 to over 40 in 2007.[17]

There are several ways these attacks unfold. In some cases, businesses receive a threatening e-mail or phone call stating if they do not meet certain demands they will be victimized. Or, the DDOS attack begins, and then the business is contacted. The perpetrator sometimes stops an attack after ten minutes or so and contacts the company to say that if it doesn't wire money to a specific account, the barrage will resume. The demands can be one hundred thousand dollars or more, but often criminals ask for smaller amounts.

"Every online gambling site is paying extortion," said Alan Paller, research director of the SANS Institute, a well-respected independent security group, several years ago. "Hackers use DDoS (distributed denial-of-service) attacks, using botnets to do it. Then they say, 'Pay us US$40,000, or we'll do it again.'"[18] DDOS attacks are also a tool in the evolving framework of cyber war. Shutting down some of a country's key links to the Internet is a bloodless way of harming or putting pressure on the country, and Internet-based DDOS attacks are very difficult to attribute to a particular source. (Chapter 5 will explore in detail the troubling issues of war in cyberspace.)

SPAM, PHISHING, AND SPEAR PHISHING ~ THE ECONOMICS OF NO~COST MARKETING

Spam is unsolicited e-mail sent in bulk. It's like junk mail, only the economics are far more attractive. Spam is not free to the sender, but it doesn't have to be printed or need postage and thus is much more cost effective. For junk mail to be profitable, typically 1 per cent or more of the recipients have to respond and generate revenue. For spam, the required response rate is a tiny fraction of that. Furthermore, unlike regular junk mail, spam can generate an additional payoff as a vehicle for spreading malware. In the third quarter of 2008, almost one in every four hundred e-mail messages contained a dangerous attachment, designed to infect the recipient's computer.[19] This is how the ecosystem of cyber crime works.

So, at a minimum, spam clogs up e-mail accounts, although most people and organizations now use spam-blocking programs. Some still gets through, though, and enough users answer the spam for it to remain highly lucrative. The amount of spam sent out is staggering; SpamCop, an organization that tracks spam traffic, counted about a billion unique spam messages (each sent to many recipients) in the twelve months ending March 2008. That is equivalent to more than thirty spams per second, and SpamCop has recorded peaks of sixty-plus per second.[20]

Earlier we mentioned the dismal failure of the U.S. CAN-SPAM Act that was supposed to curb spam. In Canada, the government tabled anti-spam legislation in early 2009. The proposed legislation would amend Canada's Personal Information Protection and Electronic Documents Act (PIPEDA), which covers online privacy in detail and contains many provisions relevant to e-mail marketing. In the EU, the Privacy and Electronic Communications Directive requires member states to prohibit the sending of unsolicited commercial communications by e-mail, fax, or other electronic messaging systems.

Early on, spammers discovered that if they sent large quantities of spam directly from their own ISP accounts, recipients would complain and ISPs would shut their accounts down. Thus, one of the basic techniques is to send spam from other people's computers and network connections. By doing this, spammers protect themselves in several ways: they hide their tracks, get others' systems to do most of the work of delivering messages, and direct the efforts of investigators toward systems other than their own.

Increasing broadband usage has given rise to a great number of computers that are online as long as they are turned on, and whose owners do not always take steps to protect them from malware. A botnet consisting of just several hundred zombies can effortlessly churn out millions of sends per day. In January 2008, an estimated 8 per cent of all spam was sent by the Storm botnet created by the Storm Worm.[21]

While spam is unsolicited bulk e-mail, phishing attacks are e-mails with enough personal information to make them appear more credible to the recipient. Generally, they aim to get the recipient to reveal personal data or to go to a corrupted Web site that might download malware onto the user's computer. Spear phishing is an even more targeted effort to personalize e-mails to specific individuals.

In one phishing attack in Sweden, criminals sent e-mails purporting to be from Visa. The e-mails directed cardholders to a Web site where they were asked to sign up for the "Verified by Visa" service and to input their personal and security details. As Visa Europe noted in a follow-up message to its customers, "Neither Visa, a bank or a credit card company will ever ask its customers by e-mail for their personal or security details. If a cardholder suspects that they have been approached in such a phishing scam or that they have given their details to an unauthorised person they should contact their card issuing bank immediately."[22] But like spam, phishing and spear phishing are numbers games: only a few people have to respond to make the effort worthwhile. An estimated thirty to forty thousand phishing-related Web sites go up every month, so even if the click-through rate is low, clearly there are plenty of victims to be gulled.[23]

Creating spear phishing messages requires some homework on the part of the bad guys. It was actually by detecting spear phishing attacks that the Monster.com data breach described earlier was identified. Symantec (a major security firm) found spear phishing messages, pretending to be sent via Monster.com from job recruiters, asking recipients to provide personal financial data, including bank account numbers. The messages also asked users to click on links that could infect their PCs. The attackers' ultimate goal in taking the data from Monster.com was to gain enough personal information to lower the guards of the target victims. "It gives these spam e-mails just a little bit of credibility," a Symantec executive noted. "These guys were trying to get financial information from people."[24]

Combining attack techniques is common in the cyber-threat ecosystem. In 2008, a group of Russian criminals known as the Rock Phish gang launched what one security researcher called a "double the trouble" attack. It not only enticed victims into giving up personal information in a phishing e-mail but also deposited a Trojan horse onto his or her PC at the same time.[25]

The Rock Phish gang is the "most competent phishing gang out there – it's very effective – and has taken phishing to the next level," Marc Gaffan, a marketing director for the security solutions firm RSA, told SCMagazineUS.com. The Rock Phish gang is unlike many because it is a closed gang operating in Russia, Gaffan said. Most groups of cyber criminals participate in the broad underground economy where credit cards are bought and sold openly. Rock Phish's "biggest fame is its ability to scale and execute thousands of phishing attacks with as little infrastructure as possible, thus making it as hard as possible to shut [them] down," Gaffan said.[26]

INSIDER THREATS

Besides outsiders attacking our systems and networks, breaking through the perimeter defences we have established, we must also worry about the "insider threat": people with legitimate access who behave in ways that put our data, our systems, and even our organizations' viability at risk. For the home user, insider threats are probably not much of a concern (though you could consider your teenager – or a hostile spouse – examining your files as an insider threat, which indeed it is). But for both private and government organizations, the insider threat shows every indication of being a major problem.

Since 2004 the annual Computer Security Institute survey has ranked insider incidents as either the first or second most commonly reported type of attack (the other being virus attacks). In 2007 and 2008, about one in four respondents said that over 40 per cent of their total financial losses from cyber attack were due to insider activities.[27] The damage is often difficult to quantify, because it can extend far beyond the actual cost of the items stolen or corrupted, especially in cases involving national security. The damage done to the U.S. by one notorious insider, FBI agent Robert Hanssen, was said to be incalculable.[28] For more than twenty years of his FBI career, from

1979 to 2001, Hanssen acted as a Soviet and then Russian spy. He sold invaluable information about U.S. and NATO espionage activities, often gathering the information by rifling through files in computer systems to which he could gain access.

Insider threats may be the most difficult of cyber attacks to discuss. The very definition of *insider* varies – is the person walking by when you've left your computer on and unattended an insider, or just a creep who is taking advantage of your carelessness? Moreover, few, for obvious reasons, like to talk about insider threats in their own organizations. Thus, while every aspect of cyber security suffers from a lack of good data, nowhere is this more evident than with insider threats.[29]

I have been privileged to perform one of the more systematic studies, a study of all cyber-insider cases prosecuted in the U.S. federal courts from 1995 to 2008. These were commercial, not national, security cases, and I was looking mainly for patterns in the types of convictions it was possible to obtain.[30]

I learned first of all that not many insider cases make it to court. For a span of thirteen years in one of the world's largest and most computer-intensive societies, I found a total of 135 cases. Insiders' motives can range from financial gain to revenge, and there are many methods of carrying out the attacks. Attacks can happen in all kinds of firms, and a firm's "insiders" can go on being threats even after they become outsiders.

In one revenge case, the victim was Art Assets LLC, a New York City firm that specializes in procuring fine art for corporate clients. A former computer contractor for Art Assets deleted and modified files and databases in the firm's system, causing financial loss in excess of ten thousand dollars (and, it would seem, considerable disruption). The contractor had been the administrator of user accounts at Art Assets and thus had access to all user names and passwords. During a meeting with Art Assets personnel to try to resolve a billing dispute, one of the owners of the firm criticized the contractor's technical abilities, telling him, in substance, "that he had done a poor job installing the Art Assets network." According to legal filings, the contractor left the meeting "very upset," and then, on the evening following, logged into the Art Assets network and proceeded to do the damage mentioned. He pled guilty and was sentenced to twelve months' probation.[31]

In other cases, insiders steal information from their employers for economic espionage or to create their own businesses. Metaldyne, an automotive parts manufacturer in Michigan, had a proprietary process for fabricating powdered metal into large, heavy-duty parts such as engine connecting rods. Three former employees were charged with theft of this process. According to the charges, two of them – the vice-president for sales and a metallurgist – left Metaldyne and began negotiating with potential competitors in China, while the third, a senior engineer and the vice-president's husband, remained at Metaldyne where he had access to confidential computer files. The indictment said the engineer made CDs of the files for use by copycat producers, while the former vice-president, Anne Lockwood, started a new company, through which all three were to receive commissions based on expected sales by Chinese businesses. The case was still pending at the time of this writing.[32]

Sometimes insiders act for direct financial gain. Philip Cummings worked as a help-desk employee at a New York–area specialized software provider, whose clients included banks and other financial institutions. The nature of its business gave the company access to consumer credit reports from the major commercial credit–reporting agencies. Cummings's position enabled him to download any consumer credit reports he wanted. After being approached by Nigerian nationals, he began selling reports to their identity-theft ring – and was able to go on doing so for two years after leaving his job. Upon conviction, Cummings was sentenced to fourteen years in prison and required to pay three hundred thousand dollars in restitution.[33]

Most experts believe that insider threats are more common and serious now than a decade ago. Nearly every employee of every organization has a computer. Universities provide their alumni with e-mail accounts, making them "insiders" even though they're no longer students. The amount and type of information on computers is vast and expanding, yet most organizations don't have a good sense of where all the information is, what is most valuable, and who should and should not have access to it.

There are no simple solutions to insider threats. Organizations come in all shapes and sizes, and so do their computer systems. What might be done to a given system by someone starting with limited access is, itself, limited only by the bounds of opportunity and imagination. And preventive measures can be hard to enforce. Workplaces have their own cultures and ways of working, which are almost never the official ways spelled out in the organization chart. Well-meaning insiders who are just trying to work around the edges to get their jobs done may resent, and actually subvert, measures to control insider abuse. In one instance I know of, a hospital installed motion detectors next to workstations. The purpose was to ensure that when a nurse left the station, he or she would automatically be logged off the computer system, thus preventing possible misuse by others. But hospital staff members found this logging back in so irksome that they placed paper cups over the motion detectors. Security staff only noticed when they saw an unexpectedly large drop in system log-offs and actually went out into the workplace to investigate.

WHAT'S NEXT?

The modes of cyber attack keep evolving, fuelled by an ever-changing mix of new technologies and new psychologies. In 2008 and 2009, one of the fastest growing modes of attack revolved around scareware. Scareware is brilliantly self-referential, feeding off people's growing fears of cyber attack. Spam e-mails went out and fake Web sites went up, all warning of dangerous new forms of malware floating around, and all selling bogus solutions that were, themselves, dangerous new forms of malware. For instance, rogue software packages such as Antivirus2009 were, in fact, built to *deliver* the latest viruses. Thousands of new scareware tricks and tools were counted, many of them purportedly coming from a mythical front company called Pandora Software – a sly allusion to classical mythology that should have been duly noted by any adult member of a Western civilization.

Sometimes new attack tools appear, drop out of sight for a while, and then resurface in another form. Ransomware is one such tool. Many people know that it's smart to encrypt the files on your hard drive so no one else can read them. In 2006, there came malware that would do the job for you, unasked, so you could not read or use your own files. The hackers would then offer to send you the decryption key, for a price. The trick soon faded from the scene, a sign that it wasn't paying off so well, at least not as a stand-alone. But ransomware made a comeback as a bundled feature in some of the bogus anti-virus software we've just talked about.

Such anecdotes may be jaw-dropping but they are mere details and footnotes in the long arc of the story. And the moral of the long arc is a short message: new security technologies alone cannot contain this burgeoning catastrophe. New policies must be tried so that we can begin to alter the playing field. Still, many people balk at policy solutions – or at the notion that cyber security is even that much of a "problem," after all.

CHAPTER 4

THE COSTS AND IMPACTS OF CYBER CRIME

We have looked at the cyber underworld and seen the tricks they throw at us. But what exactly is "the problem"? That is, how exactly does cyber crime affect you and me; how could it?

The apparent answer is that either you are hit or you are not. When and if any one of us is the victim of cyber attack, we suffer damages. Otherwise, we carry on quite well. Most people are on the Internet constantly. It may be the first place they go when they wake in the morning to read the "paper" and tackle some e-mails. At work, the business of the world gets done over the Internet. Someday there could be a real cyber catastrophe, but it hasn't happened yet, and some of us wonder if it ever will.

The apparent answer is not the right answer, for three reasons.

First, the likelihood of getting hit seems to be increasing.[1] To illustrate: Recently I was in Erie, Pennsylvania, a quiet, out-of-the-way town of the kind that seems remote from big-city hassles. I bought the newspaper, the *Erie Times-News*. On the front page was a story about a local college confirming that 10,868 Social Security numbers were stolen in a computer breach.[2]

Second, losses from cyber crime are growing so high as to be an economic burden on all nations, a burden that you share even if you are not a direct victim.

Third, we all absorb some of the "overhead" costs of dealing with cyber crime – the time and money we spend, and the frustrations we experience, in trying to keep our systems secure.

Neither the losses nor the overhead can be measured with much precision. Data collection is spotty and inconsistent, to put it kindly. It's also hard to assign a dollar cost to items like the pain and suffering of identity theft, or the general loss of trust that comes with living in an insecure cyberworld. But the rough estimates we will use here can show us the ballpark we are in, and it is clearly a ballpark where the quality of the game is being significantly degraded.

TOTING UP THE LOSSES

Lesson one: any figures you see on losses from cyber crime are probably too low. Here's a story.

Every year at Carnegie Mellon I taught a graduate seminar on cyber-security policy. The class was composed of fifteen to twenty students, intelligent, motivated men and women. I asked them to choose a particular security breach, at a particular firm or organization, for which a cost estimate had been published . . . and then to critique the methodology of the estimate. One student's approach was creative, to say the least. To quote from his paper:

> Backing myself up with the acquired skills from Kevin Mitnick's *The Art of Deception*,[3] I impersonated a representative from a fake law firm. The idea was to act as if my firm was pursuing claims against a major Internet Service Provider for all of its clients' losses, mainly due to a lack of reacting in time to the released patches one month before the Code Red worm hit. Company X, given that its main Internet access was funnelled through the same Internet Service Provider and that its losses were made public, was chosen as one of a few others that would be presented in the preliminary reports by my "law firm." A forged identity, combined with a well-crafted, buzzword-rich and highly confusing e-mail, was greeted by

open arms. [The company representative] was more proactive than I hoped he would be. It was funny how the slightest mention of compensation changed the feedback tone.

The prospect of recovering losses from the Code Red attack, by legal action, led Company X to give my student a detailed explanation of how it had gone about fixing the damage and calculating the costs. The student continues:

> After summing the numbers, a surprising value [one third greater than that publicly announced] popped up. When questioning [the company representative] about the difference, he replied by [saying,] " . . . We had to underestimate the losses in the press release . . . to avoid losing our customer base . . ."[4]

Since much of the data that we do have is self-reported – either through public disclosure of incidents (though many are not disclosed!) or voluntary responses to surveys – this story is worth keeping in mind.

Also, calculating "losses" from cyber crime is not always a simple affair. In some attacks, a large sum of money is stolen directly: for example, during 2009, criminal gangs thought to be based in Eastern Europe perfected a method of tapping the online bank accounts of small to mid-sized businesses in the U.S. Many firms had their accounts quickly drained of tens to hundreds of thousands of dollars; one plumbing supply house lost $1.2 million.[5] But in other cases, intellectual property (such as a product design or valuable business data) is stolen, for which the impact of the loss has to be estimated. And when data such as customers' credit-card numbers are stolen – or when phishing attacks glean the same kind of data from unwitting individuals – the losses are highly dispersed, because stolen or forged identification may then be used to make fraudulent purchases all over the map.

Finally, losses must include the cost of recovering from attacks. Businesses have to clean out and restore computer systems that have been breached, and *Consumer Reports* has estimated that over one million U.S. households each year must actually replace home PCs after they've been infected with malware that cannot be rooted out.[6]

Over the last few years, various attempts have been made to sum up the overall losses for a nation or group of nations. A couple of the more notable calculations:

- In 2004, the London-based security firm mi2g estimated that cyber crime was costing the OECD countries about US$500 billion per year.[7]

- In 2007, the U.S. Government Accountability Office (GAO) issued a report that listed FBI estimates on business losses in the U.S., along with estimates of losses by individual consumers.[8] The combined total, for the U.S. alone, was $117 billion. The lead author of the GAO report promptly warned that actual losses were probably much higher. Not only are many losses under-reported or unreported, he noted, but many cyber crimes are *undetected.*[9]

Then in 2009, at the World Economic Forum in Davos, Switzerland, came the global estimate mentioned in Chapter 1, from the security firm McAfee. To quote the CNET news report:

> Data theft and breaches from cybercrime may have cost businesses as much as $1 trillion globally in lost intellectual property and expenditures for repairing the damage last year, according to a new study from McAfee.
>
> McAfee made the projection based on responses to a survey of more than 800 chief information officers in the U.S., United Kingdom, Germany, Japan, China, India, Brazil, and Dubai.[10]

Note that this estimate includes only business losses of certain kinds; it is a huge figure nonetheless.

Most of us have trouble grasping the real import of numbers in the billions and trillions, so let's try to put these numbers into perspective. To start with some simple math: According to the

CIA World Factbook, global gross domestic product – the total economic output of the world – was about $62 trillion in 2008. One trillion in losses to cyber crime would be 1.6 per cent of GDP.

Similarly, the 2004 mi2g estimate for losses in the OECD countries comes to 1.5 per cent of GDP for the OECD in that year. The GAO estimate computes to 0.9 per cent of U.S. GDP, but since the report author admitted the number was low, let us assume that 1.5 per cent of GDP is closer to a fair estimate, and ask this: How would you feel if your country imposed a new flat tax of 1.5 per cent on all earnings? That's roughly what we are all paying now to cyber criminals, and getting no public services in return.

Or here is another way to look at it. I've taken the 1.5 per cent of GDP number for cyber crime, and compared it to estimates for some other types of major "costs" to society over the past decade or so: the cost of the Y2K computer fix, the cost of *all* crime, the cost of a large-scale electrical outage, and the costs of major natural disasters such as the most severe earthquakes, storms, and floods. (These other numbers are all for the U.S. only, but should be fairly typical for a developed nation.)[11]

TYPE OF PROBLEM	ESTIMATED RELATIVE ECONOMIC IMPACT (as a % of GDP)
Cyber crime	1.5
Y2K computer fix	1.1
All crime	6.5
Major electric blackout	0.1
Major natural disasters	0.6—1.15 (or more)

If the figures here are at least roughly accurate, as I believe they are, they provide some telling comparisons. The Y2K fix consumed so much time and expense that managers everywhere were glad to know it would only be a once-in-a-lifetime ordeal – and yet cyber crime is apparently costing our economies more than Y2K did, each and every year. It has become a significant contributor to the burden imposed by crime of all kinds. And even if our estimate for cyber crime is high, it is clearly in the same league as "major natural disasters." *Every year, for every nation, the economic cost of cyber crime is roughly equivalent to that of a devastating earthquake, storm, or flood in a large urban area.*

THE COSTS (AND VEXATIONS) OF "OVERHEAD"

But there is more to the picture than actual losses, as another story illustrates:

A senior colleague of mine, at a nearby research institution, spent most of January and February 2009 in Kafkaesque frustration. In early January he was informed by "some security group that just monitors wireless usage" that he had exceeded his bandwidth usage allowance. He and his departmental computer security person couldn't fathom how this was possible. They began to investigate – fruitlessly, as it turns out – whether his computer had been hacked. My friend had to swap all his files (including applications) onto a separate hard drive, sweep clean his computer's hard drive, and then reinstall everything – in the process, accidentally losing all of his e-mail bookmarks. He used a wireless connection to reload his hard drive, thereby exceeding his bandwidth quota again. He then had his wireless access denied for forty-five days. He could have fought the denial, but as he told me: "I just got tired with fighting with the 'wireless thought police.' The worst thing was that this anonymous Big Brother type group was monumentally uninterested in helping to find the reason for the initial overage. I was told that it was my responsibility to monitor my wireless usage, but the site I was directed to was hopelessly useless in helping me."[12]

With cyber crime, you don't need to have your money or data stolen in order to be a victim. My friend was most likely the victim of a surreptitious hack – someone planting a bot on his computer, to send and receive illicit messages (thus the bandwidth overuse) – combined with bureaucratic bungling by the very group charged with protecting his organization against such misuse. What he experienced was the *cost of coping* with cyber crime: the "overhead," if you will, that comes with trying to prevent it or defend against it.

This overhead not only imposes practical difficulties but also takes a psychic toll. And that toll can be significant even if we are able to avoid horror stories like my friend's.

We invest enormous sums in security measures, we take precautions that alter and hamper our behaviour.

Think of the ordeals we go through just with our home computers. Every unfamiliar e-mail or link becomes a hold-your-breath adventure: is this real or is it bogus? We worry constantly when children or teens are on the Internet. We load our machines with anti-virus software that makes our programs run slowly and erratically; we use Javascript blockers that make Web sites not work and spam filters that screen out e-mail we need to see. And still we worry – do we have the latest patches and updates? – and still we get stung. (The *Consumer Reports* "State of the Net" survey for 2009 found one in seven households reporting "serious problems" with viruses, and one in twelve having serious problems with spyware.)

These home-PC hassles are nothing compared to those endured by firms and organizations with large systems to maintain. Here the constant flow of security alerts, patches, and updates from IT vendors has become so onerous that it is a standing topic of dark humour on security-industry Web sites. One site, with morbid glee, counts the fixes issued by Microsoft in a year. A typical report noted that the April 2009 Microsoft patch release was its largest batch of security updates so far for the year: "[Installing these patches] won't be easy for many security professionals, especially in larger enterprises."[13] Another, for a previous year, cheerily noted: "Oracle has released its announcements for April . . . 'This Critical Patch Update contains 37 security fixes across all products' . . . So, if you are running Oracle, it's that time of the month again!"

All this costs money, of course. At the same time that IT budgets in business firms and other types of organizations have been going down, crunched by recessionary times, security spending as a share of IT spending has been going up. (According to Forrester Research projections for North America and Europe, security was expected to

consume about 12.6 per cent of IT budgets, on average, in 2009 –
up from 11.7 per cent in 2008.)[14]

And to put that number into terms that may help make it more
real: median corporate IT spending *per user* was $7,284 per head in
2009, according to Computer Economics, Inc.[15] So 12.6 per cent
of that would be about $918 per year, per user – just for security.

Overall, it has been estimated that cyber security is now nearly an
eighty-billion-dollar per year industry worldwide.[16] But most such
figures only include money paid to (and earned by) outside vendors
of security products and services, like McAfee and our old friend
Mudge's consulting firm. They may not include what end-user firms
and organizations spend on their in-house security staffs – or what
basic IT firms like Microsoft, Cisco, and Apple spend in trying to
make their products more secure. In total it is probably safe to
guesstimate that global spending on cyber security is well over one
hundred billion dollars per year: another chunk of GDP spent. And
again, this is just the "overhead" – expenses for security measures, not
counting losses from attacks.

We can't say that all overhead costs represent a "loss" to society.
To begin with, what is a cost to one party may be a benefit to
another. Many people make a living from cyber security, and unlike
cyber criminals, theirs is literally an honest living. Also, security of
any kind is never free. Neither cyberspace nor the streets will ever
be perfectly safe, so we'll always have to spend a certain baseline
amount on cyber security, as we do on police departments and other
physical security measures.

The problem is one of costs and returns. Ideally, we would like
to spend moderate sums on security specialists and measures, getting
a high degree of security in return. Instead, we seem to be caught in
a pattern of increased spending and anxiety for diminishing returns.

No one in the general public objects much to the overhead costs
of cyber security, or even notices them, because they are largely hidden and dispersed. Most of them are factored into the prices we pay
for things or the taxes we pay. What we do notice (if only sublimi-
nally) is the insecurity that we are left with.

Cyber insecurity is a drag on our use and enjoyment of the cyber city. As we walk down the street we have to look over our shoulders, worry which neighbours are safe to talk to, and be careful about the neighbourhoods we visit. We pay a hidden tax, whether monetary or psychic, for insecurity. Some of us begin to wonder, *Will my neighbourhood be affected? Will the problem get worse? Is this really the city that I want to live in?*

THE 'KATRINA' PROBLEM VS. THE 'DETROIT' OR 'LAGOS' PROBLEM

Looking at mass-market movies and novels, one might think that the only kind of cyber event we really need to worry about is a cyber apocalypse. Some Hollywood films[17] portray cyber attack as the electronic equivalent of Hurricane Katrina – if an entire city isn't destroyed, then it isn't news. And such a thing could happen. The probability may be low but the consequences could be high, and thus there are experts in the military and elsewhere who put serious effort into thinking about it and trying to prepare against it.

There is, however, another kind of scenario to be considered. What if year after year we just face more of what we've seen in recent years – more crime, more identify theft, more promises of the next security solution? What if our cyber insecurity problems just keep creeping up on us? Cyber crime is not just a Katrina problem; it's a Detroit problem, or a Lagos problem.

When hurricane Katrina hit New Orleans it was a true catastrophe, a great city reduced to shambles by a single incident. But a city can also be reduced to shambles by chronic low-level incidents. Inner-city Detroit, unfortunately, has become the North American poster child for this phenomenon. A neighbourhood can be so constantly plagued by run-of-the-mill crime and misbehaviour that people begin avoiding it. The costs and struggles of living there, or doing business there, are simply too great.

Conversely, there is the prospect of a Lagos problem, to cite another city often unfortunately singled out as a poster child. Much like early industrial-age London (which we'll discuss in more detail in Chapter 8),

Lagos is experiencing runaway growth, with chaos and misery also growing and running out of control. And this trend, like the Detroit trend, is not sustainable – though it can appear to have an irresistible momentum, as seen in this historian's reflection on early London:

> If London was such a rank, overcrowded sewer in the first half of the nineteenth century, then why did so many people decide to move there? . . .The tremendous growth of London – like the parallel explosions of Manchester and Leeds – was a riddle that could not be explained by simply adding up decisions made by large numbers of individual humans. This was, ultimately, what perplexed and horrified so many onlookers at the time: the sense that the city had taken on a life of its own. It was a product of human choice, to be sure, but some new form of collective human choice where collective decisions were at odds with the needs and desires of its individual members. . . . That perplexity gave rise to an intuitive sense that the city itself was best understood as a creature with its own distinct form of volition, greater than the sum of its parts: a monster, a diseased body – or, most presciently, Wordsworth's "anthill on the plain." . . . The sense, then, of London as monstrous, cancerous presence focused not merely on the smell or the overcrowding; it also included the uncanny feeling that, somehow, humans themselves were not in control of the urbanization process . . . The great city, then, could not be understood as an artefact of human choice. It was much closer to a natural, organic process – less like a building that had been deliberately constructed and more like a garden erupting into full bloom with the arrival of spring – a mix of human planning and the natural developmental patterns that emerge with increasing energy supplies.[18]

The trend, of course, to runaway growth and corresponding chaos is neither irresistible nor beyond human control. London righted itself, and one hopes that Lagos will, too. But what of our cyber city? At present, with rampant growth accompanied by rampant insecurity, it appears to be on a London/Lagos trajectory. To the average user, conditions may seem far from intolerable as yet – but the trend lines are not good and raise a number of troubling questions.

If the costs and hassles associated with cyber insecurity keep rising (as they are likely to, because the threats keep escalating), at what point might they become too burdensome for some parties to bear? At what point do they begin to limit or alter what we can do on the Internet? Might they ever reach a "breaking point," and what is it that would break?

In the eyes of some experts, these are not just speculative questions. They are questions that have been demanding answers for the past several years.

BREAKING POINTS AND CREEPING FAILURE

Experts have begun to speak of chronic security problems not as a burden to be tolerated, but as a basic weakness we can no longer live with.

In 2006, DARPA issued a Request for Ideas on new approaches to "Assurable Global Networking." The bulletin matter-of-factly stated that "it is unthinkable that commercial networks of the future could be as fragile and vulnerable as those of today," and that "it is increasingly clear that current Internet technology is an inadequate foundation" for the future. At about the same time, a high-level presentation by the nonprofit SANS Institute flatly described the entire set of cyber-security policies in the U.S. as "A Security Strategy That Has Failed."[19]

US-CERT's *Quarterly Trends and Analysis Report* for the fourth quarter of 2008 refrained from such editorial comment, merely reporting the latest bad news on the ever-growing virulence of cyber attacks. Items included a surge in "zero-day exploits" – which attack vulnerabilities in systems as soon as, or before, they are known to exist, and a growth in "blended threats" that "combine several attack methods . . . to increase the level of destruction and reach."

Security professionals still speak in the terms of guarded confidence they have long used. They call security a "never-ending battle" in which their job is to "stay a step ahead of the dark side"; they talk about the technical progress they've made and new measures to come. But in recent years they have begun to sound a bit touchy about the progress part, sometimes even using the kind of rhetoric one typically hears from those on the losing side. An April 2007 article, reporting on a speech by Scott Charney, closed with this quote from that Microsoft security executive: " . . . The bad guys are creative and they're smart and they won't go away. Still, overall I'm very bullish. The advantages we get from deploying these [information] technologies are huge and they still outweigh the negatives."[20]

Why would anyone even feel a need to argue that the benefits of information technology outweigh the negatives? This is a line of argument generally used only when the negatives are serious indeed.

Early in this book we quoted the Internet entrepreneur Phil Becker, who commented on the inefficacy of most of our security efforts by saying, "Folks, this is what things look like when a failed paradigm meets its match." We might now expand on the point by saying, *This is what creeping failure looks like.*

For a variety of possible reasons, creeping failure – not the sudden catastrophic kind, but the chronic and pervasive and, well, creeping kind – seems to be emerging as a dominant failure mode of the twenty-first century, and cyber insecurity is certainly one of its poster children. (Climate change tops the list, of course, but there are others as well: The chronic and growing water shortages in many areas of the world. Crumbling public infrastructure, in the U.S. and Canada. The health care issue in the U.S.)

For the cyber city, a true security catastrophe may or may not lurk around some future bend in the road. What may be more likely, without serious changes in policy, is nothing so darkly glamorous: just an ongoing increase in the prices we all have to pay for our Internet use – monetarily, psychically, and in terms of opportunities and enjoyment foregone. And though it is hard to envision at present, there is even the risk of an eventual Detroit-like decline. Organizations and individuals could gradually circumscribe their Internet uses to what is tolerably secure; blue-sky uses that are talked about today could fail to materialize or be stunted. It is possible that we've been living through the Internet's Golden Age – and that unless we find better ways to address security problems, we may not be able to sustain it.

BUT WHAT ABOUT THE ODDS OF A CYBER APOCALYPSE (THE 'KATRINA' SCENARIO)?

A cyber apocalypse is conceivable. It could stem from a deliberate effort to disable or destroy major portions of the Internet. We've already seen these types of efforts on a small scale, and we've seen real-life instances of cyber attack used as an instrument of war.

It could also be a case of what Charles Perrow describes as "normal accidents."[21] As technology advances, we create ever more complex systems that increase the risk of catastrophic failures – for example, in nuclear power plants, chemical plants, or aircraft and air traffic control. Perrow outlines characteristics of these high-risk technologies which suggest that no matter how effective the safety devices are, there is a form of accidental failure that is inevitable. This inevitability has to do with the way failures can interact and how the system is tied together.[22] The nuclear incident at Three Mile Island was an example of how "normal accidents" can (and inevitably will) occur in complex systems, and such a scenario is distinctly possible with the Internet.

The third prospect is a combination of the first two causes – in which some deliberate attack will in turn lead to unanticipated but serious and cascading failures. But now we are talking about cyber attack as an instrument of war or terror, which is a subject that deserves full treatment in its own right.

CHAPTER 5

CYBER WAR AND CYBER TERRORISM

In May 2007, with political tensions between Russia and Estonia rising, Estonia – a highly "wired" nation – was subject to a series of DDOS attacks[1] that certainly stand as an early example of war in cyberspace. Estonian authorities said the data floods were set off by orders from Russia or by ethnic Russian sources.

The Russian government denied any involvement in the attacks, which came close to shutting down the country's digital infrastructure, clogging the Web sites of the president, the prime minister, Parliament, and other government agencies; staggering Estonia's biggest bank; and overwhelming the sites of daily newspapers. "It turned out to be a national security situation," Estonia's defence minister, Jaak Aaviksoo, said in an interview. "It can effectively be compared to when your ports are shut to the sea."[2]

Computer security experts from NATO, the European Union, the United States, and Israel converged on the city of Tallinn to offer help, and to learn what they could about cyber war in the digital age. NATO considered the incident a possible attack on a NATO member – which raised the previously academic but now real question of what constitutes appropriate response to a national security cyber attack: You don't threaten to send in troops, do you? Or move tanks close to the border and put planes in the sky? But if you don't do these things, then what do you do?

Another fundamental question is: How does the use (or potential use) of cyberspace affect our perception of what we consider national security risks? This question too is far from academic and the answers could have far-reaching consequences. The prospects of nuclear war have shaped much of the Western world's political, military, diplomatic, and social frameworks for the past sixty years. Furthermore, since 2001, the threat of terrorism has dramatically redefined the security and social concerns of both the U.S. and Canada, forcing them to catch up with European nations that already had experience with terrorist campaigns. Cyber threats have the potential for an equal impact, in terms of redefining what war, espionage, and terrorism are, and in shaping new security concerns. These concerns already are driving massive spending and new performance requirements. (In the U.S., just one measure – Presidential Directive 54, signed in early 2008 – could cost the country as much as thirty billion dollars over seven years as it expands cyber monitoring of all Federal agencies.)[3]

Whatever citizenship we hold, we all have a stake in ensuring that national security is maintained in the face of cyber threats. But understanding what cyber terrorism, cyber war, and cyber espionage might portend, and how best to protect national interests, is far from clear. With cyber crime, we have a rich, if imperfect, picture of how the threats are developing, but we have only a few instances of actual national security incidents to point to (at least in the public record).

Prediction is notoriously difficult, too. The venerable eleventh edition of the *Encyclopaedia Britannica,* in 1912, noted that future wars would probably be of limited duration and with limited casualties – two years later, World War I.[4] And prior to that war, the French were well aware of the prospect of German attack, but grew so locked into a single view of how the war would proceed (through frontal attacks along the common border) that they ignored overwhelming evidence of what would be the major thrust: a flanking attack through Belgium.[5]

We cannot afford to share the fate of those generals who set out to fight the last war, or the wrong war. With some humility, therefore, let us consider how cyberspace has and may alter important facets of national security: espionage, terrorism, and war.

CYBER ESPIONAGE

Cyberspace has reshaped the nature, if not the intent, of espionage; stealing secrets is easier, and the scope of secrets stolen greater, through cyber intrusions.

In March 2009, researchers at the University of Toronto uncovered a vast electronic spying operation that had infiltrated almost 1,300 computers across 103 countries in less than two years. The spying operation created a botnet, dubbed GhostNet, that focused on computers in embassies, foreign ministries, and other government offices, as well as on those in the offices of the Dalai Lama. It was the request of the Dalai Lama to investigate his own systems that led to the discovery of GhostNet.[6]

Three of the four control servers behind GhostNet were located in different provinces in China; the fourth was at a Web-hosting company in southern California. The targeted computers were infected in two ways: either a user clicked on a document attached to an e-mail, which let the hackers covertly install software deep in the target operating system, or a user clicked on a Web link in an e-mail message and so was taken directly to a "poisoned" Web site. The malware could even be used to turn on the camera and audio-recording functions of an infected computer, so that spies could see and hear what was taking place in the room. A Chinese-language "control panel" allowed the bad guys to manipulate the botnet.

While the Chinese government would appear to be the logical source of the espionage, no one has yet been able to conclude that it was involved. Through its New York consulate the Chinese government rejected the idea: "These are old stories and they are nonsense."[7]

Arguably, the first major incident of cyber espionage against the U.S. came to light in 1999. "Moonlight Maze" refers to a highly classified incident in which U.S. officials accidentally discovered a systematic probing of tens of thousands of sensitive files on computers in defence and research installations. Apparently the intrusions began in 1998 and had been going on for two years before they were discovered. The Defense Department traced the trail back to a mainframe computer in Russia, but the sponsor of the attack remains unknown. Russia denied any involvement.[8]

Since then cyber espionage has become more visible and commonplace. Said Dick Clarke, who has held several high posts in national security in the U.S., "What we've seen [from March 2008 to March 2009] . . . was the U.S. Government admitting publicly that both Russia and China [have] hacked their way into secret computer systems in the Pentagon, including the Secretary of Defense's own computers."[9] As Clarke explained, even though the Pentagon has its own secure internal Internet (the SIPRNET, Secure Internet Protocol Router Network) and its own lower-security network (NIPRNET, Non-Secure Internet Protocol Router Network),

> the people working in the Pentagon on the real unclassified Internet were downloading things and putting them on their thumb drives and then moving their thumb drives over to classified computers. Well, guess what? The Russians figured that out. And the Russians came up with a virus that looked for Pentagon Internet addresses, and then looked for computers that had thumb drives on them, and downloaded a virus onto those thumb drives, and the virus then walked across the room and got into the top secret network of the Pentagon . . . and what the Pentagon did, after the fact, was [go] around with cement and actually cemented up the USB connections on their computers so that people couldn't use thumb drives.[10]

Kafkaesque indeed.

A virus, identified in autumn 2006 but not reported publicly until December 2008, infected U.S. Congressional computers with malware designed to download documents and compromise e-mails – first at the Congressional Budget office, and subsequently at eight members' offices and seven committee offices, including Commerce, Transportation and Infrastructure, Homeland Security, and Ways and Means, as well as the Commission on China (which monitors human rights and laws in China) and the Foreign Affairs Committee (where the virus compromised twenty-five computers and one server).[11]

The ensuing confidential briefing did not say where the hacker was, nor did it attribute the attack to a particular group or country; such information is notoriously difficult to ascertain. However, according to some members of Congress whose machines were infected, the attack described in the briefing emanated from China and was probably designed to steal sensitive information from lawmakers' and committee offices.

A much earlier series of intrusions, dubbed Titan Rain, was probably the most significant cyber espionage incident until the GhostNet attacks. It remains notorious in Internet security circles for the inappropriate way in which it was handled. The first of the Titan Rain intrusions was a network break-in at Lockheed Martin, a builder of military aircraft, in September 2003. A strikingly similar attack hit Sandia National Laboratories – which perform defence-related research – several months later. The scope of the intrusions was notable. Methodical and voracious, the hackers wanted all the files they could find, and they got them by penetrating secure computer networks at military bases, defence contractors, and elsewhere. Targets ranged from the Redstone Arsenal in Alabama to NASA to the World Bank. In one case, the hackers stole flight-planning software from the U.S. Army. The hackers would commandeer a hidden section of a hard drive, zip up as many files as possible, and immediately transmit the data to way stations in South Korea, Hong Kong, or Taiwan, for relay to mainland China. They moved swiftly and silently, wiping their electronic fingerprints clean and leaving behind an almost undetectable beacon that would let them re-enter the machine at their will. An entire attack took ten to thirty minutes.[12] Beyond worrying about the sheer quantity of stolen data, the Department of Defense was concerned that Titan Rain could be a point patrol for more serious assaults that could shut down or even take over a number of U.S. military networks.

While the Titan Rain intrusions were eventually tracked to just three routers in the southern Chinese province of Guangdong, and the FBI "aggressively" pursued the possibility that the Chinese government was behind the attacks, investigators never concluded whether the spying was official, a private-sector job, or the work of many independent, unrelated hands. China did not cooperate with U.S. investigations of Titan Rain. China's State Council Information Office, speaking for the government, said that the charges about cyber spying and Titan Rain were "totally groundless, irresponsible and unworthy of refute."

One engineer at the Sandia National labs, Shawn Carpenter, did much of the work in tracing the intrusions to their sources. Often he worked after hours from a home computer, and he was acting independently of official investigators. After Carpenter made his first significant discoveries about Titan Rain in March 2004, he began taking the information to informal contacts he had in Army intelligence. Federal rules prohibit military intelligence officers from working with U.S. civilians, however, and by October, the Army passed Carpenter and his late-night operation to the FBI.

Carpenter says that he was a confidential informant for the FBI for the next five months. Reports from his cyber surveillance eventually reached the highest levels of the bureau's counterintelligence division, where his work was apparently folded into that of an existing task force on the attacks. But his FBI connection didn't help when his employers at Sandia found out what he was doing. They fired Carpenter and stripped him of his Q clearance, the Department of Energy equivalent of top-secret clearance. His after-hours sleuthing, they said, was an inappropriate use of confidential information he had gathered on the job. Also, under U.S. law it is illegal for Americans to hack into foreign computers. Carpenter subsequently sued for wrongful discharge and was awarded a large settlement.[13]

The Titan Rain and GhostNet attacks revealed that cyberspace clearly provides an opportunity to expand the scope of espionage, both in terms of the number of targets and the information sought.

GhostNet, which targeted "high value" computers in 103 countries, is likely just one of numerous spy networks, says one of the Canadian researchers who uncovered it, Ron Deibert, director of the Citizen Lab, a research lab for cyber-issues in politics at the University of Toronto's Munk Centre for International Studies. "We happened to discover and publicize this particular one. But you can safely guess that there are many of these going on."[14]

Espionage had been "invented" long before the Internet, but the Internet has transformed it. Not only is cyber espionage common, it appears to be relatively risk-free. The ability to credibly identify its true source – achieve adequate attribution – is difficult when the perpetrators can remain in remote and seemingly unrelated locations. The question of attribution is central to defining the range of national security responses available – not just for espionage, but also for acts of war and terrorism.

THE CROSS-CUTTING CHALLENGE OF ATTRIBUTION

How do you know that the Internet message you've just received actually comes from the e-mail address it claims to have come from? You don't, really. While the telephone system has an effective global tracking mechanism for a call's origination point (based on the need to charge users for services on a per-call basis), the Internet's creators never envisioned this need, so it has no standard provisions for tracing where a message comes from. The Internet model was also not designed to be robust against malicious behaviour. Data is transmitted in packets, in which a sophisticated user can modify information, and it is easy for such a person to forge the source address (i.e., the sender's address) of a packet in a one-way communication. Also, common attack techniques employ a series of stepping stones, using compromised intermediate hosts to "launder" packets sent. These packets can be changed in transmission hops between hosts, so attempting to trace back by correlating similar packets won't work when you are up against a sophisticated attacker.

Consequently, even the experts just don't know with any degree of confidence where attacks are coming from. To put it into the formal language used by experts, it is very hard to "attribute" a message to its source.

In cyber-security terms, attribution means determining the identity or location of an attacker or an attacker's intermediary.[15] When you can adequately attribute the cyber attack – when you can say with certainty who's behind it – then the scope of responses and action available to you becomes clearer. However, if a nation has been the target of debilitating attacks but no one comes forward to claim responsibility for them, how much proof do you need before you can respond to the suspected source?

There is no adequate answer to this question yet.

Without the fear of being caught, convicted, and punished, individuals and organizations will continue to use the Internet to conduct malicious activities of all kinds. We need attribution to create a system of deterrence. Attribution is important in dealing with cyber crime, but the consequences of inadequate attribution or misattribution are much greater in instances involving national security.

Developing a reliable "system" for adequate attribution is very, very difficult.[16] Attribution cannot be accomplished strictly through the use of technology, and the existing technologies that do support attribution are less than perfect. Privacy is a big issue too. There are situations that make attribution highly desirable, and situations in which it would undercut open communication – for example, political dissidents in repressive regimes might not be able to use the Internet if messages could be traced to them. Hence, no common standard for attribution is desirable.

Cyber attacks often cross national boundaries, so attribution techniques require cooperation. There is no agreed-upon international right for one country's law enforcement agencies to unilaterally hack into a computer located in another country, and even if nations do cooperate, the time required to establish a working relationship may allow the bad guys to erase any evidence.

Furthermore, determining "adequate" attribution depends on the purpose for which attribution, if achieved, will be used. Attribution adequate for declaring war, or for arresting individuals on criminal charges, obviously demands a much higher standard than that necessary to block traffic from certain Internet addresses. This takes us into circular logic: attribution defines the possible scope of response, while the scope of response is, in turn, an essential part of defining adequate attribution.[17] Unfortunately, there is no established framework for monetizing cyber-attack damages or defining other levels of damage or threat, particularly with regard to the international community.

Without major policy, legal, and technical changes in the structure of the Internet, it is unlikely that we will make much headway on the challenges of attribution, and the erosion of safety is likely to continue.

CYBER WAR

Though we often misuse the term *war* (as in "war on drugs" or "global war on terror"), its correct meaning is a contest by force between two or more nations or states, which, however brutal, is at least putatively governed by an international body of law. The Spanish conquistadors, for example, before embarking in the Americas on whatever mission that invariably led to the genocide of native peoples, were careful always to have a legal justification for their acts.

The U.S. Defense Department defines cyberspace as "the notional environment in which digitized information is communicated over computer networks."[18] There are many definitions of cyber *warfare* – or information warfare, as it is sometimes called – but most are too verbose or technology-laden to be remembered, while others place a narrow emphasis on certain cyber aspects. At its most elemental, cyber warfare can be thought of as offensive and defensive operations that use computers to attack other computers or networks through electronic means, to imperil national security. It is still unclear where to draw the line between attacks on government or military cyber infrastructures and attacks on private sector-controlled infrastructures (such as banking or electric power).

Arguably, state-sponsored cyber attacks already have occurred. Russia has been accused of conducting cyber-warfare campaigns against Estonia in 2007, Georgia in 2008, and Kyrgyzstan in 2009.[19]

(Russia denies any state involvement.) Whether indeed Russia was or was not involved in such "campaigns," the threat of offensive cyber operations is a looming challenge that will continue to grow in importance.[20] For example, China is developing cyber operations as tools of warfare, tools it would likely use in any future conflict with the U.S., to exploit the nation's dependence on cyberspace.[21]

After NATO's professed accidental bombing of China's embassy in Belgrade on May 7, 1999, hackers seeming to originate from China attacked U.S. government information systems, including those of the White House, State Department, and others. I was there in the White House when these attacks were underway – in fact, I was meeting in a bunker below the East Wing of the White House to discuss them – and it is fair to say that these intrusions were regarded as one of the first government-sponsored information warfare attacks on the United States.[22]

According to government reports made public since then, the hackers' work included replacing official Web pages with protest material and offensive language, posting similar language in Internet chat rooms and news groups, and denial-of-service e-mail attacks. Pentagon computer systems were disrupted by mass e-mailing believed to have originated in China. NBC News reported that the official White House Web site was shut down after hackers attempted to break into the system operating the page. (Actually, according to what I was told, the White House site was down for a routine upgrading when the attacks began, and it was only because of this fortuitous timing that further damage was not done to White House networks.) According to the official *China Daily* newspaper, hackers also broke into the Web site of the U.S. embassy in Beijing and inserted the slogan "Down with the barbarians" on the main page. On another page, they replaced a photograph of Ambassador James Sasser with the same slogan in Chinese characters.

I believe that the bombing of the Chinese embassy in Belgrade was not accidental (after all, the bomb's target, as I understand it, was the cipher room of the embassy), and if I'm correct, then Western nations do not have clean hands. I also believe that the

Chinese government was directly behind the retaliatory cyber attacks against U.S. government systems. However, neither of these assertions is provable in the public record. Welcome to the shadowy world of national security cyber threats.

Since the 1999 Chinese incident, there have been other cyber skirmishes, such as the ones between Israeli and Palestinian interests, with each side encouraging its supporters to join in DDOS attacks against the other. But there are even more direct instances of nations attacking other nations using cyberspace.

The DDOS attacks on Estonia mentioned earlier were the first sustained attacks on an entire country's computer networks.[23] Estonia's national CERT (Computer Emergency Readiness Team) had a disaster plan in place to minimize the damage, through the installation of defensive filters on Internet gateways. Nonetheless, the hackers infiltrated computers around the world to create botnets and sent a single huge burst of data to measure the capacity of Estonia's networks. Hours later, data from multiple sources flowed into the system, rapidly reaching the upper limits of routers and switches. The tiny country of about 1.4 million is heavily Internet-dependent – its citizens go online to vote, even to pay parking tolls – and for many days, all sorts of vital communications were in chaos.

Though the attackers were never definitively identified – because of the attribution problem – they had posted their plans on the Internet before the attacks began, and investigators found detailed instructions on how to send disruptive messages and which Estonian Web sites to use as targets in Russian-language forums and chat groups. For NATO, the DDOS attacks in Estonia sparked a discussion of the need to modify its commitment to collective defence, enshrined in Article 5 of the North Atlantic Treaty.[24] U.S. government officials said the nature of the attacks suggested that they were initiated by "hacktivists," technical experts who act independently from governments. (When such people take their own country's side in international disputes, like those that had been simmering between Russia and Estonia, they are also called "patriotic hackers.") Moscow offered no help in tracking down hackers who the Estonian government believed might have been involved, and a spokesman for the Kremlin denied Russian state involvement, adding, "The Estonia side has to be extremely careful when making accusations."

In July 2008, before Russia entered into armed conflict with Georgia, there began a series of DDOS attacks that overloaded Georgia's Internet infrastructure and effectively shut down crucial servers. The Web site of the Georgian president Mikheil Saakashvili was put out of commission for twenty-four hours, according to researchers at the Shadowserver Foundation, a group of voluntary professional security experts who monitor malicious online activity (or, as they put it, "the darker side of the Internet"). The researchers said the command and control server that directed the attack was based in the United States and had come online several weeks before the assault. The cyber attacks looked as if they might have been designed as a probing or softening-up tactic prior to physical conflict – or, as some theorized, a dress rehearsal for an all-out cyber war once the shooting started.[25] It was certainly the first time – but doubtless not the last – that a known cyber attack coincided with a shooting war.

Here again, no one knows exactly who was behind the cyber attacks. The Georgian government blamed the Russian government, which issued a denial, adding that individuals in Russia or elsewhere might have taken it upon themselves to launch the attacks. "I cannot exclude this possibility," Yevgeniy Khorishko, a spokesman for the Russian embassy in Washington, said. "There are people who don't agree with something and they try to express themselves. You have people like this in your country."[26] This is a rationale that we've heard before from both the Russian and Chinese governments, and one we'll likely hear again from any of a number of countries.

Simply put, DDOS attacks are cheap to mount and difficult to attribute. As one expert put it, "It costs about 4 cents per machine. You could fund an entire cyber warfare campaign for the cost of replacing a tank tread, so you would be foolish not to."[27]

National security missions are increasingly experiencing attempted cyber attacks, and, by their own admission, they are vulnerable to them in myriad ways. In 2003, John M. Gilligan, then Chief

Information Officer for the U.S. Air Force, described a "nightmare scenario" in which hackers could potentially "ground our Air Force" at a crucial time by getting into the unclassified systems used for mundane but essential functions such as aircraft maintenance, supply, and back-office support.[28]

As early as 2000, the CIA agent John Serabian stated, "We are detecting, with increasing frequency, the appearance of doctrine and dedicated offensive cyber warfare programs in other countries. We have identified several, based on all-source intelligence information, that are pursuing government-sponsored offensive cyber programs. Foreign nations have begun to include information warfare in their military doctrine, as well as their war college curricula, with respect to both defensive and offensive applications. They are developing strategies and tools to conduct information attacks."[29]

According to Chinese military writings, the People's Liberation Army (PLA) is developing information-warfare capabilities designed to cripple high-technology weapons and support systems. By the early 1990s, China's military began exploring cyber attacks as asymmetric weapons – as a means of countering an otherwise superior adversary. [30]

The Chinese military theorists coined the term "Integrated Network-Electronic Warfare" to outline the offensive use of electronic warfare, computer network operations, and kinetic strikes against key military communications centres.[31] Pre-emption is a fundamental core of their "active defence" strategy.[32] Beijing's intelligence services continue to collect science and technology information to support the government's goals, while Chinese industry gives priority to domestically manufactured products to meet its technology needs. The PLA maintains close ties with its Russian counterpart, but there is significant evidence that Beijing seeks to develop its "own unique model for waging cyber warfare."[33] In 2005, the PLA began to incorporate offensive computer network operations in its military exercises, primarily in first strikes against enemy networks.[34]

China and Russia are not the only the nations working on the capability to knock out vital computer, information, and electronic systems. The U.S. has publicly acknowledged that it has both cyber-attack and cyber-defence capabilities. Canada and most other Western bloc alliance countries (e.g., NATO members, or the informal alliance that includes Canada, the U.S., the U.K., Australia, and New Zealand) have been more reticent, though it's obvious that all of them are working together in developing offensive, defensive, and espionage-based uses of cyberspace.

In 1997 the U.S. Defense Department conducted a mock cyber-attack exercise, Eligible Receiver, which revealed dangerous vulnerabilities in U.S. military information systems.[35] A later exercise, Eligible Receiver 2003, indicated a need for greater coordination between military and non-military organizations to deploy a rapid military computer counter-attack.[36] Meanwhile, the aptly named Digital Pearl Harbor exercise (2002) concluded that the most vulnerable infrastructure was the Internet itself, along with the computer systems that are part of the financial infrastructure.[37]

However, continued bureaucratic shuffling characterizes the U.S. approach to military cyber-operations. The U.S. Government started to formally develop classified guidelines for offensive cyber operations and warfare with the July 2002 release of National Security Presidential Directive 16 (NSPD-16).[38] Another classified NSPD, issued in 2004, directed the establishment of U.S. policy for offensive cyber operations.[39] Within the armed forces, the creation of the Air Force Cyber Command was announced in 2006. It would have been one of ten Commands (with a capital C) in the U.S. military, but later was downgraded to a numbered unit within Air Force Space Command, where parts of it had resided before. In 2009, Defense Secretary Robert Gates approved the creation of the new, unified Cyber Command, though skeptics promptly raised questions, including a fundamental one posed by *Wired* magazine in a lengthy commentary: "[W]hat does cyber defense really mean, these days?"[40]

Of course, the form and purpose of nation-state cyber military action is still evolving. For instance, such attacks could be used to soften up targets in advance of kinetic (physical) attack, or a slow attack might be launched, gradually degrading infrastructures or penetrating information systems over a protracted period of time.

And, the cyber-warfare competition is shrouded in secrecy, making it difficult to determine national vulnerabilities and threats – and therefore to gauge whether a purely defensive strategy is appropriate, or whether offensive capabilities are needed to create a credible deterrent.[41] A recent, and somewhat frightening, statement by the head of the U.S. Strategic Command, responsible for military cyber operations, implied that his country favoured a wide-open approach: "I don't think you take any response off the table from a [cyber] attack on the United States of America."[42]

So we return to the question: What is the justification and appropriate form for military action in cyberspace?

Many are wrestling with this question. The U.S. is already engaged in bilateral discussions about the military use of cyberspace. Press reports say that Russia supports forging an international treaty that would ban countries from engaging in military cyber war, similar to past chemical warfare negotiations. The United States advocates improved cooperation among law enforcement agencies under the Convention on Cybercrime. The U.S. position is that by declaring cyber attacks illegal for criminal purposes, it will also make military attacks illegal.[43]

Still, the U.S., Canada, and other allies need to establish and communicate – to allies and possible opponents alike – clear national policies and a military doctrine for military action and response in cyberspace. These policies and doctrine should address the point at which military cyber action might spill over into kinetic action, and under what circumstances proactive actions in the face of perceived threats would be justified. Policies also must address what role the private sector or non-state actors should play (for example, should private firms, if attacked, have "hack-back" capability – the cyber equivalent of a door rigged to a loaded shotgun?).

Several factors make this goal perhaps uniquely challenging.

First among the challenges is the attribution problem we've already noted. In addition to the technological difficulty of tracing an attack to its source, the prevalence of criminal groups and so-called patriotic hackers, who may or may not be carrying out attacks for a nation-state, further clouds clear identification of the attacker. Then, even if we can attribute an attack to a particular individual or organization, defining an appropriate response will entail dealing with our uncertainty in linking those sources to a nation-state.[44] In cyberspace, non-state actors could try to foment a war between nations. It has even been theorized that terrorist hackers could trigger a nuclear conflict by spoofing the warning signals that tell a country when an adversary has launched missiles.[45]

The target of the attack, and the severity of its consequences, are other considerations in determining whether an attack calls for military response. For example, at what point do cyber attacks on civilian networks become acts of war? Attacks on key infrastructures such as financial and transportation systems, or power grids, can both disable a country and hamper military support and supply.

National policy can look to the laws of war to help answer these questions for more "historical" (read "kinetic") acts, but they are inadequate or undeveloped when applied to cyberspace. We have to resort to two different perspectives: what is generally considered the law of war, and what are established international conventions, particularly those of the United Nations and NATO.

Traditional just war theory operates from a "will to peace" and is divided into ethical considerations of just recourse to war (*jus ad bellum*) and just conduct in war (*jus in bello*). According to Christian or Western just war tradition, *jus in bello* actions are those that are discriminate and proportionate. "Discriminate" means that destructive actions are aimed at the adversary and that non-combatants and the innocent are not targeted. "Proportionate" means that the effects of destructive actions are not out of proportion with the ends we seek to achieve.[46]

The Charter of the United Nations is the acknowledged mechanism for determining the lawfulness of the resort to force by nations.[47] Countries like Canada and the U.S. are also bound by the NATO Treaty, which states that an armed attack occurring against any member in Europe or North America will be considered an armed attack against all.[48]

However, recent examples like Estonia indicate the matter still is not clear when it comes to defining the justification and form of military action.[49] While Estonia was under DDOS attack, NATO first had to wrestle with the issue of whether there was sufficient confidence that the DDOS attacks ultimately originated with the Russian state, or whether it was organized crime or independent patriotic hackers who were responsible. Then NATO had to consider what might be an appropriate response. In the end, apparently, nothing was resolved, but the threat also disappeared.

We need a policy, with supporting doctrine, which outlines both military and diplomatic responses. A major challenge to this goal is that cyber war (and cyber terrorism) in the future might extend to hostile attacks whose form or targets we have not yet seen. For instance, in 2009, the world's largest particle accelerator, the Large Hadron Collider, near Geneva, was infiltrated by hackers identifying themselves as Group 2600 of the Greek Security Team. A few scientists had already worried that experiments with the Large Hadron Collider could inadvertently create a planet-swallowing black hole. Physicists called this impossible, or at least extraordinarily unlikely. Even so, the hack raises a different sort of worst-case scenario: if hackers were to disrupt or get control of a sensitive scientific experiment, what could the consequences be?[50]

On a less universe-shaking level, computer hackers in China have not only penetrated U.S. government information systems, but in a few cases gained access to electric power plants in the United States. They could possibly have triggered recent widespread blackouts in Florida and the Northeast U.S. and Canada, according to U.S. government officials and computer-security experts.[51]

Attacks against critical infrastructures such as power grids, transportation systems, and communication systems are not new. Military action for centuries has included knocking out bridges and (since the nineteenth century) rail lines. (One Confederate general in the U.S. Civil War was noted, perhaps apocryphally, for saying, "We'll burn that bridge when we come to it.") What is new are questions about the impact cyber attacks against critical infrastructures might have, and about how we will defend and respond to them.

There is considerable effort directed toward defending critical infrastructures. In Canada, Public Safety Canada has explicit responsibility for protecting physical and IT infrastructures, which, if disrupted or destroyed, would have a serious impact on the effective functioning of the nation.[52] In the U.S., the National Strategy to Secure Cyberspace (NSSC), complemented by a vast array of Presidential Directives and National Plans, states:

> Our Nation's critical infrastructures are composed of public and private institutions in the sectors of agriculture, food, water, public health, emergency services, government, defence industrial base, information and telecommunications, energy, transportation, banking and finance, chemicals and hazardous materials, and postal and shipping. Cyberspace is their nervous system – the control system of our country. Cyberspace is composed of hundreds of thousands of interconnected computers, servers, routers, switches and fiber optic cables that allow our critical infrastructures to work. Thus, the healthy functioning of cyberspace is essential to our economy and our national security.[53]

However, many critics dispute whether either country actually has a workable plan.

Moderately successful attacks against both the Internet and critical online functions (finance and banking, telecommunications, transportation, and so forth) have occurred, though all at a less than hair-raising scale. In 1988, the Worcester, Massachusetts, Airport was disabled, accidentally, by some teenage hackers; luckily there were no serious consequences. In 2000, a hacker – who had helped to design the target system – broke into the computers of an Australian sewage plant and leaked raw sewage into rivers and parks. Numerous fish died, but no people.[54] Then on January 25, 2003 (Super Bowl weekend in the U.S.), the Slammer worm, also known as the Sapphire worm, hit the Internet at 5:30 a.m. GMT. Exploiting a software vulnerability in servers running Microsoft SQL Server 2000, Slammer was the fastest-propagating cyber attack in history. According to a team of researchers from the University of California at San Diego, Lawrence Berkeley National Labs, and Silicon Defense, the number of infections doubled every 8.5 seconds, and within the first ten minutes following its release Slammer had already done 90 per cent of its damage. Among other things, the worm took down parts of the Internet in South Korea and Japan, disrupted phone service in Finland, and slowed airline reservation systems, credit-card networks, and automatic teller machines in the U.S.

To disrupt the global Internet *for an extended period* would require coordinated attacks against routers and servers at many different physical locations, and at different levels within the network of networks that make up the Internet. That requires real work, though the vulnerabilities (for example, in the Border Gateway Protocol, which controls the routers that act as traffic cops for the Internet) do exist.

Taking down the whole Internet is very, very hard; taking down just 25 per cent of the Internet is hard. However, taking down the segment that supports, say, the Culinary Institute of America (the other CIA) is probably relatively easy. Many services are now provided exclusively on the Internet – it's getting hard to deal with any major business or institution without going online for at least part of the interaction, or for information that you need – while other services piggyback off Internet connectivity. (Most long-distance calls, even if they aren't officially VOIP [Voice Over Internet Protocol], are routed over the Internet.) Despite their reliance on the Web, many of these functions have enough "redundancy" and backup that an Internet disruption would result merely in degradation of their performance, not complete shutdown. However, this is not always the case and there are a lot of situations, from public-safety emergencies to the everyday bustle of commerce, in which just a "mere" degradation of performance might lead to major problems. Internet disruption for brief periods would probably not cause the irreparable economic harm that colours some descriptions of a "cyber Pearl Harbor," but it could be significant.

Also, attackers have twice launched denial-of-service attacks against the Domain Name System (DNS) root servers. The first attack occurred in October 2002 and disrupted service at nine of the thirteen root servers. The second attack occurred in February 2007 and caused disruptions at two of the root servers.[55] These machines provide service to all Internet users, and thus the attacks could be classified as attempts to take down the entire Internet – except that it is unclear what the attackers' true motivations were.

So, yes, it appears that important economic and public systems can be disrupted through cyber means. Such disruptions have been a facet of war and raiding since Sumerian times; there is nothing new about the targets. It is the method that's new – and the unlikely prospect of being able to identify the originator of the attacks.

CYBER TERRORISM

A typical view of cyber terrorism comes from the *Daily Mail*.[56]

> At first it would be no more than a nuisance. No burning skyscrapers, no underground explosions, just a million electronic irritations up and down the land. Thousands of government web pages suddenly vanish to be replaced with the Internet's version of the Testcard – that dreaded screen '404 – Not Found' or, more amusingly, some pastiche or parody. Then the Labour website starts to promise a wholesale renationalisation of the railways. The popular response this generates turns to amusement then bemusement as everything from Jaguar to BT is, the sites claim, to be taken back into state hands. When conservatives.org.uk starts to promise compulsory repatriation and the return of capital punishment, bemusement turns to alarm.
>
> Britain under attack: Cyber-terrorists could cripple the country. The disruption continues: thousands of popular websites, from eBay to YouTube, start malfunctioning or are replaced by malicious parodies. Tens of millions of pounds are wiped off the share price of companies like Amazon as fears grow that the whole Internet credit card payment network is now vulnerable and insecure. Eventually, reports start to flood in that hundreds of thousands of personal bank accounts have been raided overnight. Panicked bank chiefs and PR men go on TV to try to reassure, promising that this is no more than

an electronic glitch, but thousands of anxious citizens take to the streets, many in tears, and pour angrily into the banks to demand their savings in cash. When the ATM system goes down, the government steps in. A task force is appointed. There is a rush on hard cash that leads to a shortage of notes and coins.

Soon, it is clear that the United Kingdom (and much of Europe) has been subjected to a sustained and effective cyber-terrorist attack. Disaster is narrowly avoided when a series of sophisticated viruses disrupt the workings of the National Air Traffic Control System. Slowly, the computer network is disinfected; the viruses, botnets and worms that are the electronic versions of bombs and bullets are defused and rendered harmless. No one has died, but the attack has cost Britain £10bn, and share prices take months to recover.

Such a scenario, say some experts, is not only possible but likely in the near future. But hysteria is easy. Let's go back a few steps.

The word terrorism dates from the era of the French Revolution, when supporters of the Reign of Terror were called *terroristes,*[57] and today the term commonly describes actions that have the ultimate goal of creating a general sense of dread and terror in the target populace. Interestingly, terrorism lacks a universally accepted legal definition. In Canada, the Anti-Terrorism Act[58] defines it as an act that is committed for a political, religious, or ideological purpose with the intention of intimidating the public, or of compelling someone to do or refrain from doing an act. Its intention is to cause death or serious bodily harm to a person by the use of violence, to cause a serious risk to health and safety of the public, or to cause serious disruption of an essential service. In the U.S. the State Department defines terrorism as premeditated, politically motivated violence perpetrated against non-combatant targets by subnational or clandestine groups usually intended to influence an audience.[59] This last definition captures today's common understanding, that terrorist acts are not committed by another state.

By these definitions, we have yet to see an act of cyber terrorism – and the *Daily Mail* piece, while dramatic, doesn't quite fit the definition either. If we consider the root concept of terrorism as acts that induce a state of terror or dread in the population, I would argue that cyber threats are incapable of producing terror. The effect of random bombings, kidnappings, and assassinations is fundamentally different in its impact from that of having one's computer systems hacked into, or even losing vital services like electric power. Bombings create terror; losing electricity is just a major hassle. In his book *Spies Among Us,* security expert Ira Winkler argued that "cyberterrorism" wouldn't work well because it literally does not sow terror. That, he said, is best done with physical attacks that disrupt a society by making people afraid they'll suffer *mortal harm in the course of everyday activities* – afraid to get on an airliner or go to public places, afraid (as with the post-9/11 anthrax attacks) to even open the mail.

I believe that cyber terrorism, if it occurs at all, will be a minor element in our terrorism concerns. Attacking critical infrastructures would threaten some lives, and certainly result in substantial economic loss, but the effect of such actions is in a different league than the effect produced by random bombings or the systematic killing or kidnapping of civilians – what's more, these actions require much more technical sophistication and planning. So I think that the role of cyberspace for any terrorist campaign will be to help it inflict economic harm and inefficiencies on the target population, rather than to induce terror or fear.

Many discussions of "cyber terrorism" report, breathlessly, that Al Qaeda (or whoever) is already using the Internet and computers to communicate, store information, recruit members, and publicize its cause – and that, therefore, cyber terrorism is already taking place.[60] But we don't refer to terrorists using the telephone as telephone terrorism. Using cyberspace as anyone else would isn't terrorism. In fact, in considering the prospect of cyber terrorism, it seems a global takedown of the Internet is unlikely to occur simply because terrorists want access to cyber networks just like everyone else does.

A CYBER PEARL HARBOR?

Much of the discussion about cyber and national security has been framed, at least in the U.S. context, in terms of the prospect of a "cyber Pearl Harbor" – a coordinated set of electronic attacks that cause economic damage, weaken our national security, or sow widespread panic and unease among the citizenry along the lines of the *Daily Mail* article. Some of this concern is hype, but some of it is valid. It is certainly possible that we will experience coordinated attacks against national security systems and critical infrastructures, and the possibility of economic harm is real. But I do not believe that it will result in alarm and terror.

Moreover, the metaphor "cyber Pearl Harbor" is misleading and distorts our thinking. Unlike the attack on Pearl Harbor, which was intended to destroy the American Pacific fleet and free the Japanese for unlimited action in the Pacific, attacks in cyberspace, however severe, are more like throwing sand in the gears. They are a drag on the system, a constant annoyance and inefficiency that will at times make things run pretty rough, but we'll deal with it and learn to live with it – as we have already done. Major electric blackouts, or communications systems failures, are not unknown in North America, though of accidental origin, and we've survived. There is no indication that our response would be any different were these disruptions to be the consequence of deliberate cyber attacks.

Some experts disagree and suggest that a cyber attack could bring an advanced Western economy to its knees. One scenario for a successful attack against the Western financial system would be to attack Fedwire and Fednet. Fedwire is the financial funds transfer system that exchanges money among U.S. banks. Fednet handles financial transactions. The system has one primary installation and three backups. As one expert noted, "You can find out on the Internet where the backups are. If those are taken out by a mix of cyber and physical activities, the U.S. [and Western] economy would basically come to a halt."[61]

Another problem with Pearl Harbor as the metaphor for cyber terrorism or war, however, is that it presumes that an attack will be a unitary, organized event. Not all serious incidents, in military or civilian life, are Pearl Harbor-like, resulting from a perfectly executed strike or a single fatal flaw. Perhaps the reason we haven't yet had a major cyber catastrophe is that it will take a perfect storm to produce one, and these are rare. Certainly, at any moment, there are large numbers of malicious hackers combing through all kinds of systems looking for all kinds of flaws they can exploit. But to do spectacular and fateful damage might take the right hacker – one with the right skills – finding the right flaw in the right system, and exploiting it in such a way as to trigger a *cascading series of failures.*

Often the perfect storm develops from an unexpected cascade of little things. In March 1979, the main feedwater pumps failed at the nuclear reactor generating electricity at Three Mile Island near Middletown, Pennsylvania. Despite the plant having been engineered with multiple redundant safety systems and run by skilled operators, it lacked an instrument directly measuring the level of coolant in the reactor core. Other instruments misleadingly showed that conditions were normal. As a result, when warning lights went off, operators made a series of decisions that worsened the problem, causing a melt-down of the reactor core. The resulting accident was the most seri-ous in U.S. commercial nuclear-power-plant history, though it led to no deaths at the plant or in the surrounding communities.[62]

In August 2003, a massive power outage – the largest blackout in North American history – affected parts of the Northeastern and Midwestern U.S., and Ontario in Canada. One-third of the popu-lation of Canada, and one-seventh of the U.S., lost electric power. The cascading failure started with a Cleveland generating station going offline during a heat wave that was causing unusually high electrical demand. Other key high-voltage power lines subsequently went out of service after contact with "overgrown trees." System-wide controls designed to manage power over the extended regional grids failed, including those engineered after the 1965 Northeast outage. Along with human error, a computer software bug in the electric-grid-control alarm system was one of the faults.[63]

In October 1987, prices on the New York Stock Exchange (among other exchanges) collapsed in what the chairman of the Exchange called a near "meltdown." The Dow Jones average of leading industrial stocks fell by over 22 per cent, nearly double the amount of the famous 1929 collapse that sparked the Great Depression. The head of the Securities and Exchange Commission discussed the possibility of a government-imposed halt in trading. In retrospect, we can see that a confluence of factors led to this totally unexpected market collapse (I had just started working at a Wall Street investment bank at the time): the market was generally viewed as greatly overvalued, and a variety of recent economic news had caused disquiet, but the unanticipated role of newly developed computerized trading schemes was a critical factor.[64]

Each of the foregoing cases exemplifies the failure of a critical system that had been actively overseen to ensure its reliability. Each failed in unanticipated ways, in spite of the attention and best efforts directed to making it fail-safe. But as critical as these events were, things got back to normal; people didn't stop using electricity or trading stocks. Equally important, each event led to massive re-engineering of the systems involved so that we could learn from the failures and prevent similar ones in the future.

It is easy to imagine a cyber incident cascading out of control, and impossible to prevent it with 100 per cent certainty. Thus it is far more likely that what we will see is a cyber Three Mile Island rather than a cyber Pearl Harbor. What we can try to do is minimize the chances, though our present policies and approaches make this difficult and arguably put us at greater risk than we ought to be. For instance, the lack of good incident-reporting makes it hard to even characterize the threats that could lead to a catastrophe. We may not know how many near misses there have been. We may not grasp what a near miss consists of, since our ability to compare and analyze incidents is fragmentary.

NATIONAL SECURITY IN THE FACE OF CYBER THREATS

To sum up: How does the use of cyberspace affect our perception of what we consider national security risks?

A student of mine recently commented that "no one has ever died from a cyber attack." To which I answered, "Yet." Cyber attacks do have the potential to cause loss of life, though those fatalities would probably be incidental to the economic harm and the interruption of routine societal functions caused by disrupting critical infrastructures. And here again, the greatest damage could come from a cascade of errors and actions producing an unintended and unimagined outcome. Such an event is at least as credible a possibility as a highly coordinated, unitary cyber attack.

Of equal consideration is the fact that cyber attacks are simply not mainstream instruments of terrorism. Cyber "warfare" can be used to extort or scare smaller groups, but the havoc it wreaks doesn't create terror in the way that bombings and killings do. As a tool for expanding the scope and ease of espionage, however, there is no doubt that cyberspace will play a major role.

Of far greater import to our national security concerns is the problem of attribution, the possibility that we will be unable to pinpoint the source of cyber attacks. Even in the most extreme types of attacks (should they be possible) there may be a period – of hours or days – when we (the target) simply may not have sufficient confidence to name the source of the attacks. Such was the case in Estonia, or earlier, in attacks against U.S. government systems that seemingly originated from China.

In the future, therefore, our national security environment will be shaped by events for which, because we lack attribution, our immediate response may be limited to purely defensive actions. It is increasingly difficult to believe that cyber attacks will not be part of or precede any future conflict. In this future world, we will need to define what "adequate" attribution is, and define what the appropriate suite of responses might be. Both the definition of adequacy, and our range of responses, may depend on the nature of the threat – is it an act of war, or a terrorist attack, a hostile act by another nation-state that falls below the threshold of war, or is it something else? Equally, we will have to shorten the time required to sufficiently attribute the source of a cyber threat.

The line between war and crime is not always clearly drawn – consider the act of granting letters of marque to privateers, a measure that redefined a crime (piracy on the seas) as an act of war. And the distinction between terrorism and crime is even less clear – one side's "freedom fighters" are the other side's "criminals." In cyberspace, there is even more blurring of the lines. Criminal networks can be used in cyber war and terror. They may have been used in Titan Rain, and were surely involved in Estonia, where botnets were rented by the Russians to launch their attacks.

Based on our existence in the physical world we separate crime, war, and terrorism into distinct categories. But because we cannot reliably distinguish among them in cyberspace, our old ways of thinking and responding may be inappropriate. We have distinct agencies, and distinct laws and methods, for dealing with national defence, crime, and terrorism. The difficulty of knowing who is behind a given attack affects and complicates all our decisions about how to structure our agencies, deploy our resources, and cope with the threats. Most of these issues have yet to be sorted out, and it would seem impossible to ever resolve them with perfect clarity.

CREEPING TO DEFEAT?

Regardless of how well we address the issues of doctrine and attribution, one more question remains. Are our current capabilities for cyber war and anti-terrorism *good enough*?

To citizens of the U.S., Canada, and allied or aligned countries, this is the question that ultimately matters. Are we as able and prepared as we can be – as we need to be – to defend against cyber hostilities of various kinds; do we have the cyber-offensive powers to disable or deter an adversary?

In terms of offensive capabilities, it's hard to say. Development of the U.S. cyber arsenal is done in secret, of course, and we get only glimmers of what some of the tools and tactics might be. For instance, it was revealed in 2009 that initial plans for the 2003 invasion of Iraq had called for U.S. intelligence forces to hack into, and freeze, Saddam Hussein's bank accounts, thus tying up his country's financial system and weakening its defences. (This was not done, out of concern that ripple effects from the attack could disrupt global financial systems.)[65]

But as to whether our own defences are adequate, the answer for the U.S., according to one panel of experts, is: absolutely not. In

2008, the Center for Strategic and International Studies (CSIS), an independent think tank in Washington, released a stinging and thoroughgoing critique. Here is an excerpt from the Introduction to the CSIS report:

> Many people know the story of Ultra and Enigma. Enigma was the German military encryption machine in World War II. Ultra was the British program to crack the German codes. The British, through a combination of skill, luck, and perseverance, were able to collect and decrypt sensitive German military communications and essentially became part of the German military network. This gave them an immense advantage and made allied success more rapid and assured. The outcome of an invisible struggle between Britain and Germany in a precursor to cyberspace gave one side an immense advantage.
>
> The United States is in a similar situation today, but we are not playing the role of the British. Foreign opponents . . . have been able to penetrate poorly protected U.S. computer networks and collect immense quantities of valuable information. . . .
>
> America's failure to protect cyberspace is one of the most urgent national security problems facing the new administration . . . [This] is, like Ultra and Enigma, a battle fought mainly in the shadows. It is a battle we are losing.[66]

The main purpose of the report, produced by a special CSIS commission of IT and security experts, was to recommend new policy approaches. But in criticizing results to date, the report made clear that intrusions into defence-related systems (like the ones described in this chapter) are by no means the only threats to "national security." Whereas the Enigma-Ultra battle was all about secret military communications, in cyber war the theatre is much larger – any and all of a nation's online systems, including non-defence business systems, are liable to be targets:

> The immediate risk lies with the economy. [Because in today's world] competition will usually not take the form of traditional

superpower confrontation . . . Fleets, armies, and military alliances will not be as important in this competition as the ability for a nation to accelerate its technological progress and economic growth, to create new ideas and products, and to protect its informational advantages.

Furthermore, the report notes, should armed conflict ever develop, cyber war on civilian systems will almost surely be part of it, with the intent of damaging "our ability to respond and our will to resist."

In other words, in cyberspace one cannot draw a hard-and-fast line and say that national defence against cyber war or cyber terror is one set of tasks and concerns, while plain old cyber security (protecting everyday systems) is another. Everything is so interrelated that if you fail at the latter you are likely to fail at the former, too. And as previous chapters have amply shown, failing at the latter we most certainly are – all of us – in the U.S., Canada, and like-minded nations everywhere.

Failing – not catastrophically, but creepingly. Accepting a state of affairs in which day-in, day-out vulnerability to ever-growing volumes of malicious attacks and malware is somehow seen as normal. This is creeping failure that could send an entire nation, or several, creeping down the path to defeat.

Now let us see why the root of the failure lies not in the technologies we are using, but in the policies we are using – and in those we are neglecting to use.

CHAPTER 6

IT'S POLICY FAILURE, FOLKS

Throughout modern history, public policies have helped, hindered, or shaped the course of progress through technology. The airplane was invented in the U.S., yet during World War I, the American ace Eddie Rickenbacker and his Army Air Service squadron flew French biplanes. Why? Because disputes over the Wright brothers' patents in the U.S. had tied up innovation so badly that their home country built no aircraft able to perform on a level with European fighter planes. The government stepped in, creating a shared patent pool that allowed the U.S. aviation industry to move forward again in the years ahead.

Here's another example. After World War I, a new mass-market electronic industry emerged: radio broadcasting. It flourished in nearly all countries but took shape differently depending on the policies in place. While some countries allowed radio stations to sell advertising, England's BBC network was funded for many years by fees from the listeners. Anyone buying a radio receiver in a store had to buy, and renew, a licence to "operate" it. In the U.S, where licensing was lax even for broadcasters, the early days of radio were chaotic. When you tuned the dial you might find competing stations at the same frequency, producing a jumble of noise as they tried to over-power each other's signals. Better allocation of frequencies wouldn't come until the late 1920s.

Policy of course has played a major role in the exploration of space. In 1957 the Soviet Union stunned the world by launching Sputnik. The Soviet space program – which not only put Sputnik in orbit, but scored a long series of firsts in human space flight and interplanetary probes – grew from a long series of policy measures. The Soviets diligently funded research and education in rocketry; they came up with good methods of coordinating the brainpower to put together a space mission. Tellingly, however, Soviet policy-makers had less success in other vital fields of technology, such as computing. The Eastern bloc countries educated many good computer specialists, but they chronically lagged the West when it came to actually producing world-class computer systems for general use. Progress in computing seemed to require marketplace interaction and fluidity, which weren't exactly hallmarks of the Soviet approach.

Perhaps the best example of public policy working in concert with technology *and* the marketplace is one we're all familiar with: the automobile. A car is a marvellous collection of technologies, reflecting more than a hundred years of work by inventors, entrepreneurs, and other private enterprisers. From the start, the car has been more than a paradigm-changing product; it has been one of the few products that inspires genuine emotion. Do people write songs about their computers?

But also from the start, public policies have aided the development of the automobile and guided its use. Early motor vehicles were called "horseless carriages" because they were mainly seen as a replacement technology, with motors replacing draft animals. But the improvement of roads, and then the building of controlled-access highways, turned the motor vehicle into something more: a trans-former of society, a new mode of high-speed transit without rails, an enabler of new patterns of urban and suburban living. And in every case, road building was a public policy decision.

Public policies have made cars and driving safer. Drivers have to be licensed for competence, vehicles must be registered and in many places inspected regularly. Whenever good new safety features have been invented – turn signals, brake lights, seat belts, and more – governments around the world have usually moved to require that vehicles have them. Governments and engineering bodies set standards for the construction of cars and roads. Governments and independent testing labs rate the different makes of cars for safety so buyers can make informed choices.

Every advanced nation has a universal system of auto insurance, to help car users bear losses, as well as highly trained police and emergency units to deal with traffic law violations and accidents. Standards are set for the *performance* of cars (fuel efficiency, emissions, etc.), and these standards, plus a host of other policy measures, are constantly being tweaked to balance market demand with other needs, such as protecting the environment.

None of the policies described here is perfect. The policy-making process is often controversial and contentious. The point is that technologies alone, even the most potent, do not necessarily change things or solve problems. There often has to be some kind of policy involvement – some kind of collective, public action – that helps to bring the technology into wide or full use. And as technologies do take hold, new needs and behaviours emerge that often then have to be managed at the policy level.

This brings us back to cyber security, where it seems this history lesson hasn't quite sunk in for many of us. On the Internet, we are used to new technologies (new "solutions") appearing as if by magic. From seemingly nowhere the cyber-world springs to life on our screens when we log on. We can "call up" a Web page as if we were sorcerers conjuring what we need with a click of the fingers. And always there are new wonders to be found, new Web sites and services, new applications and upgrades. We know that somebody has to make these things, certainly. Yet once they are made they just seem to materialize everywhere, and they are usually pretty easy to access or download, and in many cases they are *free*.

All of this creates what I call a "Field of Dreams" mindset. It is the expectation that if we have a need or a problem, someone will create a technology for it, which gets deployed without much pain on our part: they will build it, and the solution will come.

It's not surprising to find the Field of Dreams mindset applied to security, nor is it only naive users who see the issue mainly in terms of technology. By far, most of the funding and effort for research in cyber security goes into security technologies, to such an extent that when someone speaks of "doing research" in this area, it's typically just assumed they are working on new technology. A good bit of that work goes on at Carnegie Mellon's CyLab, across the parking lot from my old office. You may not find any computer scientists or engineers at CyLab who actually think they can build a bulletproof technology that will close the case, but tremendous effort is spent in this building (and many others) on technologies to create more hassle for the bad guys or less for the users.

Likewise, the greatest share of the security money on the market goes to protective technologies, or technology services, or to consultants who help you tune up your technologies: when chief information officers tote up their security budgets, these are the purchases that predominate. Even home users, through a mix of purchase and freeware, can now have quite an array of security technologies. You can outfit your computer and network with virus scans, firewalls, packet filters, Secure Socket Layers, Virtual Private Networks, and certificate authorities. Coming soon are Domain Name Server security protocols and technologies (DNSsec) and Internet Protocol security (IPsec). If your systems are kitted out with all of these, you might ask, then what's the problem?

The problem is that the technical kit-out approach hasn't been sufficient. Instead of a Field of Dreams protected by a Great Wall of Technology, the result tends to be more like the Maginot Line: impregnable to frontal attack by known methods, but whoops, they attacked from the flank and with methods we hadn't seen.

The Field of Dreams/Wall of Technology mental model has some inherent flaws. The Internet is a vast network of interconnected, interdependent systems and users, which means you can't simply fortify your own bunker and expect to seal yourself in tight. A lot of "secure" technologies and protocols have to be adopted network-wide (or to a certain critical-mass extent) in order to be effective. But adoption of some key security tools has ranged from not-enough to almost nonexistent. Ingress filtering is a method that Internet service providers can use to combat the trick of launching spam and other attacks from spoofed addresses. It is deployed by many ISPs but far from all. And remember that it took *ten years* for IPv6 (Internet Protocol version 6) to reach a usage rate of a small fraction of one per cent.[1]

Protective software, the kind that security vendors sell, is only a first line of defence. It can be of little use if your underlying "working" programs – the operating system and applications – are full of security vulnerabilities, as they tend to be. There are ways of writing the programs so that they have far fewer defects, and some software teams follow these practices; sadly, many do not.

Moving good things into wider use, through a mixture of carrots and sticks, is one of the classic roles of policy. Unfortunately, that mixture has seldom been tried in cyber security.

Cyber-security professionals are usually quick to point out that no security technology can be an ultimate solution, because there will always be bad actors on the Internet, and it's likely they will eventually find ways to hack through just about any defence. Thus we hear the oft-chanted mantra that "all we're trying to do is stay a step ahead of the bad guys" – meaning, coming up with new security technologies faster than they come up with new attacks.

The job is difficult. In 2002 and 2003, the anti-virus unit of Symantec created about twenty thousand new "malicious code signatures" each year. This means that about twenty thousand different viruses, worms, and the like were detected and digitally fingerprinted for inclusion in the firm's anti-virus software. The count has gone up astronomically since then. In 2008, Symantec created *over 1.6 million new malicious code signatures*. Granted, not all of the viruses, worms, and so forth that the company detected were actually newly written strains of malware that had never been used before by the black hats. Far from it. In many cases hackers had just made slight alterations to existing malware – often to the "encryption keys" used in disguising the stuff. But the point is, legions of hackers around the world are easily able to keep tweaking their products to evade detection and blocking, while defenders are left with a Sisyphean task that verges on becoming both infeasible and useless.

Technology is best at solving problems that tend to stay solved. Good air brakes will stop a train every time, a problem solved in the 1800s. If you need a way to regulate the temperature in your house, a thermostat will do it faithfully, and if you need a way to look up information on the Internet, a search engine will do that. Technical solutions like these may be enhanced or refined over time, with added features like zoned climate control or slicker search algorithms, but the solutions are basically long-standing, persistent, and reliable. This is not the case in cyber security and we need to reframe our thinking. Instead of viewing the cyber-security issue as a "problem" to be "solved," it is more sensible to think of it as *a condition to be managed.*

This brings the human side, the policy side, into play. Instead of just installing software to fight off other people's software, we should also look for better ways to influence activity on the Internet, to reduce exploitive behaviour and increase secure behaviour. Along with redesigning computer systems to resist attacks, we might try to create better human systems to mitigate the outcomes; we could think seriously about better ways to police and prevent.

Technology is the coin of the cyber-realm and a lot of business has to be transacted through it. Its hegemony will not decline. But to change the dynamics of this losing game, the chief option is to play the policy hand more actively, a hand we've been holding behind our backs.

THE ASSUMPTION OF NO (OR VERY LITTLE) REGULATION

One definition of "policy" is "an attempt to define and structure a rational basis for action or inaction."[2] Cyber-security policy has long tilted to inaction. An underlying assumption has been the need to avoid regulation – to avoid even the appearance of it. The precedents were set in the U.S., during my years in Washington. Under the Clinton administration, the 1997 report *A Framework for Global Electronic Commerce* urged a laissez-faire approach toward the Internet generally. A key passage reads:

> Though government played a role in financing the initial development of the Internet, its expansion has been driven primarily by the private sector. For electronic commerce to flourish, the private sector must continue to lead. Innovation, expanded services, broader participation, and lower prices will arise in a market-driven arena, not in an environment that operates as a regulated industry. Accordingly, governments should encourage industry self-regulation wherever appropriate . . . Even where collective agreements or standards are necessary, private entities should, where possible, take the lead in organizing them. Where government action or intergovernmental agreements are necessary . . . private sector participation should be a formal part of the policy making process.[3]

That no one regulates the Internet is often cited as one of its great strengths. One of the oldest veterans of the Internet, the researcher and entrepreneur Steve Crocker, propounds this view. In 1968 Crocker helped to launch the Internet's precursor, the ARPANet, which connected a few research computing sites in the western U.S. Though just a graduate student then, he was able to join the communal group that became the Internet Engineering Task Force. Writing recently in *The New York Times*, Crocker praised the process by which this group set technical standards for design and operation of the fledgling network:

> Instead of authority-based decision-making, we relied on a process we called "rough consensus and running code." Everyone was welcome to propose ideas, and if enough people liked it and used it, the design became a standard . . .

[T]hat culture of open process was essential in enabling the Internet to grow and evolve as spectacularly as it has. In fact we probably wouldn't have the Web without it. When CERN physicists [in Switzerland, the originators of the World Wide Web] wanted to publish a lot of information in a way that people could easily get to it and add to it, they simply built and tested their ideas. Because of the groundwork we'd laid . . . they did not have to ask permission, or make any changes to the core operations of the Internet. Others soon copied them – hundreds of thousands of computer users, then hundreds of millions, creating and sharing content and technology. That's the Web.[4]

But as the Internet grew, so did the security issue. In 2003, we found the Bush administration publishing its National Strategy to Secure Cyberspace. The document notes that "federal regulation will not become a primary means of securing cyberspace" and that "the market will provide the major impetus."

The Bush strategy did list some areas where federal involvement is warranted, such as "research and technology development." Ominously, the list of areas where it's okay for government to tread also included some rather grey areas, reflecting the confusion and muddle that had already begun to hinder policy-making. For instance, one area was protecting "systems critical to national security" – aren't an awful lot of systems critical? Another was protecting against "organized attacks capable of inflicting debilitating damage" on the nation's economy – who decides when attacks have reached that level? By the time you know, might it not be too late?

Two very different administrations set the pattern of keeping hands off *except* in cases commonly agreed to be basic duties of government anyway. It's a pattern that has been followed in most open democracies. One could say this approach is in line with the standard philosophy of limited government, the notion that all rights and responsibilities lie with citizens unless otherwise specified. But the scope that's been drawn for public action in cyber security is limited in the extreme.

Protecting "security" has never been construed to mean only the security of the nation at large and its major institutions. It has always included the duty to protect the security of individuals. Adam Smith himself wrote that it includes "the duty of protecting, as far as possible, every member of the society from the injustice or oppression of every other member."[5] In today's world, that would seem to include going pretty far to do something about malicious hacking.

Furthermore, even the most laissez-faire nations have long recognized the need to make trade-offs with individual liberty and free enterprise in matters such as security, safety, and public health. That's why you need a licence to drive, for example. Yet the Internet is considered off limits to government in areas for which, in other sectors, public involvement is seen as both normal and necessary.

With automobiles, the basic policy framework sees auto safety as having three foundations – safe drivers, safe vehicles, safe roads. There are policies that work from all sorts of angles to achieve each one. In cyber security the equivalent would be policies to work toward the goals of secure users, secure products for the users, and secure networks. But let's turn the analogy around: what if our auto safety policies mirrored what we have in cyber security? Here's what you would see: no safety requirements for cars or even heavy trucks, only the hope that manufacturers would make safe vehicles. Investment in safe roads would be at the convenience of whoever owns the roads. Speed limits would be advisory and people could drive however they pleased. Happy motoring!

I am not advocating that everything on the Internet be regulated, or that everyone earn a secure user's licence before they are allowed to log on. I am suggesting we have more active *policies* for working on fundamental security issues, which in some cases could include regulation.

There are quite a few policies now in place in various countries. None are very successful and many don't address key issues at all.

AN APOLOGY FROM THE AUTHOR

You are about to enter the murky world of policy description. It has the rare distinction of the potential to be deadly dull and hectically confusing at the same time. If you do not play role-playing games such as Dungeons and Dragons or World of Warcraft, and have ever had a serious player try to explain the arcane intricacies to you, you know what I mean: after a while you just don't care that the Qwesting Beast defers to the Sword of Power except in the Dungeon of Eternal Flame where Hulga rules.

Worse, policy people speak in acronyms. (I used to, until the day at the White House when I gave a presentation after which a kindly private-sector colleague leaned over and whispered, "Do you know that at least 75 per cent of your talk was in acronyms, and not in English?")

There are two reasons to join me on this upcoming tour nonetheless. There will be no organization charts. And nowhere else will you get a whirlwind review of cyber-security policy in less than one chapter; it's your only chance.

I am going to be critical – not of the many good people who work in cyber security, but of the dunderheaded game plans that have somehow emerged and under which they have to work. It is very hard to make and implement good public policy. It's nothing like the clean-cut intellectual exercise often taught in schools. In the real world, politics and messiness intrude. The best-laid plans get caught up in endless rounds of interagency meetings. They get caught between conflicting pressures from interest groups and their lobbyists, legislators, and top administration officials. Your own coalition, the people on your side, can be exasperating.

A lot that should take place gets lost in this process. As the economist Paul Krugman wrote, "Policy tends to move things in a desirable direction, yet to fall short of what you'd hoped to see." The challenge, he said, is to strike a balance: deciding "how many compromises, how much watering down, one is willing to accept" but also not being too picky – not "making the perfect the enemy of the good" and missing an opportunity for action.[6]

To compound the problem, when Internet security surfaced as an issue it was a new kind of issue and an ideal course of action was not clear at all. As a result, our policies in cyber security have not merely fallen short of the mark; they have aimed at the wrong targets and missed those. And, worse, we haven't learned from those failings, for which there can be no apology.

PLANS MADE AND ENTITIES FORMED: AN ALPHABET SOUP MORASS

Cyber security is an issue of many agendas. It is a part of protecting "critical infrastructures" from terrorism and other threats, part of the defence and war-fighting agendas of many countries, and an element of economic and social functioning for parties ranging from big corporations to you and me. Dealing with cyber security is in part domestic policy and in part a matter of building and managing multinational frameworks and, of course, the global Internet itself.

Prosecution of the actual commission of cyber crime, for example, falls under the purview of many laws criminalizing activities such as fraud that occur in the physical as well as the cyber world. In the U.S. only one statute – the Computer Fraud and Abuse Act – criminalizes unauthorized access to a computer.[7] In many (U.S. Federal) prosecutions other common charges include "'Theft of Trade Secrets," "Fraud by Wire, Radio, or Television," and "Unlawful Access to Stored Communications." An international treaty, the Convention on Cybercrime, further calls for countries under the Convention to "harmonize" their laws regarding cyber crime. Yet the EU notes that "there is no agreed definition of cyber crime."[8]

This all creates diffusion, if not confusion. A multitude of organizations are involved within the United States alone; overlaps and gaps abound. In the U.S., entities with responsibilities for pursuing cyber crime – just one aspect of security – include the Secret Service (part of DHS, the Department of Homeland Security); the FBI (part of DoJ, the Department of Justice); and the FTC (Federal Trade Commission) – and did I mention CHIP (the Computer Hacking and Intellectual Property Unit), which is part of DoJ but not of the FBI? Did I mention that the Defense Department operates its own set of computer response teams, as do a number of private organizations – and that Defense also owns NSA, the National Security Agency, which has a big hand in cyber security and aims to have a bigger one?

The complexity eases up when we look at other OECD nations. Most have some type of cyber-security policy, whether formal or informal. Canada does not have its own separate national cyber-security policy,[168] although the National Security Policy of 2004, the Emergency Management Act of 2005, and the Department of Public Safety and Emergency Preparedness Act of 2005 integrate functions including the National Crime Prevention Centre and the Office of Critical Infrastructure Protection. The Canadian Cyber Incident Response Centre was launched in 2005.[10]

The U.K. had developed the U.K. Government Strategy for Information Assurance, with the Central Sponsor for Information Assurance, a unit within the U.K. Cabinet Office, providing strategic direction. Critical national infrastructure (CNI) sectors are partnered with equivalent government agencies, with the Home Office having core responsibility for these infrastructures but with a number of departments playing a role, including the Centre for Protection of National Infrastructure (CPNI), the National Infrastructure Security Coordination Centre, and several mechanisms for information sharing and partnering with the private sector.[11]

Since criminal groups can operate in multiple and scattered locations across the globe, national law enforcement agencies cannot investigate most cyber crimes without either investigative support from their foreign counterparts, or the authority to unilaterally search and seize evidence from computers in other countries in pursuit of cyber criminals. Prosecution requires that countries cooperate in locating and holding or handing over the actual cyber criminal. Thus, multilateral cooperation, or authority to conduct cross-border searches, is essential for effective cyber law-enforcement.

Multilateral cooperation against cyber crime operates through three mechanisms: informal cooperation, formalized cooperation through the G-8, and the Council of Europe Convention on Cybercrime.[12] Informal cooperation is crucial and does not require lengthy treaty processes, but it is uncertain. Moreover, extradition of cyber criminals is difficult in the absence of a treaty.[13]

Both the Council of Europe Convention on Cybercrime and the G-8 Subgroup on High-Tech Crime create frameworks for cooperation between officials in the originating state (of the cyber crime) and those of the target state in investigations. The G-8 Subgroup does this unofficially. The Convention on Cybercrime more comprehensively counters cyber crime through harmonizing national legislation, enhancing law enforcement and judicial capabilities, and improving international cooperation. The Convention deems cyber crimes to be extraditable offences, and permits law enforcement authorities in one country to collect computer-based evidence for those in another. It also calls for establishing a twenty-four-hour, seven-days-a-week contact network to provide immediate assistance with cross-border investigations.[14]

Right now, though, the U.S. is the only nation outside of Council of Europe members to have ratified the Convention on Cybercrime.[15] Canada has signed but not ratified the Convention. Notable missing parties include China, India, Russia, most of Africa and South America, and other Asian and Pacific Rim countries. Thus, the Convention doesn't have the critical mass it needs to be effective. Also, we do not now have an effective method of dealing with non-signatories – neither voluntary understandings with these nations nor a framework for sanctioning countries that are havens for cyber crime.

Whatever the country or convention, it's a bewildering array of overlapping responsibilities, ripe for bureaucratic territoriality and confusion.

Since U.S. policy provides the de facto framework, if not the details, of cyber-security policy for the rest of the OECD, we will concentrate mostly on the U.S. from hereinafter. Despite its limited-role intent, the U.S. definitely has made up for the paucity of formal planning documents from other countries. Here is a *selected* list of major reports and plans since cyber security/critical infrastructure protection became an important issue in the mid-1990s.

- (1998, White House) *Presidential Decision Directives (PDDs) 62, 63,* and *68* establish the national goal of protecting critical infrastructures, particularly information systems;

- (2000, White House) *National Plan for Information Systems Protection, V. 1.0* is initial national plan for cyber security;

- (2001) *Office of Homeland Security and Homeland Security Council* is created;

- (2001) *Presidential Executive Order (EO) 13231* establishes President's Critical Infrastructure Protection Board;

- (2002, Federal legislation) *Homeland Security Act* creates the *Department of Homeland Security (DHS),* giving it lead responsibility for preventing terrorist attacks in the U.S., and creates a new lead against cyber crime, the Undersecretary for Information Analysis and Infrastructure Protection (easy bonus question: does this complicate things?);

- (2002, White House Office of Homeland Security) *National Strategy for Homeland Security* is developed;

- (2002, Federal legislation) *Federal Information Security Management Act* sets standards for U.S. government agency cyber-security;

- (2002, Federal legislation) *Critical Infrastructure Information Act* provides some protections to the private sector for cyber security/critical infrastructure information shared with the Federal government;

- (2003, White House) *National Infrastructure Assurance Council* is created;

- (2003, White House) *National Strategy for Physical Protection of Critical Infrastructures and Key Assets* is developed;[16]

- (2003, White House) *National Strategy to Secure Cyberspace* (NSCC) lays out the follow-on plan for cyber security by the Bush administration;

- (2003, White House) *Homeland Security Presidential Directive (HSPD) 7* establishes a national policy of key federal departments, working with corresponding economic sectors, to identify and prioritize critical infrastructures and to protect them from terrorist attack;

- (2004, White House Office of Science and Technology Policy/Department of Homeland Security Science and Technology Directorate) *National Plan for Research and Development in Support of Critical Infrastructure Protection* is created;

- (2005, Department of Defense) *Strategy for Homeland Defense and Civil Support* [17] outlines the role of the Defense Department, distinct from DHS, in protecting against cyber threats as one component of homeland defence; an Assistant Secretary for Homeland Defense is created.

- (2006, Department of Homeland Security) *National Infrastructure Protection Plan*[18] attempts to roll up all previous plans into a comprehensive framework for critical national infrastructure protection;

- (2008, The White House) *National Security Presidential Directive/HSPD 23* establishes the (classified) Comprehensive National Cyber Security Initiative (CNCSI). Michael Chertoff, then head of Homeland Security, touts CNCSI as a "Manhattan Project" for cyber security but the claim is met with much scoffing;[19]

• (2008, Department of Homeland Security) *National Cyber Security Center* is created within DHS to coordinate all U.S. government cyber-security efforts.

There are seventeen listed here. This list does not include the passage of criminal laws and other laws pertaining to cyber security, nor does it include key initiatives from the private sector. In 2009, the Obama administration released its own initial review of cyber-security policy, sure to be followed by further plans and directives.

THE COST OF THE SHUFFLE

What gets lost in the shuffling and the muddling? Here are a few examples.

In the U.K., the National Hi-Tech Crime Unit was formed in 2001, primarily to deal with cyber crime. But in 2006 the NHTCU was dissolved and many of its duties transferred to the "e-crime unit" of the U.K.'s new SOCA, the Serious Organised Crime Agency, which also has a mandate to deal with such matters as drug trafficking. Many criticized the SOCA e-crime unit as being under-resourced and poorly structured. (For instance, businesses could report cyber crimes in confidence to the old NHTCU, an arrangement meant to encourage reporting. But the "confidentiality charter" was suspended for the SOCA unit.)

So, late in 2008, a supplementary move was announced: the creation of a new Police Central e-crime Unit, the PCeU, linked to the London Metropolitan Police Service and a newly created National Fraud Reporting Centre, the NFRC.

Meanwhile, in the U.S. in 2008, there was good news: a new office was created, the National Cyber Security Center (NCSC), to coordinate all U.S. government efforts in cyber security. Better yet, a private-sector luminary, the high-tech entrepreneur and author Rod Beckstrom, was recruited to direct the Center. But early in 2009, Beckstrom resigned, citing a lack of funding. He said that his office had received about five hundred thousand dollars during the first year, enough to fund about five weeks of operation. He also claimed that the NSA, the National Security Agency, had too much influence over federal cyber-security decisions. Others rose to NSA's defence, arguing that it, and not Homeland Security, should have primacy in cyber security . . . [20]

Between them, the U.K. and the U.S. have spent years trying to resolve one high-profile case, that of the Scottish hacker Gary McKinnon. McKinnon, a.k.a. SOLO, was accused of hacking into a series of U.S. military and NASA computers in 2001–2002. In 2002, he was arrested by the U.K.'s National Hi-Tech Crime Unit for violating the U.K.'s Computer Misuse Act. But much more serious charges against him were levied in the U.S. Attempts were begun to extradite him to the U.S. for trial, but as of mid-2009 he had fought off extradition for seven years and gained an army of supporters across the U.K. (McKinnon has been diagnosed with Asperger Syndrome, and it seems that part of his motive for hacking into American systems was to look for suppressed evidence of UFOs.)

None of what we've reviewed here is surprising or even necessarily bad. Extradition disputes do occur. More to the point, it's not at all unusual for a single country to have multiple agencies dealing with a single issue. When it comes to matters like security and policing, some even consider this a good thing, a healthy separation of powers. And when a new issue emerges, as cyber security did, it's not surprising for there to be some initial confusion over whom the issue "belongs" to – especially when it's an international issue.

In fact, various governments have started to recognize their shortcomings. In November 2008, the EU's Council of Ministers adopted changes to the European Program for Critical Infrastructure Protection of 2005,[21] proposing a series of operational measures, such as cyber patrols, joint investigation teams, and remote searches to become part of the fight against cyber crime. Reports on crime across EU states would now be pooled for cross checking by Europol.[22]

But the real trouble in cyber security is that while all this shuffling of deck chairs has gone on, the adversary – the cyber underworld – has been evolving and adapting literally at Internet speed. While bureaucrats and politicians wrangle over who should be in charge of what in their respective countries, criminals react rapidly to any defensive move or strike at their capabilities. They even react quickly to changes in the underground "markets" for various kinds of stolen data. The public sector just can't keep up. Nor, it seems, can the private sector.

CRIME STOPPING IN THE PRIVATE SECTOR (AND ELSEWHERE)

In some of the best cases of voluntary cooperation, private entities have teamed up to shut down cyber criminal operations, with little or no involvement from law enforcement or official government agencies. One such string of cases happened in 2008. Key players were the nonprofit group HostExploit.com (which bills itself as an "open-source resource" for research on cyber crime, and has many volunteer workers from the cyber-security industries), other independent security groups, and the *Washington Post* reporter Brian Krebs, who writes an influential blog called "Security Fix."

HostExploit, with publicity and reporting from Krebs, exposed the workings of the McColo Corporation, a U.S. firm that provided Web hosting for a number of international outfits known (or found) to be spammers. McColo's upstream Internet providers then cut it off. HostExploit also published a report on Atrivo, a.k.a. Intercage, an ISP in Concord, California, that was providing services for many illegitimate and quasi-legitimate enterprises (including a number that had been linked to the Russian Business Network). Atrivo's upstream providers eventually cut it off as well.

And, in a related move, HostExploit and Krebs exposed EstDomains, a domain-name registry used by criminal enterprises. Krebs published a column pointing out that the EstDomains CEO, a twenty-seven-year-old Estonian named Vladimir Tsastsin, was in prison in his home country for fraud and other crimes.

Subsequently, ICANN decertified EstDomains – whose clients had been doing business with Atrivo, and which was believed to be linked to cyber-crime czars in Russia.

Altogether it was nice work, chopping off some major tentacles of the cyber underworld without a single court case other than Tsastin's imprisonment in Estonia. But it's unlikely to have lasting effects. As noted before, global spam volume dropped after McColo was shut off but climbed back to normal within a few months. And as for putting Atrivo and EstDomains out of business, Krebs himself noted that all the good work may be in vain.

I asked a couple of sources what they thought of this development, and whether it would have any long-term impact. Suresh Ramasubramanian, head of anti-spam operations at Hong Kong–based Outblaze.com, sees this action as a mere speed bump for the bad guys, who won't soon make the same mistake of putting all of their criminal domains in one registrar's basket.

"While the Russkie mob might resurrect EstDomains with a different patsy than Tsastsin, my suspicion is that they'll do something I have observed for quite a while – shift to spreading the load among a large number of dumb registrars," Ramasubramanian said. "I think there will be no further big juicy targets. No Intercage/Atrivo, no Estdomains, no recognizable entity called the Russian Business Network. These guys got cocky and were allowed to operate that way, but they can just as easily spread the load around and operate hidden in plain view."[23]

There have also been some big busts made by actual, official cyber cops. In the two largest known thefts of credit-card numbers and customer data, the TJX/T.J. Maxx case and the Heartland Payments Systems case, likely perpetrators have been identified and arrested. But many more gangs have eluded capture – and news of the data breaches they performed haven't been publicly reported.

A software expert told me he felt sure that his own credit-card information has been stolen at least twice: once in the TJX breach, because after that breach, he was issued a replacement card for the one he'd been using at a local TJX store. And once more, a couple of years

later, in an incident unknown to him – because he received a replacement for another card, which he'd been using at various *other* retail
outlets – and this card had not expired, and there was no reason given
in the brief and discreet notice that came along with it, just "here is
your new card."

Records generally show that many arrests are of low-ranking or
penny-ante hackers. In my district, for instance, a couple of university students rather inexpertly ran a little cyber racket that (according to the prosecutor) appeared to be part mischief hacking and part
let's-see-if-we-can-steal-something. There have been few cases of
insider threats coming to court and I have yet to find a major one.

But policing cyber criminals is only one component of cyber security. A review of other components shows progress being made in several areas, although again it has not been enough to turn the tide.

POLICY EFFORTS TO DATE:
A BRIEF PERFORMANCE REVIEW

One key policy goal since the early days has been setting up pub-
lic/private mechanisms to share information on cyber attacks and
coordinate responses. The most significant institutions created for
this purpose are the CERTs – Computer Emergency Readiness (or
Response) Teams – and the U.S. system of ISACs.

The U.S. CERT, which we've mentioned earlier, dates from
1988.[24] A host of other countries now have CERTs or CERT-like
organizations as well, including many European nations, India,
Pakistan, Argentina, Brazil, and Chile. The setups vary: Germany
has multiple CERTs, while France has one operated as a nonprofit
centre by major industries, and another run by the government. All
more or less follow the U.S. operating model, whereby private and
public entities can report major cyber incidents or vulnerabilities
to the CERT, which may then help out in any number of ways,
from analyzing threats and disseminating alerts to helping defend
against an attack in progress.

The CERTs are routinely valuable and have had some spotlight
moments – for instance, when global CERTs worked with the Estonia

CERT to deal with the DDOS attacks on that country. A major limitation is that many incidents are not reported to CERTs[25] – and indeed, if all were, the CERTs would probably be hard pressed to process them.

The ISACs (Information Sharing and Analysis Centers) in the U.S. are independent entities meant to help inform and protect specific "sectors" of the society, such as particular industries, or state and local governments. Run by and for their members, they were created in the wake of the 2000 National Plan that I helped to draft, and though little known to the general public, ISACs have made significant contributions to overall cyber security.

The most prominent is the Financial Services ISAC (FS-ISAC),[26] serving mainly the large financial institutions. The FS-ISAC operates a secure database and lets members report information to it anonymously. Specialists then analyze the nature of each incident or vulnerability and potential solutions. The FS-ISAC is both secretive and seemingly everywhere. I attended a conference on insider threats, and a representative of the FS-ISAC was there. He said nothing about his members' interests or concerns, did not encourage any additional contact or collaboration, but paid very close attention to the proceedings.[27] Other notable ISACs include NCC, the National Coordinating Center for Telecommunications. A holdover from the days when AT&T and the U.S. government worked together closely, it serves as the telecom industry's ISAC along with fulfilling other duties.

All told, ISACs play a central, but problematic, role in the government–private sector partnership. Their performance in that regard has been less than totally satisfactory, for two very different reasons. First, while being necessarily secretive – no ISAC wants bad guys to know what it knows – the highly confidential nature can get in the way of sharing information more widely. (For instance, the rules for sharing between the ISACs and the U.S. government have never been fully worked out.) Second, the ISACs vary widely in structure and effectiveness. The FS-ISAC, the NERC/ISAC (for electric power) and the NCC are actual operating entities, but other ISACs are essentially industry associations given new names, with not much real capability.[28]

Two other long-standing goals of U.S. policy are to have the government itself set high standards for cyber-security practice, and to encourage best practices and solutions in the private sector. One can hardly say that the first has occurred. Here, for instance, are the detailed grades from the Federal Computer Security Report Card cited in Chapter 1:

GOVERNMENTWIDE GRADE 2007: C (2006: C-)

	2007	2006
Department of Justice	A+	A-
Agency for International Development	A+	A+
Environmental Protection Agency	A+	A-
National Science Foundation	A+	A+
Social Security Administration	A	A
Housing and Urban Development	A	A+
Office of Personnel Management	A-	A+
General Services Administration	A-	A
Department of Energy	B+	C-
Department of Homeland Security	B	D
Department of Health and Human Services	B	B
Small Business Administration	B-	B+
National Aeronautics and Space Administration	C-	D-
Department of State	D	F
Department of Education	D-	F
Department of Commerce	F	F
Department of Transportation	F	B
Department of Labor	F	B-
Department of Defense	F	F
Department of the Interior	F	F
Department of Treasury	F	F
Nuclear Regulatory Commission	F	F
Department of Veterans Affairs	F	N/A
Department of Agriculture	F	F

These grades were issued in 2008, covering the previous year; later report cards are not available. There is no simple explanation why some agencies should do so well and others so poorly, nor why grades in some cases should change so greatly in the space of a year. Agencies differ dramatically in the quality of their chief information officers and their personal and organizational attention to security; I suspect these are the real distinguishing factors. Also, the mixed results suggest the ineffectiveness of trying to impose standard security measures across the board – a point we will return to later, when we ask what the appropriate role of government should be in improving cyber security in the society at large, outside of government itself.

As for results from the private sector, certainly this sector can boast a much larger security *apparatus* than it had in, say, the 1990s. Whereas few IT firms or end-user firms then had in-house security departments, virtually all now do. Security products and consulting have become major industries for McAfee, Symantec, and countless other firms worldwide.

Also, some of the best data-gathering-and-sharing entities are neither CERTs nor ISACs, but private international groups started in grassroots fashion. Spamhaus, a global nonprofit based in Geneva and London, tracks spam worldwide and issues useful spam-blocking lists as well as a rogues' gallery called ROKSO, the Register of Known Spam Operations (complete with photos and personal details on the masterminds). The Anti-Phishing Working Group (APWG), supported by industries, studies and helps to combat phishing globally. Spamhaus and APWG can be seen as sterling examples of the "let the private sector do it" policy approach.

THE BOTTOM LINE

We could go on at great length, looking at policies and entities in various countries. They all sound good and some work well, for their intended purposes. But they haven't given us the results we desperately need. Despite a lot of good work in both the private and public sectors, the tide running against us in cyber security has not been reversed. Whatever we are doing, then, must not include what really needs to be done.

A lot of things that could help make us *fundamentally* more secure aren't being attended to. Instead we are playing endless games of catch-up, or conducting isolated exercises in catch-the-bad-guy. Altogether it's a failed paradigm, a losing proposition.

Many security improvements in the private sector have gone unmade or poorly made because we have trusted market forces to bring them about, and the incentives just aren't there. It takes time and investment for a software company to write software that's more secure, or for an ISP to deploy the best possible security features. The markets are fiercely competitive on the basis of price: home users jump from one ISP to another to get cheaper connectivity, and corporate buyers of software and hardware have tight IT budgets. Although quality matters, too, what most customers care about is how the stuff works: how fast and reliably it runs, whether it has new *functional* features they can use.

In such markets it's difficult for any one company to spend more than its competitors on security, or use security features to justify a premium price. Enhanced security can be a tough sell. Your customers may not experience the benefits directly or notice an appreciable difference. They may not understand your security claims, or believe them, and the Oracle debacle of the early 2000s didn't help. (Oracle advertised its corporate software as being so secure that hackers "can't break in." Of course this inevitably backfired, since security can never be perfect. Holes were quickly found and the ad campaign became a laughingstock.)

The security marketplace is full of complex perversities. Even when a software company makes its own products more secure, or an ISP makes its services more secure, customers may continue having problems because other products and services they're using remain less secure, leaving them open to attack in other ways. Or they may persist in using the Internet unwisely.

In every such case, it's clear that the whole market must move in a certain direction but doesn't because it fails to drive each of the individuals in the herd appropriately. These "market failures" are classic cases that call for policy intervention – to provide the incentives (or frankly, the coercion) needed. But *that* isn't tried either, because any proposal to expand or alter government's role in cyber security has been seen as leading to Big Brother and the end of Net freedom. Yet it is clear that voluntary action is not enough. Nations must assess and prioritize risks and set minimum standards for securing cyberspace. A path needs to be charted that avoids burdensome regulatory mandates that could add cost and stifle innovation, but we can no longer continue to over-rely on market forces, which have shown themselves inadequate to meet national and public security requirements. And since cyber security is not just a single-country issue, a pressing question is: How can engaged countries (Canada, the U.S., and the U.K., to name a few) operate more effectively together? The U.S. particularly needs to untangle the bureaucratic spaghetti that is its cyber-security policy, and tame the internal turf wars.[29]

A ROUGH OUTLINE FOR NEW POLICY: THE THREE I'S

The number-one salient fact is this: The cyber underworld has evolved into a finely tuned and marvellously adaptive ecosystem for doing harm, while our ecosystems for maintaining order just haven't kept up. So here again it helps to think of cyberspace as a city, one much like early industrial-age London or the burgeoning megacities of the developing world today. In each case we have a new *kind* of city where the harmful side effects of growth are spinning out of control, because the mechanisms for dealing with them haven't been invented or put into place yet.

What kinds of "mechanisms" would improve security in our cyber-city? To put it as simply as possible – using a mnemonic device, even – what we'll lay out here are the three I's: *institutional infrastructure and incentives.*

Institutional infrastructure means a proper set of social "systems" for cyber security, including both public and private entities. At present we have only a partial set, and some systems that we do have aren't very well developed. Needed are:

• A system for managing or coordinating the adoption of new technologies. The communal-style bodies we now have do good work but aren't adequate – given that it took ten years just to get a less-than-one-per-cent adoption rate of the new Internet protocol, IPv6. Work is now underway on a full "clean slate" redesign of the Internet architecture – in order to, among other things, fundamentally improve security. But if this is ever to be done well and implemented globally, we'll need some sort of international coordinating mechanism that can do much more than was done with IPv6.

• A system or systems for gathering good, consistent data on cyber incidents, the damage they do, and the effectiveness of various defensive measures. Without better data than we now have, we are operating in dim light.

• Better systems for global policing of cyber criminals and cyber terrorists. (Which may also require a better and more consistent body of law, both at the national and international levels . . . along with clear multilateral agreement on the "rules" for responding to apparent cyber terror or cyber war.)

• A well-developed system for insurance against cyber attack.

"Incentives" are measures that induce firms and people to do (or not do) things that would improve security for all. Incentives can take many forms. For instance, a set of financial incentives might include subsidies, credits, or public investments for desired behaviour, and/or fines, tariffs, or other sorts of penalties on undesired behaviour. Incentives can also include things like precedents at law (which, through court decisions, encourage or inhibit certain kinds of behaviour), or widely accepted review-and-rating systems. (The Underwriters Laboratories ratings of product safety have long carried a good bit of weight, as have consumer-product ratings like those from the nonprofit Consumers Union, or the vehicle safety ratings done by government agencies in various countries. An example of a rating system that has *not* worked well recently is the system for rating bonds and securities on Wall Street.)

Whatever the forms, in cyber security we could use, for instance:

- Incentives for software firms to write software that's more secure, with fewer vulnerabilities.

- Incentives for firms such as ISPs and other network-management companies to deploy better security across their networks.

- Incentives for end-users – firms and organizations, as well as individuals – to follow better security practices and avoid being negligent or just plain stupid.

So that's a short list of what is needed – and of course it's not such a short list. We are basically talking about re-inventing how cyberspace is run, while (a) somehow getting the world's 220-or-so nations on board with the program and (b) avoiding damage to the freedom and vitality of cyberspace. We will never get the job done perfectly or completely. But we can certainly do better than muddling along on the present course – a course on which we're likely to keep losing ground, at increasing risk and cost to you and me, despite the hard work of many in the cyber-security and IT communities.

The final question we must ask in this chapter is a big one. We're calling on governments to become far more active than they have been, implementing the three I's and so forth. But how, exactly, would they best do that? What kinds of tools should they try for which kinds of tasks; what kinds of things should they *avoid* doing? And how do they justify what they propose to do, to the many who will be skeptical or outright hostile to expanded policy action?

WHAT IS THE APPROPRIATE ROLE FOR GOVERNMENT?

At least two models have been cited as possible precedents for developing a better cyber-security framework.* One is the response to the Y2K problem. The other is public health and safety.[30]

The Y2K problem provides an interesting parallel. What does Y2K-compliant mean? Neither the Canadian nor the U.S. government specified a standard of Y2K compliance. What both nations did was to take action along two lines, information sharing and raising awareness – in the U.S., through a special advisor to the President, who worked with industry and international bodies (including the UN) to encourage awareness and action in advance of the new millennium. And perhaps even more importantly, in the U.S. the Securities and Exchange Commission (SEC) required that public companies report on what, if anything, they were doing to prepare for Y2K. The SEC left it up to investors and the market to determine whether a company was Y2K-compliant or not and whether their actions were sufficient. This disclosure requirement was a powerful incentive for effective private-sector action.

In public health and safety, we do impose certain performance requirements. Some of these, interestingly, are the result of private action. We do not as a matter of law require people to get an annual checkup, or visit the dentist, but many insurance policies require at least an initial physical, and some companies require their employees to have annual checkups. In other cases, government plays a role in requiring measurable and specific performance requirements. Most countries enforce driver's licensing and speed limits, and virtually all have public health regulations that say one must (or must not) do certain things.

In general, what distinguishes these specific performance requirements is that there is a direct link between the required action and the desired outcome. Restaurant employees must wash their hands because they handle food for the public; the rest of us are encouraged to do so, but since we generally endanger only ourselves if we don't, there are no laws requiring everyone to wash their hands.

---

* I am indebted to Dr. Shari Lawrence Pfleeger for much of what follows here.

In cyber security, this linkage between specific performance requirements and the desired outcome (better security) is usually not very direct. The abysmal record of the Federal Report Cards and Government Accountability Office reviews in the U.S. suggest that government agencies have not taken implementation very seriously, or have botched it. Consequently a program of required standards has not resulted in the desired outcome – better security.

In the private sector, there are many organizations that take seemingly appropriate actions – security audit, organizational standards and policies, appointment of a chief security officer, training for their employees – and yet it is hard to see that the systems are measurably more secure than before. The point is that the link between most "good security practices" and better security is not as clear as the link in public health and safety, and thus requiring a general set of security standards to be adopted for most organizations is an inappropriate role for government.

There are three tests for the appropriate role of government. Do requirements link (more or less directly) to desired outcomes? Can we measure these outcomes? Are there other means by which we can create mechanisms which let those closer to the problem "sort out" what is the appropriate set of actions (as in Y2K)?

One signal feature of public health and safety is that the government's role is in both prevention and response. This role is based on a system of creating an infrastructure, defining what is to be of concern for that system, and defining where there is a direct linkage between action and desired outcome as the basis for regulations.

In other cases, government should let other mechanisms define the exact specifics of how an outcome is to be achieved, rather than doing it through regulation.

Ensuring the quality of the medical profession is a good example. Doctors regulate themselves through medical school and residency, and then through standards created by their own profession. This system is not perfect – the bottom 10 or 20 per cent of those who become doctors are probably only minimally competent – but there is no "perfect system." And it works well enough.

But additionally we control the quality of doctors by licensing them. They are also ranked by their reputation and the quality of the institution that they are attached to. And as a last resort there are liability and malpractice suits. Whatever one thinks about malpractice suits, they have the effect of weeding out truly incompetent doctors.

So here's the point: the desired outcome – high-quality doctors – is hard to measure. Therefore, the role of government is to provide some baseline framework of licensing, to gather and disseminate data on the relative quality of different institutions to which doctors may be affiliated, and to provide mechanisms that let people measure and act on the results (by selecting doctors with better reputations or attached to better institutions, or through malpractice suits).

Now consider environmental regulation, where the outcome – release of pollutants – can be readily measured and where there is a direct link between a specified government requirement – reduce or limit the release of pollutants – and the desired outcome – a clean environment. Over time we have witnessed the transformation of government action in this area from one of dictating specific processes to focusing on outcomes: you (factory, company) choose whatever mechanisms you want, but we (government, society) determine what level of releases is allowable or not. Furthermore, the government provides data (the Toxic Release Inventory) that creates the additional mechanism of public reputation to further encourage companies to take action beyond that required by the specifics of the law.

There is a similar type of linkage, creating pressure to take action, in the various data breach notification laws that now exist in thirty-some states of the U.S. Deirdre Mulligan is a legal scholar at Berkeley who helped to craft the original California law, the first of its kind in the U.S. and a model for legislation elsewhere. As Mulligan has noted, "The purpose of the law was to improve security practices" – not by spelling out the practices to be used, but just by requiring companies to notify customers whose personal data has been exposed in a security breach. And, she went on, "Research and anecdote both suggest that [the law] has improved practices along many dimensions."[31] It remains to be seen whether data-breach laws will lead to the ultimate desired result, which is having fewer and less severe breaches over the long run. But here we at least have an example of how appropriate action can be encouraged.

There are probably a small set of performance requirements – the equivalent of speed limits or requirements that restaurant employees wash their hands – where there is a more direct linkage between the action and the result, and thus where a *specific* action should be required collectively, though any individual institution may not have the incentive to adopt it. One example would be requiring all ISPs to filter messages entering their network to ensure that each has a valid source address for that network entry point. This is called ingress filtering, and its widespread use by all service providers would greatly limit the ability of an attacker to send packets using spoofed source addresses, thereby making tracing the attacker a much easier task.

Another legitimate role of government is to promote data collection and dissemination. Since, unlike crime or speeding, we don't have good definitions for "cyber attacks" or "quality software" this is an area where the role of government is to establish a reporting requirement and let other institutions sort out what the metrics need to be.

One possibility would be for the Financial Accounting Standards Board to require that audits or financial reports list all "material" cyber attacks or security breaches. That leaves it up to auditors to determine "materiality," but there are well-established parallels in other spheres that could be brought into play. It's not a perfect system, and curiously, would put the government tax and revenue agencies in the position of being the collector of a lot of information about cyber attacks. But it would avoid putting government in the position of defining what a cyber attack was for many different kinds of organizations and businesses.

It is impossible to produce "perfect" software. Vulnerabilities reported to the CERT should be grouped by software product and made publicly available by software product. Software and hardware manufacturers should also be subject to tort negligence liability. Right now they are generally viewed as immune from such suits and this immunity has even been codified in two U.S. states. Liability could be limited both in terms of the judgments awarded and the types of suits that could be filed, but the exposure to liability would still provide an important incentive to nudge software and hardware manufacturers to pay attention to security.

There is a role for government in cyber security, and the appropriate role is to create incentives or require actions that result in (ideally) measurable outcomes. Even more so than in areas of public health and safety, however, output metrics are difficult to create in cyber security; equally, the link between a specific action and the desired social collective good is not as direct. We can measure how many (statistical) lives are saved by enforcing speed limits or by investing in additional road improvements. We cannot, in general, achieve the same level of precise causal linkage in the case of cyber-security actions.

The risk, therefore, is that government involvement takes the form of onerous requirements for specific actions – say, adoption of certain software development practices or required adoption of security standards – that end up achieving little in the way of real improvement in security. We suspect that it is the fear that government involvement in cyber security will take this form that motivates much of the political resistance to a greater role for government.

It need not be that way.

CHAPTER 7

BETTER SOFTWARE AND BETTER USERS

The two major sources of cyber insecurity are vulnerabilities in software, and those damn(!) users. Quite a bit can be done to make software considerably less vulnerable. Unfortunately, quite a bit less can be done to make users behave so that they don't open the door to cyber attack, but it is important to understand what *can* be done.

WHAT IS SOFTWARE?

Software is a set of computer instructions or data, as distinct from hardware, which includes memory, processing, and display devices. A microprocessor that Intel makes is hardware; Microsoft Word 2007 is software. More specifically, Microsoft Word and other programs that enable us to *do* things on a computer – write documents, manage spreadsheets and databases, edit pictures, and so on (either with human input or automatically) – are applications software. Windows 7 and Vista are examples of underlying systems software – including the operating system – that enables the computer to function and "run" your applications.[1]

Software is everywhere, and connects everything with everything else. "Software is the new physical infrastructure of the information age. It is fundamental to economic success, scientific and technical research, and national security."[2] Your car has more computing power than the Apollo space missions; the elevators, and heating, cooling, and lighting systems in your office are software-controlled. Increasingly these systems are linked together, which means that problems in one software system affect others – oftentimes unexpectedly. In August 2003 a programming error in the management of the (North American) Northeast power grid caused multiple systems trying to access the same information to get the equivalent of a busy signal. The resulting alarm failures contributed to a major electricity blackout.[3]

Software is typically written in a "source code" based on a particular coding language. In my high-school years I was taught to program in BASIC; today, examples of high-level languages would be C++ or Java. Another computer program, a compiler, transforms the source code into the object code or machine language that the computer actually operates on. No one in their right mind writes in machine language; as part of a hellish computer-science course I took in college, I had to do so, and have been scarred ever since.

A simple example of software is a program that prints out the lyrics of "Ninety-nine Bottles of Beer on the Wall," in this case written in FORTRAN IV:

```
C Allen Mcintosh
C mcintosh@bellcore.com
  integer bottls
  do 50 i = 1, 99
  bottls = 100 - i
    print 10, bottls
10 format(1x, i2, 31h bottle(s) of beer on the wall.)
   print 20, bottls
20 format(1x, i2, 19h bottle(s) of beer.)
   print 30
30 format(34h Take one down and pass it around,)
   bottls = bottls - 1
```

```
    print 10, bottls
    print 40
40 format(1x)
50 continue
    stop
    end
```

The first C means "Comment" and identifies the author. Then the program spells out the instructions for printing, successively: "99 bottles of beer on the wall, 99 bottles of beer, take one down and pass it around, 98 bottles of beer on the wall," and so on.

Software is the most important handmade product in the world, yet visiting a software developer and looking at software being produced is actually like watching paint dry – a bunch of mostly youngish men (and some women) sitting in front of workstations and drinking coffee. There are automated tools to assist in evaluating and testing software, and libraries of existing software functions that can be plugged into a new program. In fact, most "new" software is actually developed by modifying an existing program.[4]

As well as being handmade, software is devilishly complex, if only because the programs are in general becoming bigger and we have increasing expectations of what they should do. Software size is measured in lines of source code. To put this in physical terms, one thousand lines of code can take up thirty printed pages. Windows Vista has over fifty million lines of code.[5] And, at least for the desktop market, we expect the operating system to support a multitude of applications: word processing, data sheets, games, video and image processing, and e-mail and Internet connectivity, to name just a few.

It is not surprising, therefore, that software contains lots of defects.

Here's the ninety-nine bottles of beer code again, this time with an introduced defect, shown in bold:

```
C Allen Mcintosh
C mcintosh@bellcore.com
```

```
integer bottls
do 50 i = 1, 109
bottls = 100 - i
   print 10, bottls
10 format(1x, i2, 31h bottle(s) of beer on the wall.)
   print 20, bottls
20 format(1x, i2, 19h bottle(s) of beer.)
   print 30
30 format(34h Take one down and pass it around,)
   bottls = bottls - 1
   print 10, bottls
   print 40
40 format(1x)
50 continue
   stop
   end
```

In this case, there will be 109 verses of the song rather than 99, with the last ten extra ones having negative bottles of beer on the wall. This defect comes from assigning the wrong value to a variable (the number of verses in the song), due either to a typo or an outright mistake. But defects have multiple ways of occurring – others include logic errors (not getting the flow of instructions right), and incorrect or unchecked input fields.

Not all defects will cause the program to misbehave every time, and those that do are often obvious enough to be caught and fixed before the software is released for use. But a lot of defects can cause problems sometimes, under certain conditions. And defects that can be exploited – in order to make that program and/or other parts of the system do unintended things – are security problems waiting to happen.

Software defects in the delivered product are quite common. On average, for *delivered software* there are about 7.5 defects per thousand source lines of code (known by the acronym KSLOC, the standard measure of the defect rate), even after the developer has gone through its own quality assurance process. This product testing consumes on average 40 per cent of the total effort spent on producing software.[6] Yet the range of defects we can expect commercial software to contain is between six and thirty per one thousand lines of code. The software is considered good if it is near the low end, and companies are usually delighted when their code contains fewer than five faults per one thousand lines of code.[7]

One day recently I was sitting in the office of Rich Pethia, head of the CERT at the Software Engineering Institute. He's the expert I met in late 1999, when we had our initial discussion of DDOS attacks, just prior to the first major shutdown of major e-commerce sites. We're talking about software, and he observes that "software is mostly pretty bad today. And my intuition is that this situation hasn't changed much in the past twenty years."[8]

"Easter eggs" are playful examples of the fact that massive numbers of defects – or massive amounts of all sorts of weird code – can lie hidden in delivered software without many users even noticing. In the first release of Microsoft Excel 2000 was embedded an entire video game called Spy Hunter (in which you drive an armoured sports car while gunning down tanks and assorted bad guys). There was a flight simulator in Excel 97, Pinball in Word 97, Tetris within the Mac OS X terminal, and yet another flight simulator embedded in Google Earth in 2007.[9]

Less playful is the list of fixes included in Windows XP Service Pack 2 (as of June 2008) that ran to forty-four printed pages of small type.[10] And Vista was released without the necessary drivers for many printers, scanners, and other hardware peripherals to work with it; one Microsoft executive had to continue to run Windows XP on a second machine just so he could use his peripherals.[11]

WHEN SOFTWARE FAILS

Not surprisingly, software can fail, or fail to perform appropriately – sometimes catastrophically, and sometimes not until years after its release. Among other things, failure can be induced when software is used in ways for which it was not designed (which it often is), or as part of a larger set of connected programs in ways that, again, were not anticipated in the original design specifications.

The most spectacular failures occur in "real time" systems for operating missiles and aircraft. In 1996 the European Space Agency's unmanned Ariane 5 rocket exploded after launch because of a software error due largely to using the same software that had controlled the Ariane 4. The program tried to stick a 64-bit number into a 16-bit space, causing an overflow. This was in a part of the guidance software dealing with the rocket's sideway velocity; at 36.7 seconds after launch the computer tried to convert this velocity measurement from a 64-bit format into a 16-bit format; the number was too big.

Why did this happen? The original programmers decided not to add the extra code that would allow the system to recover gracefully from this sort of error, assuming that the velocity figure would never be big enough to cause a problem. That may have been true for the Ariane 4, but the Ariane 5 was a faster rocket. The calculation with the bug actually served no purpose once the rocket was launched; it was intended to align the rocket prior to takeoff. Engineers decided, however, to leave the function running for the first forty seconds of flight, a special feature that would make it easy to restart the system in the event of a brief hold on the countdown. There was a backup system designed to take over in the case of failure, but it was running the same software and suffered the same error.

In response, the guidance system shut down, confusing the onboard steering computer into making an unneeded course correction, which then led the rocket to self-destruct.[12]

Also in 1996, and much more tragically, a software defect in the flight systems of a Boeing 757 caused the airplane's flight computers to malfunction in ways never anticipated. The resulting crash, into the Pacific Ocean off Peru, killed seventy people. Noted Peru's Transport Minister: "It is not the first time that one of these planes has had this kind of fault. We have to find out why the computers went crazy."[13]

In 1991 during the first Gulf War, the Patriot missile system, designed to shoot down enemy aircraft, was found to have software that performed defectively when the missile was used to shoot down incoming Iraqi Scud missiles instead. As a government report explained, "after about 20 hours [from last rebooting the Patriot's guidance system] the inaccurate time calculation becomes sufficiently large to cause the radar to look in the wrong place for the target. Consequently, the system fails to track and intercept the Scud."[14] These inaccurate calculations were the result of truncation errors, an accumulation of round-off errors over time that did not affect the Patriot system's ability to shoot down aircraft but did seriously affect its ability to shoot down supersonic missiles.[15] In February 2001, a Patriot missile system operating at Dhahran, Saudi Arabia, during Operation Desert Storm failed to track and intercept an incoming Scud. This Scud subsequently hit an Army barracks, killing twenty-eight soldiers.

Most software failures are more mundane – though they can be potentially dangerous. A software problem caused some 2004 and 2005 Toyota Prius hybrid cars to stall or shut down while driving at highway speeds. Owners of some 23,900 Prius cars received a service notice advising them to bring the cars to dealers for an hour-long software upgrade.[16] In 2003, Microsoft released a patch for flaws that could cause Word 2003 to crash when printing or saving some documents, or cause text to disappear.[17] Some Macintosh users who downloaded the latest version of iTunes in 2001 found that a bug in the installation program completely deleted their hard drives. According to Mac experts who examined the code of the buggy iTunes installer, the problem arose from a forgotten quote mark.[18] Another defect surfaced in BlackBerrys, where a typical complaint posted on the Web recently was:

> When I end calls (on my BlackBerry 8830) the screen goes blank and the phone becomes useless until I reset the phone by removing the battery. Or when I push the send button to get to the call screen to dial a number – the screen suddenly closes and goes back to the previous screen . . . It sounds like there is a memory leak somewhere.[19]

One software expert confirmed to me, "Yep, the fix is usually to 'take out the battery.'" Then he added: "They've improved the newer models. It's easier to get the battery out."[20]

Apple suffered extensive network gridlock in 2008 when many of the six million users of the original iPhone simultaneously tried to upgrade their software – while the first buyers of the new iPhone 3G were trying to activate their purchases. As a *New York Times* reporter commented, "The setback was a classic example of the problems that can follow when complex systems have single points of failure. In this case, the company appeared to almost invite the problems by having both existing and new iPhone owners try to get through to its system at the same time."[21]

The problems that defective software imposes upon us continue: Alcohol breath analyzers used by police are found, on inspection of their source code (as a result of a two-year lawsuit), to inaccurately average results, and to have disabled any indication when the microprocessor may be malfunctioning.[22] Two months after a new bus line is opened, passengers still can't purchase or validate tickets at the stations because of software glitches in the ticket vending machines.[23] Microsoft patches an "insane" number of bugs.[24] And so on.

Defective software also causes a lot of disappointments. For large software projects, only 32 per cent are delivered on time, on budget, with the required features and functions. Twenty-four per cent are cancelled prior to completion, or the software is delivered and never used.[25] Sometimes these failed projects end up costing billions with nothing to show for the spending. The U.S. Federal Aviation Administration (FAA) spent fifteen years overhauling its computer systems for air traffic control, and ultimately wrote off $1.5 billion of its $2.6 billion investment. "The FAA's Advanced Automation System (AAS) project dwarfs even the largest corporate information technology fiascos in terms of dollars wasted," observed a Congressional aide.[26]

In the classic software-junkie book *The Mythical Man-Month*,[27] the author, Fred Brooks, presents a series of famously dire observations on big projects. The best known of these is a dictum called Brooks' Law: "Adding manpower to a late software project makes it later." Brooks knows whereof he speaks; he was the IBM director who developed the operating system software for the IBM System/360 computer line. Overall, the 360 software project was one of IBM's first major efforts to run far beyond planned budgets and schedules. The cover art for the book captures the story: ground sloths struggling to free themselves from the La Brea tar pits.[28]

DEFECTS CAUSE SECURITY VULNERABILITIES

A *security vulnerability* is a defect in software that prevents you from being able to enforce whatever security policy you have chosen.[29] Not all defects are vulnerabilities, but all vulnerabilities are rooted in defects. For example, one user found a defect in the home shopping site QVC.com, by which she learned that she could place an order, cancel it at a specific time, and never be charged. However, the order would still be sent to her. Four hundred thousand dollars and eighteen hundred items later, she was eventually caught – but only because eBay buyers became suspicious that items were being sold there with QVC packaging at less than QVC prices.[30]

New security vulnerabilities are found all the time; a number of Web sites and e-mail security newsletters have constant updates on the most recently discovered vulnerabilities. Manufacturers are pretty good about fixing defects once they are reported, though it is unclear how proactive they are in fixing these defects before they become public. In 2002, a major vulnerability was discovered in switching equipment software that runs the Internet, years after the software was first released. Vendors and network operators raced to fix this vulnerability before it was exploited by hackers. U.S. government officials reportedly made efforts to keep information about the vulnerability quiet until patches were installed.[31]

Based on what's going on – with security vulnerabilities being constantly reported and fixed – one would think that software must be getting more secure all the time. But software is not getting more secure. Some classic bugs continue to be written into new code and, maddeningly, these defects persist as the sources of vulnerabilities year after year. The top-ten known defects that cause a security vulnerability account for 75 per cent of all vulnerabilities, and more than 90 per cent of all security exploits are due to attackers exploiting a known defect.[32]

A short list of all-time classic vulnerabilities that persist in code would include *buffer overflows.* These are among the top-two security vulnerabilities. They are the easiest to exploit and can have devastating consequences, often resulting in the complete takeover of the host computer.[33] A buffer is a space in the program in which data can be held. A buffer overflow is the computer's equivalent of what happens when you try to pour two litres of water into a one-litre pitcher;[34] some of it is going to spill out. However, the potential overflow causes a serious problem only in some instances. Depending on what is adjacent to the buffer, overflows may result in the program trying to compute with a faulty value or to execute an improper operation.

Buffer overflows were first notably exploited by the Morris Worm in 1988,[35] and for a long time they were simply a minor annoyance, causing errors and sometimes system crashes. More recently, attackers have used them as vehicles to cause controlled failures, with serious security implications. Buffer overflows have for several years been among the top-twenty security flaws that the SANS Institute publishes. The now infamous "Code Red" worm exploited buffer overflows to make headlines when it began to wreak havoc throughout the Internet in such a short period of time starting on July 12, 2001.[36]

Cross-site scripting (XSS) is another classic vulnerability, typically found in Web applications. It allows malicious Web users to inject code of their own into the Web pages viewed by other users.

You come across several auctions that someone has posted and would like to see more items that the same person has for sale; let's assume this person is a "bad guy" (though you don't know it) and call him BG12345. You click on BG12345's website and see a listing of his auctions. You click on a link on his page that interests you and are taken to auction.example.com's site displaying that item. You scroll down to place a bid, and the auction site prompts you for your name and password to sign in. You enter all the information and hit the submit button. Everything looks fine, but in reality, the information that you submit is getting sent back to BG12345. How can this be? The answer is that auction.example.com has what is known as a cross-site scripting vulnerability.[37]

This example is dated 2001 – which merely goes to demonstrate again that some major vulnerabilities have been around for a very long time. In recent years XSS surpassed buffer overflows to become the most common of all publicly reported security vulnerabilities.[38] Likely at least 68 per cent of Web sites are open to XSS attacks on their users.[39]

Incomplete mediation involves entering data values in a form other than what the program expects – it expects a date, or a number, but something else is entered instead. For example, an online retailer, in its ordering procedures on the customer Web site, left the price of the items ordered as an input parameter on an otherwise irrelevant screen (where the shipping options were chosen). While not transparent to the normal user, this created the opportunity for a sophisticated and malicious attacker to order in any quantity at any price. This code was running on the Web site for a while before the problem was detected! Fortunately, in this case a consultant hired for a routine inspection of the code found the error. Nonetheless, the question remains: How many similar problems are there running in code today? Will they ever be found out?[40]

These are only some examples of vulnerabilities. There are so many vulnerabilities that there is now a lexicon for cataloguing different types of vulnerabilities – the CVE, or Common Vulnerabilities and Exploits, which provides standard names for all publicly known security exposures.[41] The CERT's reported software security vulnerabilities give one view of the overall number of vulnerabilities – and the need for a CVE to organize them:[42]

2008	8,077 (annualized from first three quarters – since then, data is no longer reported)
2007	7,236
2006	8,064
2005	5,990
2004	3,780
2003	3,784
2002	4,129
2001	2,437
2000	1,090
1999	417
1998	262
1997	311

The number of reported vulnerabilities has increased more than twentyfold in eight years, and this reporting may include only a fraction of the true number of vulnerabilities out there. The director of security strategy at IBM's Internet Security Systems estimated that in fact over 130,000 software vulnerabilities were found in 2007; in other words, only 5 per cent were publicly reported (the rest presumably were found in proprietary software and thus not reported publicly).[43]

MAKING MORE SECURE, LESS BUGGY SOFTWARE

Why is it so hard to build software that has few, if any, defects, and few, if any, vulnerabilities?[44]

Certainly, automated software development tools are getting better. Compilers, editors, interactive development environments (IDEs), debuggers, and run-time and static-analysis tools have been improving. Microsoft, for example, believes that it has what it takes to "commoditize common problems" and thereby enable average software developers to write above-average programs.[45] An entire industry now has emerged to build better development tools.[46]

But defect-free software remains elusive in spite of better tools. Unlike most physical products, which can work perfectly well as long as they're manufactured within certain tolerances (allowable margins of error), software is a product in which every keystroke of the code says something. Writing it is like dialling a telephone number – it's either exactly right, or it's wrong. And given the length of many programs, you are looking at the equivalent of dialling thousands or millions of phone numbers.

Making the task even harder is that we expect a lot from our software. We expect our desktop software to support a variety of applications – it's a bit like expecting our lawn mowers to also be food processors.[47] And we do expect software to work in situations for which it was never designed. The software supporting the Internet is the mother of all examples: the Internet was certainly never designed with its current uses in mind.

But the real underlying reason why defect-free software remains so elusive is that most software is produced without much consideration of ensuring that robust and repeatable development processes are in place. Good processes recognize the tension of managing an inherently handcrafted creation while building in practices that reduce the number of defects being created, setting up a repeatable and sustainable environment for software production. However, as Robert Seacord of the federally funded Software Engineering Institute at Carnegie Mellon told me, "the way software gets written today is every which way."[48] And two of his colleagues wrote in a recent paper: "Most software engineers do not plan and track their work, nor do they measure and manage product quality. This is not surprising since engineers are neither trained in these disciplines nor are they required to use them. The dilemma is that until they try them, most software engineers do not believe that disciplined methods will work for them."[49]

Aggravating the lack of process is that software manufacturers don't have to care much about producing defect-free software. The market simply doesn't demand it. When buyers look at software features, they're typically most interested in *functional* features – the kind they can use to get things done – and many will go for the product that offers the latest functionality at the best price. So a typical business model for producers is to produce software quickly, but with lots of defects. As one expert noted, "I'm always amazed that every new generation of software vendors has to learn the lesson of threats and vulnerabilities the hard way. If you put code on the Internet, it will be attacked. Period."[50]

The prevalent way of improving software quality remains, frustratingly, "test and patch." Basically, testing involves taking a completed program (or modules of it), compiling the software so that it is operational on a computer, and then running the software under different test conditions. It normally catches only about 50 per cent of the total defects.[51] Sometimes testing involves a top-quality "tiger team" to test the system's security by attempting to make it fail, or to break its security. The test is considered proof of security if the system withstands the attacks. I was recently in correspondence with a top scientist at NSA, who is thinking about ways in which an auction of outside tiger teams can be constructed to provide incentives to test various programs being considered by NSA. While the specific approach is novel, it rests on the old paradigm that testing for vulnerabilities until one is found is the way to prove a system's security.

But testing is hard, expensive, and fundamentally incomplete. Often, too, it is very hard to trace unexpected testing outcomes back to the actual *defects* in the lines of code. And the possible combinations of test cases and variations of input can quickly explode in number.[52] The problem is that we have to look not just at the one behaviour the program gets right, but also for the perhaps thousands of ways in which the program can go wrong – particularly if there are malicious attackers bent on exploiting a vulnerability. Any testing process can only identify and fix the defects encountered in running those specific tests. Many program defects are sensitive to the program's state, the data values used, the system configuration, and the operating conditions. Consequently, the testing *footprint* (the range of values and conditions tested) is often constrained; *happy path* testing describes the process of testing only under the conditions that the system is supposed to run, rather than exploring possible conditions under which the system might very well be run.[53]

These limitations are carried over into the post application release, leading to the pattern of continuous patch-and-fix that is prevalent today. A *patch* is simply a program, usually built by the original software developer, which replaces some of the source code in the original release with other code. Patching after release is both frustrating and expensive. Finding and fixing a software problem after delivery is often a hundred times more expensive than finding it and fixing it during the requirements and design phase.[54] All this is made worse for the end-user by the software industry's well-earned reputation for ineffective or time-consuming customer support.

Patching after release also leaves users in danger of being attacked before the patches get to them. For instance, in April 2009 Microsoft issued a collection of security patches for its software that one researcher called "insane." Insane, because of the twenty-three vulnerabilities fixed, nearly half were already being exploited by attackers.[55]

The problems inherent in producing defect-free software have not gone unnoticed, and there are a few different approaches out there for producing higher quality software. All are based on the recognition that the majority of IT vulnerabilities today stem from the initial stages of software development – its design, coding, and implementation.[56]

OPEN SOURCE SOFTWARE

So far we have been discussing software development as a project that a particular company or organization has taken on, for which it creates a team and delivers a product. This is a closed or proprietary source model. Its opposite, the open source model, has grown in prominence over the past fifteen years. Open source software is developed by groups of volunteers (generally global in scope) operating under a special form of licence that provides open access to the software source code, and generally unlimited ability to use the resulting product. Under a closed development model, the source code is carefully protected to maintain a company's competitive advantage – and its profit potential. With the open source model, no one is economically benefiting from helping to write or review the code. The Linux operating system is perhaps the best-known example of open source software. (Companies like Red Hat sell Linux but argue that they provide special, additional services that justify their selling what is actually available freely to any interested user.) Popular open source application programs are the Mozilla Firefox Web browser and the Apache Web server software.

Some security experts argue that open source software is more secure because it's open to review by a broad range of individuals.[57] However, open source software provides no guarantee that the software is reviewed for security, or that those reviewing it understand either the program's context in a larger system or the program's external interactions. In other words, just being able to read the code doesn't mean you have the wherewithal to do anything with or about it. On the other hand, attackers have also become adept at reverse-engineering software programs, so that not releasing the source code only slows attackers down. An analysis of CERT/CC vulnerability reports shows vulnerabilities accruing in both Windows and Linux operating systems at similar rates.[58] There is no evidence that open source results in fewer defects or in a more secure end product.[59]

AGILE DEVELOPMENT

Agile development is not a single approach, but an overall term for a range of methods that have some key features in common. As the name implies, agile methods are iterative and interactive. They break big software projects into smaller chunks, each of which can be done in a week to several weeks; and they use a minimum of long-range planning and formal documents. Instead, these methods rely upon frequent face-to-face exchange and feedback among team members and with the customer.[60]

For instance, one popular agile approach is called Scrum. It's carried out by software writers who work in self-organized teams. They write code in "sprints" that typically last fifteen to thirty days, with the goal of producing a working module or block of code at the end of that time. They hold a planning meeting before each sprint and review meetings at the end, along with daily progress meetings – the "scrums" – which are often done standing up and are usually no longer than fifteen minutes.

A particular coding technique often used in agile development is pair programming. Here, each programmer sits at the keyboard with a partner. One person in the pair (the "driver") actually writes code while the other (the "navigator") observes and reviews the work; the two switch roles from time to time during the day.

Other agile approaches have names like Extreme Programming (XP). They all aim to make code writing more efficient and adaptive. How well they do at producing code with fewer defects is hard to say, in part because there are so many different agile methods and they are applied with varying degrees of rigour. One overview study, by the U.S. Defense Department's Data and Analysis Center for Software, concluded that agile development reduces defects per thousand lines of code by an average of about 32 per cent.[61]

Critics say that reductions in the range of 30 per cent – or even 40 per cent, 50 per cent, or more, as have been found on certain agile projects – are not good enough. Some point to yet another method that seems to promise results much closer to actual defect-free software.

This other method is a family of approaches centred on the *Capability Maturity Model Integration (CMMI)* and the related *Personal Software Process/Team Software Process (PSP/TSP)* developed at the Software Engineering Institute at Carnegie Mellon University.

CMMI is not itself a process for writing code; it describes the *characteristics* of effective processes and the organizations that have them. The basic goal is for software teams to have a stable process model, so that practices that are proven by experience to be effective can be reliably adopted and repeatedly used.

The *Personal Software Process* and accompanying *Team Software Process* (PSP/TSP) are approaches software engineers can use to plan and track their work, identify which practices work best to produce fewer defects, and adhere to timelines and budgets. Teams also learn how to replicate those practices reliably.

A key to the PSP/TSP approach is actual inspection of the code, line by line, looking for specific known defects – first by the individual programmer, and then by peers. Inspection means more than just reviewing the code for things that don't look right. It is done from prepared checklists of commonly found defects: each programmer keeps a record of (and looks for) the kinds of errors that he or she has made in the past, while peer inspection is based on errors that are prone to be made in that type of code generally. Ideally, the result is a learning process in which the sources of error are systematically weeded out. The code is still run and tested after inspection, and when the whole job is done properly, software quality is quite good.

In the same Defense Department study that found agile methods reducing defects by an average of 32 per cent, PSP/TSP was found to reduce defects by an average of *98 per cent*. Results published by the Software Engineering Institute itself show similar results – and also show that while inspection takes time, it can actually shorten the overall software development time by drastically cutting the time needed for testing:

MEASURE	TYPICAL PROJECTS AVERAGE	CMMI/PSP/TSP AVERAGES
Defects before testing (in KSLOC)	15	0.4
Defects in the delivered product (after testing and quality control)	7.5	0.06
Percentage of total effort in software development going into final-stage testing	40%	4%

According to Bill Nichols, a Senior Member of the Technical Staff at SEI who, among other things, travels the globe teaching PSP/TSP:

There is a pervasive opinion in software development that software defects cannot be prevented. Our data show that this is not true. Studies[62] reported a sample of TSP teams delivering roughly 60 defects per MILLION lines of code. That's a factor of 20 better than best of class results and a factor of 100 or more better than typical. Inspections are the most powerful removal technique. Not using them or only applying them to "critical code" should be considered professional malpractice.[63]

Moreover, Nichols points out, agile methods and PSP/TSP are not mutually exclusive. There have been Scrum teams that combine the two approaches, with excellent results. "The *agilistas* have some good ideas," he says. "I would simply insist that they do some other things in addition. What we add is the measurement and tracking of defects, at a level of data that no one else gets, and then the use of that defect data to improve. This ties into the concept of 'deliberate practice' . . . [and] these data-driven inspections, combined with testing, give you the multiple filters you need to achieve very high levels of quality."

Whatever the method used, some defects are still likely to end up in the finished software. Consequently, the need to patch will always be with us. It's just that with few defects in the released product, there will be far fewer patches.

None of this will significantly reduce costs, at least in the short run. The benefits will be in a higher quality product.[64] And that quality is free, in the sense that it doesn't cost more than producing a defect-ridden product; however, it doesn't drive immediate cost savings – an important factor when we consider why such methods have not been more widely adopted.

IT'S THE MARKET, STUPID

So what stands in the way of the seemingly simple choice to produce a better product? Is the software industry really as blind as the North American auto industry was in the 1980s when it ignored the evidence that Toyota and other Japanese manufacturers had figured out a means of producing much higher quality cars at costs equal to or lower than those the North American producers were making?

Unfortunately, probably yes, although thus far there are no equivalents to the Japanese automakers on the horizon. PSP/TSP, for example, has been used by teams at major software vendors such as Adobe and Intuit, and is being exported to countries outside the U.S., but as of mid-2009 it was licensed to just fifty-eight software development entities and academic institutions.[65] Adoption figures for other approaches seem not to be available.

Why such a low adoption rate? For one thing, although software process improvement (SPI) methods can save time and money over the long run, they take time up front for training and implementation. And in the world of software – where new releases are rushed to market and companies push their coding teams to keep up the pace – many firms aren't willing to make that upfront commitment. Some prospective users of PSP/TSP, says Bill Nichols, have asked that the standard two-week initial training be cut back to one week. In other cases, new methods have been only partly adopted, for instance, by software teams that pick and choose only the features they like from an agile approach. And half-hearted preparation and practice, in turn, can have a negative ripple effect. When people don't get the results they expected, they conclude that the methods don't work and they give them up.

Thus the default approach is to rush to production rather than to seek perfection – or as the entrepreneur Guy Kawasaki put it, in his famous maxim for the software industry, "Don't worry, be crappy."[66]

The typical business model for software developers is to wait for users and attackers to find additional defects, and then to develop fixes (patches), which the system's users then apply. According to studies, 90 to 95 per cent of all defects are harmless; they're never found by users and they don't affect performance. It's much cheaper for a company to release software with defects and fix the 5 to 10 per cent of defects that people complain about.[67]

Moreover, if you buy a physical product, and get harmed because of a manufacturer's defect, you can sue and win. But software is sold without any liability whatsoever. Software manufacturers don't have to produce a quality product because they face no consequences if they don't; thus the marketplace does not reward real security. Real security is harder, slower, and more expensive to design and implement, and the buying public has no way to differentiate real security from bad security. The way to win in this marketplace is to design software as insecure as you can possibly get away with. Smart software companies know this, and know that defect-free software is not cost effective. Even standards groups reflect this orientation. Referring to an industry/academic initiative focusing on standards for C, a common programming language, one expert on the group noted that "even the C standards group really isn't interested in security. They'll accept security if it doesn't cost anything. They compete on performance and speed to market."[68]

THE ROLE OF PUBLIC POLICY

So here's what's going on. Neither software developers (as a corporate entity) nor software engineers (thinking about their culture and way of working) have much if any incentive to change their ways of doing their work. The market doesn't reward highly secure software; software engineers don't like feeling that they are being bossed around. Multiple approaches do exist for producing software with higher quality (and presumably higher security). The underlying truth, the distinguished computer scientist Dave Farber told me, is that "there really is no magic in what any of these methods do. Producing high-quality software requires work – sometimes a lot of work – and people want a silver bullet. They seek to avoid the discipline of having to do real planning, real design, and the effort of reviewing and inspecting their product."[69]

The data supporting claims of improved quality is spotty, but taken as a whole it is persuasive that better ways of producing software exist.

In short, we know we can do better but have no silver bullet to help us nor any market incentive to spur us on.

So here is an instance where policy can be bold in helping to shape the markets. The key is changing the incentives facing software producers. Here are several steps that would help, some to be examined more closely in Chapter 8:

Software producers need to be made liable for defective products. Unlike most other products, software is exempt from legal challenges on grounds of defects. Software is a new *type* of product in jurisprudence terms and the law is still in a state of flux regarding producers' liability. And software is notoriously hard to evaluate for quality and security, so it's hard to demonstrate conclusively that its producer was negligent in production. There are also powerful political forces behind maintaining the status quo. Two American states have passed legislation formalizing the exemption of software from product liability suits, and software producers further protect themselves by loading their licences for use with as many disclaimers as possible.

Extending liability to software producers would be a powerful economic and social incentive for better software. Public policy requires that responsibility be put wherever it will most effectively reduce the risks inherent in defective products.[70] Software producers are better able to anticipate defects and flaws and guard against their effects than users, and are in a better position to bear the cost. Producers can insure against the risk of injury or adjust the price of the software so that the expense is distributed across consumers as a cost of doing business.

One way to make producers responsible is through legislative reform, by requiring that strict liability be applied to software products. Alternatively, the courts could build on long-established theories of warranty of fitness, misrepresentation, abnormal danger, negligence, fraud, lack of clarity, and unconscionability to find liability for software security failures.[71]

Governments should require publicly reporting companies to disclose what efforts they are making to ensure that their software is secure. This simple action would focus both management and investor attention on the issue. It would bring out information that the market could then use, to judge who is taking security seriously. A company's security standards could be factored into overall investor perceptions, including the ratings by the likes of Standard & Poor's, Moody's, and Finch.

Government standards for purchasing secure and reliable software should be made more stringent, and applied. In the U.S., the Federal Information

Security Management Act's requirements for federal procurements of software are vague, and it seems that many waivers from these requirements are granted. Federal governments in Canada and the U.S. should require that software be acquired from producers who have demonstrated compliance with established, well-documented software development processes (the Capability Maturity Model Integration and PSP/TSP approaches make up one set of candidates). Required levels of performance could be ratcheted up over time. Although government procurement makes up only a fraction of the total market for software, its share is significant enough to drive necessary change.

This step does not need to be limited to federal governments. Individual states like California, or provinces like Ontario, could also set and enforce high procurement standards. There is ample precedent; California, for example, already has more stringent emissions standards for automobiles than does the rest of the U.S.

A requirement that software (particularly for consumer use) be marked with a security seal or rating would create further market incentives for better software. Such programs work well in other areas: there are crash-test safety ratings for cars, and regulations in the U.S. require major appliances to display their energy efficiency prominently. Such programs for software, if ratings were based on the use of good development methods, would be easy to implement and would provide valuable information and education to consumers.

Finally, there is a need for more research on techniques to produce and measure secure, defect-free software. We need better development and evaluation tools, better ways of evaluating and fixing legacy software, and further work to improve the entire process of software development and maintenance.

Together, these actions would signal to software producers that security and quality matter in the marketplace.

THE OTHER (GENETIC) SOFTWARE - THOSE DAMN USERS (!)

Users may be the biggest vulnerability of all. It may be possible to produce defect-free computer software but, unfortunately, making defect-free genetic software (i.e., the perfectly security-conscious user) is, well, impossible. Some users are malicious, while others are simply misguided. Attackers exploit users' behaviour, while users do things unintentionally that infect their own systems. In an organizational setting (a business, a government agency) these are considered insider threats, even in the absence of malicious intent – because you have *an insider's action that puts an organization or its resources at risk.*[72] The problem is particularly serious because of the amount of direct damage that can result.[73]

In one example of a non-malicious insider threat,[74] a senior employee of a small company was fired for "misconduct" and instructed not to return to the office after she had taken part of a company computer home for the weekend to work on a customer presentation. In a subsequent lawsuit, the company claimed she removed the hard drive without permission, and that the removal had crippled the company's operations and placed vital company data at risk. From the employee's perspective, she was preparing for an important meeting and she chose to remove the entire hard drive to use with her compatible home computer, rather than take additional time to transfer the files to a disk. At the time, the company had neither a policy about taking work equipment home nor established computing protocols. So who was at fault? (Eventually the courts ruled in the employee's favour.)

In early October 2007, Alex Greene was changing jobs. In preparation for the switch, he wanted to update his subscription to a U.S. Department of Homeland Security intelligence bulletin by changing his designated e-mail address. Rather than type in the DHS address *to which he was sending his notice,* he replied to an e-mail he had on file – but apparently, he mistakenly hit "reply all."[75] This touched off a listserv free-for-all when his request arrived in the inboxes of several thousand government and private-sector security specialists.[76] What ensued – joke e-mails, angry e-mails, requests to unsubscribe, and even an e-mail from an employee of Iran's defence ministry, asking if the unusual number of e-mails was a joke – created a mini denial-of-service attack. There were more than 2.2 million e-mails pinging among approximately 7,500 recipients before the e-mail server was forced to shut down. Worse than the temporary shutdown was the potential national-security breach. While the information contained in the bulletin was unclassified, and the subscription list open, when individual subscribers with security classifications hit "reply," their messages often contained automatically generated signatures including titles and phone numbers. One poster to this listserv pointed out that armed with the information contained in auto-signatures, he was one fake letterhead away from impersonating a Defense Department employee.

These are instances of insider threats where there was no malice involved. But insiders can be malicious, too – and sometimes very clever at exploiting poor decisions or lax oversight by others in the organization.

Harriette Walters, the perpetrator of the largest embezzlement in the history of the U.S.'s District of Columbia, was sentenced to more than seventeen years in prison.[77] Until her arrest, said one news report, "Walters was a 26-year tax employee known among her colleagues as a problem solver with a knack for finding solutions by using the department's antiquated and balky computers or finding a way around them."[78] The court found that she used her position to produce fake cheques for bogus tax refunds with fictitious names; the total stolen was said to exceed fifty million dollars.

The scheme involved Washington, D.C.'s new Integrated Tax System, built by Accenture to handle the city's income, business, and real-estate taxes. Walters was consulted when Accenture designed the system, and she "contributed to the decision that her unit, which handled real estate tax refunds, be left out of it."[79] At the time, the decision seemed to make sense. D.C. had spent one hundred million dollars to implement the business and income parts of the system, and it had only five million dollars left for implementing the real-estate tax portion. So the system's perimeter was defined to omit real-estate tax processing.

That design decision allowed Walters and her co-conspirators to create the bogus tax refunds to the fictitious names that were not checked against actual real-estate records. Some refunds were issued multiple times; the recipient (often someone's boyfriend) would claim that the cheque was never received, so that a new one was issued – with interest to compensate for the long delay. The schemes exploited several loopholes: each cheque was under the forty-thousand-dollar threshold for requiring a supervisor's approval, and no action was taken to cancel the first cheque or confirm that it had not already been cashed. As the *Washington Post* reported,

> "Our system has got a plethora of internal controls on it," said tax office head Stephen M. Cordi hired to replace managers cleared out when the Walters embezzlement scandal broke. "On top of that, we have manual controls. But you're always vulnerable to an enterprising employee who knows how the controls work."[80]

Oftentimes malicious insiders are simply motivated by anger at their employer (or ex-employer); in other cases they are motivated by greed. Either way, at least in the U.S., very few of these people are prosecuted. Indeed, some of these malicious users act in ways that seem beyond the reach of the law because it is so difficult to collect evidence of their actions.[81]

HOW ATTACKERS FOOL USERS

Meanwhile, attackers who are malicious *out*siders can be very clever at exploiting user behaviours to infect target machines. Want to infect the computers protected by a corporate firewall? Just drop a lot of memory sticks (a.k.a. dongles) around the corporate parking lots early one morning. As one expert notes, "They are almost irresistible for someone to pick up."[82] Out of curiosity or a desire to find the rightful owner, people load them onto their work computers. A given computer may then auto-log onto any specially named program (e.g., autolog.exe) on the dongle and execute it. As easy as that, the attacker has gained access and compromised at least one computer behind the corporate firewall.

Spam, phishing (e-mails tailored to a group), and spear phishing (e-mails tailored to an individual) were mentioned earlier. Though targeted to small groups or individuals, coordinated large-scale phishing attacks now occur. Canadian and American financial institutions recently were warned about the exploitation of valid banking credentials belonging to small- and medium-sized businesses. The scammers have an established routine: they send a targeted e-mail to the company's controller or treasurer. The message contains either a virus-laden attachment or a link that surreptitiously installs malicious software designed to steal passwords. Armed with these credentials, the crooks then proceed to transfer money out of bank accounts. Multiple small transactions are done so as to avoid alerting the banks to possible malfeasance.[83]

Many spam or phishing attacks, of course, have the added goal of building a big botnet to be used as the base for further attacks. The easiest way to do this is to get a lot of users to download malicious software and let the malware "sit around quietly until enough computers are corrupted."[84] Classic attacks, where the attacker is actually sitting in front of a computer breaking into another computer, are now quite rare. It's dangerous for the attacker, because these types of attacks are much easier to pin down than attacks that originate from innocent users' computers.

And it is startling how many users can be fooled. In 2005, the state of New York decided to educate its employees about phishing by sending out a *simulated* phishing e-mail – designed not by an actual attacker, but at the behest of New York's chief information officer. Nearly 10,000 state employees received this bogus e-mail. The idea was that those who responded would get, instead of a malicious download, a warning message and brief lesson on the dangers of phishing attacks. About 15 per cent took the bait, clicking on a link and typing in their state-system passwords for "verification."[85]

In a similar exercise, the U.S. Military Academy at West Point had a bogus phishing e-mail sent to more than five hundred of its cadets. This one was signed by a fictitious colonel. Among the cadets – drawn from America's best and brightest, and instilled with a sense of duty – about 80 per cent responded.[86] One would hope that users have gotten smarter recently.

But worse yet, a lot of Web sites actually make it easier for attackers. How many times have you gone to a Web site and been told that you have to enable JavaScript, or ActiveX, or have cookies enabled? When you enable any of these programs, you are also putting your computer in an open configuration setting. If the Web site's server has been compromised already, then the mere act of visiting it means that the HTML language that makes the site look so nice on your screen also contains a lot of hidden instructions to infect your computer.[87] Most users don't know this, and cheerfully go on enabling plug-ins or JavaScript or any functionality that makes visiting Web sites more enjoyable – and potentially corrupting.

So what can be done? There are a variety of approaches designed to save us from ourselves. In August 2009 an industry group representing some of North America's largest banks (FS-ISAC, the Financial Services Information Sharing and Analysis Center mentioned in Chapter 6) advised commercial banking customers how they could help secure their online banking accounts. The recommendation was draconian – customers should "carry out all on-line banking activity from a standalone, hardened, and locked-down computer from which e-mail and Web browsing is not possible."[88] Some security steps, on the other hand, are very simple. Systems administrators can prohibit users from having their computers in an open configuration while visiting external Web sites. Organizations can at least try to restrict their employees from using the Web or perusing personal e-mails on company computers.

In fact, one avenue for dealing with user behaviour is simply to remove choice through technology. That's what Trusted Computing is all about. The Trusted Computing (TC) or Trusted Platforms approach has many detractors (some say TC stands for Treacherous Computing), but its goal is to provide a computing platform – your computer – that obeys a defined "security policy." You or others can't tamper with the application software, and to use the dry language of computer scientists, your computer ends up in a *predictable state*.

I didn't understand what "state" meant until some kind soul told me to think of a Coke machine. (Every time you put in a coin, the vending machine goes into a different "state," registering how much money has been put in so far and what still needs to occur. Eventually, once you've inserted enough coins, you hope that you will get your drink. But this will happen only if every state along the way is predictable – i.e., well defined and reliably achieved by the machine – including that very important give-this-person-a-Coke state at the end.) The machine's designers want it to always do the right thing while also *not* responding to, say, counterfeit money or other attempts to trick it. Similarly, the Trusted Computing folks want to assure that your computer is always in a predictable state (or states) of maxumum resistance to intrusion.

Trusted Computing requires that special technology be built into your computer. A number of major chipmakers and personal-computer makers have released TC-enabled products, but the approach remains controversial. At a research seminar in 2008, one agenda item was "Trusted Platforms: Who Do They Protect?" Cynics believe that the original motivation for Trusted Computing was digital rights management (DRM). Under DRM, the music industry will be able to sell you music downloads that you won't be able to swap, or CDs that you'll only be able to play three times, or only on your birthday. But TC's professed interest is to make it much harder for you to run unlicensed software. That may be a good thing, if it keeps malware off your system.

Depending on your point of view and belief about the future, technologies like Trusted Computing can either make your computer the lackey of Big Business, or make your computer, and others', much safer and more secure. This is a key point – technologies can either be bad or good. It all depends on who controls what and how the technologies are deployed. Keep in mind, however, that removing choice from the user in the name of security is what many of the technologies under consideration would do.

A NEW SOCIAL CONTRACT

Ultimately, however, user behaviour will only really change when we as a society have come to adopt a new "social contract" for cyber security.* Right now, the social contract for the Internet is essentially "the Internet is free, and I'll do whatever I want to do on it (except if the place where I work forbids it, and even then I might not listen)." But in both Canada and the United States, the areas of public safety and public health offer alternative models on which we could build an approach for addressing Internet security. All three areas of interest share these characteristics: There will always be bad actors and naive victims. There will always be new threats. The level of bad outcomes will never drop to zero. Technology can assist in addressing problems, but it will never solve the problem.

In public health and safety, societies recognize the collective need to sacrifice some aspect of personal flexibility and privacy for the common good. Some of the steps required are individual, and others require collective action. Collectively we build and maintain safe highways and have traffic laws; we provide health care and pass sanitation laws. Collectively we sacrifice, paying taxes for roads and medical services, or when we concede latitude of choice in following certain laws.

A new social contract for the Internet will not solve all user-based cyber-security problems, just as our social contract for public safety doesn't stop all auto accidents. But I do believe that some acceptance of shared responsibility is an important, though imperfect, means of ensuring that users behave responsibly and securely when on the Internet. Meanwhile, technologies can assist in limiting the damage that Internet users can do, just as anti-lock brakes and air bags technically reduce or limit the damage from an auto accident. A new social contract *combined* with new technologies could greatly reduce the problems related to "those damn users" – a phrase frequently used by security professionals to express frustration about why security technologies alone don't work.

---

* I am indebted to Dr. Shari Lawrence Pfleeger of the RAND Corporation, whose thinking and joint work contributed greatly to this section.

CHAPTER 8

NEW FRAMEWORKS

I've said repeatedly that the Internet is a city like early industrial-age London, a new kind of city, vital and growing but plagued by problems yet untamed. By seeing how problems in London spun out of control in areas such as fire and sanitation – and more important, how these problems were eventually brought under control, by Londoners and others around the world – we can shed light by analogy on what it would take to improve cyber security.

Learning from history is tricky. The last war doesn't always teach generals how to fight the next, and here we'll be not only comparing the past to the present, but also drawing analogies between a physical city and a cyber city. Nonetheless, the parallels are too striking to be ignored. And in each case the story line follows the same arc:

We humans are very fond of changing how we live. By inventing, exploring, and organizing ourselves along new lines, we change the settings and the patterns of life. When the results are good, as they often are, we call it "progress." But even then we notice a curious fact. While we have been busy making some things better, other problems take on new forms or multiply. Call it what you will – the price of progress, the law of unintended consequences – it usually happens because our changes have upset an old balance or over-strained old capacities, causing a *systemic* disorder that will persist until we arrive at some new "system" for putting things aright.

So it is with the Internet. With this technology we've created a new setting for life – one which, among other things, changes the calculus of crime and chicanery. Old tricks can be played in new ways and have greater reach than ever, thanks to the connectedness of cyberspace. Our frailties and errors leave us open in ways we didn't expect. And so it was in early modern cities like London. As London grew from a medieval walled town to a metropolis, vast numbers of people poured into and across it to ply their trades. Fire, crime, filth, and disease – all of which had been chronic problems before – found new footholds, and were able to spread more virulently. The threat levels were soon growing much faster than the ability to cope with them.

What turned the tide? Historians speak of the "reform movements" in London and elsewhere in the early 1800s (though some key steps came before then, or much later). Many kinds of people were involved and many things done, all now the subjects of many a head-splitting college course. None of it was simple, but step by step people created new systems for dealing with their problems. And those reformed systems were more effective than the systems we've created thus far in cyber security, for reasons best made clear by some stories, starting with the story of fire.[1]

FIRE

Our primeval ancestors may have learned to use fire before they learned spoken language, and people have been finding thousands of new uses for it ever since. It is one of the core technologies of civilized life. But in today's world, where fire is so concealed and controlled that one can go for long periods without seeing an open flame anywhere but on a stovetop, it is hard to imagine how ubiquitous those flames once were. They were open sources of light and heat; they burned merrily in the shops of the blacksmiths and bakers and soap-makers; they were as common as computers are today.

And the more that fire was used, the more dangerous it became, especially in towns and cities. Although it is unlikely that Nero fiddled, large parts of Rome did burn in 64 AD. So did much of medieval London, several times. Measures were taken. The Assizes of the first mayor of London, in 1187, included a building code with specifications for hearths and chimneys and firewalls (the original kind, made of stone, between buildings). Like many best practices in cyber security, these standards might have had some effect if they had been widely adopted. But they were not, and in 1212 a wide swath of the city burned again.

Yet London kept growing. By the mid-1600s, Greater London, the old walled city plus a welter of adjoining districts, had a population of nearly half a million. That was about ten times its medieval size. But many of the streets were still narrow, twisting medieval-style lanes, and along those streets, houses and apartments were built to leverage every square foot of land space. The upper storeys were cantilevered out beyond the ground floor until the top floors often nearly touched those across the way – perfect for spreading a fire. (And in that respect, much like the Internet, which is insecure partly because it runs on infrastructure and protocols that weren't designed for security.) Scattered all through the dense urbanity of London were commercial establishments that either worked with fire or stored flammable goods: the blacksmiths and bakers, the tailors and wool merchants, the dealers in gunpowder and oils and chemicals.

Codes and regulations were now stricter, but in the face of hectic growth they were winked at. And just as in cyber security, with fundamental prevention lacking, the fallback was piecemeal defence. Parish churches were stocked with firefighting supplies. The night watches were entrusted to watch for outbreaks of flame; citizens were to pitch in and help with the quenching. Wiser heads saw gaps and inadequacies, but as they mulled how to fix them they were outrun by the adversary.

One difference between the past and the cyber-world of today is the time scale – usually, things happen much faster on the Internet. The Great Fire of 1666 is worth dwelling upon because here the difference was reversed. In only four days, the lifespan of the Great Fire, many things went wrong that have eerie parallels with what has gone wrong in cyber security over the course of years. Not all of the parallels are perfect but the whole episode is a capsule portrait of failure. Technical weaknesses were compounded by flawed plans and decisions, and all were exposed by a threat that grew too rapidly. Defences were overwhelmed or rendered useless by the perverse interlinking of events.

In 1666, shortly after midnight on September 2, somehow a fire started in a baker's shop on Pudding Lane. The baker and his family (who lived upstairs) got out and roused the neighbours. Constables and night watchmen rushed to the scene; the mayor himself arrived. As flames jumped along the lane, some men urged pulling down buildings in the path of the fire to try to contain it. Fatefully, this was overruled by the mayor, who explained his decision in the name of private interests: many of the buildings were rental properties. Finding the owners to get their assent would be impossible late at night, and the fire was not so great as to justify such action. ("Pish, a lady could piss it out," the mayor reportedly said.)

By morning things were out of control. Although the term "critical mass" hadn't been coined, the fire had reached it. The tools and strategies at hand – bucket brigades, primitive hand-drawn fire engines with water nozzles, fire hooks, and demolition – were barely adequate for smaller fires when well deployed; now they were being flung at a behemoth amid the hot fog of crisis. The mayor soon found to his great dismay that houses couldn't be torn down fast enough. The Duke of York took to the streets with his personal fire crew, but time and again they were foiled, and in many places the residents could not be pressed into firefighting service. When people saw the walls of flame advancing, their first thought was every man for himself: they fled with as many belongings as they could carry. Bankers scrambled to save their gold coins as the blaze swept through the financial district. Wharves and buildings along the Thames caught fire, hampering efforts to draw water from the river or to put goods out upon it in boats.

St. Paul's Cathedral, one of the gems of London, was reckoned to be a safe haven, a stone-walled structure in the midst of a broad plaza serving as a firebreak. But the incineration all around created updrafts and cross drafts that carried burning "fire-drops," like viruses. Unluckily, renovations were in progress at the cathedral, and the updates had created a vulnerability. The exterior was laced by wooden scaffolds. They became staging platforms from which the flames wormed their way in. Worse yet, the city's printers and booksellers had tried to rescue their wares by carting them into the cathedral: the crypt was filled with great mounds of combustible data. When these ignited, the effect was staggering. St. Paul's crumbled; molten lead from the roof and the stained-glass windows flowed out across the plaza.

We have no accurate death toll. It is thought that few died in the Great Fire itself but many more succumbed during the winter months that followed, as thousands, now homeless, camped in makeshift shelters. Most of the city's houses and shops were destroyed, along with buildings from guild halls to prisons. Recovery was slow and arduous – a special Fire Court, convened to settle disputes over rebuilding, remained in session for more than five years.

STEPS TOWARD A SYSTEM, AND A SOCIAL CONTRACT

In the aftermath, a comprehensive system of fire protection began to take shape at last. At this point the time scale reverts to pre-Internet speed; the process would go on for centuries. But the first step came quickly. In 1667 an entrepreneurial citizen of London, Nicholas Barbon, started a new kind of company. He sold fire insurance. And then he expanded the offering. If you bought insurance, you also got the services of a fire brigade, a company crew that would come hustling to your home or building in case of fire, to try to minimize the damage: a win for the policy-holder and insurer alike.

Fire companies of this type gradually proliferated in London and elsewhere. (Ben Franklin famously started one in Philadelphia.) A protected building had a "firemark" on the façade – a tile marked with the emblem of the company, often a mythical beast or heraldic device, much like the logo that pops up on your screen when the anti-virus program or Javascript-blocker is running. The firemark advertised the company and also served a practical purpose, for when the company's brigade showed up at a big fire, they could quickly see which buildings it was their duty to save.

The private fire brigades were seen as a great leap forward, but like your anti-virus program they turned out to have limited value. Not enough people bought the service, and when a whole neighbourhood is ablaze it's hard to protect buildings one by one. In the early 1800s a better approach surfaced in Scotland. The city of Edinburgh deployed a *municipal* fire brigade, with well-trained crews responding in concert to all fires city-wide. To us it may seem obvious that such a thing was needed all along. Indeed, Nero's Rome had had such a brigade (manned by intrepid slaves); more recently, Paris had tried its own version. Still, in London and many other places it was either not obvious or not tried for centuries – just as, in cyberspace, it has taken a while to spread the notion that a more comprehensive approach to security might be needed.

In 1833, London followed Edinburgh's lead. Ten independent fire companies pooled their brigades to form the London Fire Engine Establishment. James Braidwood, who had led the Edinburgh venture, was recruited to run the LFEE, which eventually became a true municipal brigade under public authority.

And from here the story branches out in many directions. Insuring against fire and firefighting were on the path to becoming distinct specialties, each with a narrower focus but more fully developed and more broadly available. The days of patchwork coping were coming to an end. Building codes, in London and elsewhere, came to be better written and more widely observed – a process helped by the development of both insurers and professional firefighters. (Insurers would inspect properties before insuring them, and set rates proportional to the risk. Firefighters – the smaller-town volunteer kind as well as the paid kind – became on-the-ground experts, educating and advising and watching for problems.)

Underlying these steps was a key development: a new social contract was emerging around the issue of fire. Everyone had long understood that a common threat required a common response – if your neighbour's house caught fire, clearly you had good reasons to join a bucket brigade or do something to help – but now there was a difference. As the old systems kept falling short, people grew more willing to have their common responses institutionalized in new ways. Paying for insurance, supporting a fire department, became an accepted part of the deal. People got to the stage of expecting these things which previous generations hadn't imagined.

People also began seeing that other institutions were needed to fill out the system. Skip back to 1828, in London, shortly before the fire brigades merged. The brigades were doing their best to quench fires and protect property – but what about rescuing people inside the buildings? The brigades would try, but it didn't seem to be part of the mandate and they carried no equipment for that purpose. So, concerned Londoners formed the Royal Society for the Protection of Life from Fire. The RSPLF had escape ladders. They placed them in every neighbourhood and trained people to use them. Today you may have an escape ladder, the flexible toss-down-from-the-window type, in your house. Your local fire department certainly has ladders and other rescue gear. You expect them to – but somebody somewhere had to see the need and set the precedent; somebody had to institutionalize it.

Leap ahead now to 1894, in Chicago. A young man named William Merrill was part of a new profession: he was an electrical engineer. He knew that as the use of electricity grew it posed new kinds of fire hazards, and he founded an organization called Underwriters Laboratories – supported, initially, by fire insurance underwriters – to test electrical and other products for fire safety. Today UL is worldwide, and there are legions of other entities that do similar product testing, including independent labs and government agencies. We now expect that every product we buy (even pajamas) will be reasonably fire-safe, and that if any product isn't, it will be promptly flagged or recalled from the market. This too has become an institutionalized part of the social contract.

As I write, I am looking up at the ceiling of my office, at a sprinkler. This built-in fire protection wasn't part of the original building, erected in 1900. It has been added since, and automatic sprinkler systems are now everywhere because somebody saw, and others agreed, that they could play a worthwhile role in our ever-evolving system for fire protection. Nor is the system confined to technologies and products. It addresses the human factors, too. Schools and companies hold fire drills. Extensive public education campaigns have taught us to avoid behaviours like smoking in bed or leaving campfires burning.

With the advent of the industrial age, industry itself became a major hazard. The boilers on steam engines exploded with alarming frequency, in factories and trains and boats. (In the worst incident the big steamboat *Sultana* burned on the Mississippi River in 1865, killing an estimated 1,200.) Fires in textile factories, where legions of workers and goods were gathered, could be far worse than a fire in a country handweaver's workshop ever was; chemical warehouses went up in pillars of flame. The boiler explosions were tamed by better engineering, to standards hammered out over the years by a mix of government agencies and professional groups. And today almost every industry has a full portfolio of fire safety standards and programs.

Fires still occur, but the threat is greatly reduced. In most of the developed nations, nothing on the scale of the Great Fire of London, or the Chicago Fire of 1871, has occurred for many years unless caused by war or earthquake. And even in a "small" fire that could destroy a home, the psychological balance has shifted. We are careful about fire, as we should be, but not many of us dread it chronically or lie awake worrying about it, as was common in the not-too-distant past.

CYBER SECURITY: COMPARISONS AND ARGUMENTS

For cyber security we do not yet have a system such as the one that evolved for firefighting. One could argue, quite properly, that there just hasn't been time. Whereas modern fire protection evolved over centuries, cyber security has only been a serious issue for a decade or so, during which an emergent system has been created – with some pieces that look a lot like certain parts of the fire system. A number of the cyber-security pieces haven't worked well, but the fire system took trial and error, too.

That is a reasonable argument. The problem is, there just isn't time. Of course we can't and probably wouldn't spend centuries building out the system; there won't be an Internet by then, there will be something else. A reasonably adjusted fraction of the time it took for fire (twenty years to a fuller system?) might be a reasonable estimate, except for other problems. One such problem is that recent efforts haven't shown the focus or the drive needed to get there even that fast. Another problem is that the adversary is different in cyber security. Because malicious hackers are conscious and fire is not, cyber crime and cyber threats evolve quicker than the threat of fire does; they are much faster at finding new ways to "start" and "spread." Too much of our current system is devoted to playing catch and patch, a losing paradigm. We *particularly* need elements that shift the paradigm and come at the issue from other angles (as the fire system has done).

Yet there haven't been many signs of change in the underlying social contract for cyber security. Most of the action is within the bounds of the old contract, and most of the agitation is about clinging to it: government should keep its place and keep doing the kinds of things it's been doing, only better and maybe packaged differently. Ditto for the IT industries – and the rest is up to you, the users. This approach has not been working and is not a good basis for going forward.

When people talk about paradigm shifts and social contracts the discussion can start to get very abstract, so I will give you another very real example of the kind of shift I think is needed in cyber security.[2]

PUBLIC HEALTH: BEYOND THE GREAT STINK

By the 1840s, London's population had tripled from what it was less than a century earlier. The twin impulses of industrial revolution and land reform were pulling in thousands more people each year.

Disease and unhealthy conditions were rampant; in *Bleak House,* Dickens described one poor (albeit fictional) denizen of the City during these times: "Jo lives, that is to say, he has not yet died." A central problem was that the social contract for public health was still that of a village. For example, human and animal waste was directed to cesspools, which were supposed to be cleaned out periodically. In reality, scavengers fished their hands through the waste looking for items of value that people had possibly lost or tossed in the process, and sewage frequently flowed into cellars, street drains, or worse. (In fact, until 1815 it was illegal to discharge raw waste into existing sewers, which were meant for rainwater.) Enumerating all the other horrors would be too much, so I will just mention that runoff from slaughterhouses and factories flowed into the same soup, and a lot of it wound up in the Thames.

These conditions were certainly noticed and commented on, and from them people died young and quickly. But this state of affairs was viewed as a problem, not as a crisis. No equivalent of the Black Plague killed a sizeable portion of the city at once. People died of diseases for which the science of the day had no explanations. The city stank, and that was that.

Yet in a short time, a new social and physical infrastructure was created. In 1842, Edwin Chadwick, a pioneering social reformer, made his first great mark, not by organizing rallies but simply by writing and releasing a carefully detailed report. It was a report on sanitation among the labouring classes, describing the repellent state of waste disposal, and making a case that doing something about it could directly alleviate the rates of death and disease. In 1844, the Metropolitan Building Act required that new construction have sewer connections. Further pressure by Chadwick and others led in 1848 to the Public Health Act, which established a three-member Board of Health, and to the Nuisances Removal and Contagious Diseases Prevention Act, which created a Commission of Sewers that required both existing and future buildings to drain into the sewer system. For this to be possible a vast new public infrastructure of sewers would have to be built, and here was an implicit mandate to do it.

In the space of a decade, London's social contract had changed. As Steven Johnson, the modern writer on science and society, puts it, the idea that individual responsibility was enough when it came to issues affecting health had been largely replaced by a new set of ideas: that "the state should directly engage in protecting the health and well-being of its citizens, particularly the poorest among them; that a centralized bureaucracy of experts can solve societal problems that free markets either exacerbate or ignore; that public-health issues often require massive state investment in infrastructure or protection."[3]

How did such radical rethinking of individual and collective responsibility take place? The answer has several elements. Since the problem was seen (and smelled) as chronic but was not yet a crisis, it didn't require a state-of-emergency response: the call was to move quickly, but time was available to reflect on the problem and evaluate many possible solutions. Additionally, an economic perspective suggested that the waste could be put to good use, improving English agricultural lands. And there was indeed a reform movement, raising the visibility of problems and possible solutions. The movement was led by category-crossing people like Edwin Chadwick – a barrister turned social scholar and thinker (his report grew famous for promoting "the sanitary idea"), turned activist and then administrator (he went on to head the Board of Health). Victorian England was infused with unending optimism, convinced that any problem could be solved. Perhaps it was the spirit of the time: almost simultaneously in the United States, the first state board of health was created.

However, the problem of action still remained, and it was a political problem. Building a new sewage system for London would be expensive, especially if done right. For years, despite cholera and stench, despite petitions from notables, Parliament dithered and debated the possible solutions – how the new sewers should be built, whether they should be built, what else could be done. After all, one should not commit too hastily.

The summer of 1858 is credited with tipping the scale. It was a hot summer. The Thames ran high with sewage and various unspeakable floating objects. Bacteria, though not well understood and only recently named, clearly knew that flush times had arrived and responded vigorously. It was not thought that London could stink any worse than it had, but this stink made it difficult to think of anything whatsoever. It was frightening. The Prime Minister described the river as "reeking with ineffable and unbearable horror"; many at the time still believed that cholera and typhoid could be caught by breathing foul air, and the House of Commons stood by the river.

The members now debated earnestly what to do. When hanging the windows with curtains soaked in chloride of lime did not help, they considered adjourning to a place outside London, then settled for moving to the landward side of the building. The Great Stink, fully deserving its capitalization, had moved Parliament. And not long after, a select committee was appointed and approval gained for a new sewage system designed to the highest specifications, which was then constructed by 1865.

One of the biggest obstacles that London faced in implementing reforms was neither engineering nor medical; it was establishing political jurisdiction. Early Victorian London was guided by a Byzantine assortment of over three hundred local boards whose authority had been established over the centuries by 250 separate acts of Parliament. Outside of the inner core (the "City," in today's parlance), municipal government hardly existed.[4] Until 1855, the only bodies having jurisdiction over all of London were officers appointed under the Metropolitan Building Act, and by the Commission of Sewers. One reform led to another: in 1855, the Metropolis Management Act was passed, creating local governments responsible to taxpayers and, incidentally, defining the jurisdictions of London as equivalent to those used by the Sewer Board. It also created the Metropolitan Board of Works as the central authority for both sewers and the Building Acts. Changes in the city's political governance made possible the master planning for financing and building out the public health infrastructure. Without these inherently political changes, the rest of the reforms would have been for naught.

Building a sewage system by no means completed the public health "system." The reform movement went on to do much more, becoming global. Campaigns against specific diseases, notably yellow fever and smallpox, spanned decades and many countries. Today you can literally see signs of the public health system everywhere. The signs in restaurant rest rooms, instructing employees to wash their hands, come from that jurisdiction's health department. When you see news reports on the global progress of the H1N1 flu virus or carry a Yellow Card (an international certificate of vaccination) on your travels, you are looking at the work of the World Health Organization (WHO), the public-health arm of the United Nations.

Again, you expect these things. They are parts of the worldwide social contract that you participate in, and a worldwide system that you help to pay for. And the system, though not perfect, actually works. Smallpox was a terrible scourge as recently as the 1950s and 60s, but you are extremely unlikely to ever have it, because in 1980 smallpox became the first contagious human disease to be declared completely eradicated. The London sewers worked in 1865 and they are still working. In various cities around the world in the early 1900s, the first campaigns to lower infant mortality did just that, and more recently the fluoridation of drinking water was found to greatly reduce tooth decay. Efforts in public health continue, but a lot of what the global system has done so far has worked.

One can't help wishing for a cyber-security system that could be half as effective. Arriving at such a system would have to involve arriving at a new social contract, in which cyber security is regarded as a public good, much as health is. Part of this contract would be, in Steven Johnson's words, that "the state should directly engage" in correcting the market's failures to address security issues. Users would understand their responsibilities to one another, and stupid cyber-behaviour that can infect others would be regarded and treated as what it is: behaviour that can infect others. For software vendors, releasing an insecure product would have consequences.

Is this a harsh mindset? Not at all. It is the mindset we already have for health, for fire, for auto safety. It is a *reframing* of the issue in order to handle it effectively, and Londoners did not arrive at it by dwelling overmuch on consciousness-raising. They set out to look for what could work – a proper fire brigade, a proper sewage system – and in the process, sometimes in great leaps and sometimes with great difficulty, they changed their thinking little by little, then their systems, and their world.

REFRAMING THE FRAMEWORKS OF CYBER SECURITY

What will work in the cyber city? The recommendations here are not exact parallels to system elements that have been put in place for fire protection and public health: I don't think the Internet needs more sewers, for example. But they do draw on the nature of those systems, coming at the security issue from multiple angles and involving shifts in the social contract. The list is not a complete list, just a few big items that I and others judge to be high priorities. In Chapter 6, I outlined briefly some of the needed reforms in terms of "institutional infrastructure and incentives." Here we will look at four:

- A new framework for Internet governance
- Tort liability – for software vendors and network service providers
- A robust insurance market
- Better data collection systems

If you are not a lawyer or an actuary, these reforms may sound mundane and clinical, lacking in dramatic strokes and short on magic bullets. In fact, if they were to be carried out, they could go a long way toward changing your experience of the Internet, for the better. And they could turn the tables on the bad guys without even touching them, by shoring up our side.

A NEW FRAMEWORK FOR INTERNET GOVERNANCE

The Internet has technical standards or protocols that among other things ensure interoperability and dictate how data is transmitted. And it does already have a governance structure. The Internet

Engineering Task Force (IETF) provides the forum for technical coordination.

But, as we've seen earlier, adoption of new security technologies across the Internet has been very slow. IPv6 has yet to be widely adopted, a decade after its release. A year after a major serious vulnerability (the Kaminsky vulnerability) was discovered – one that would allow attackers to actually give you an incorrect Internet address from the Internet's "address book," the Domain Name System – one in four of the DNS servers was still unpatched.[5] Securing another Internet protocol, the Border Gateway Protocol (BGP),[6] has been a priority since at least 2003, yet a senior U.S. government official recently noted, "The real barrier to securing BGP is that we just haven't had a serious enough attack. If people start losing significant money because there's some type of attack on the routing infrastructure, I think you'll see a whole lot more interest." In other words, something has to go really wrong before this item gets done right.

The problems here stem from the fact that the IETF does not, in the strict sense, govern. It is a communal-style body, descended from the Internet's earliest days, that provides a forum for coordination and cooperation among the many entities that actually build and run the Internet's equipment. So how could this be improved?

The International Telecommunications Union (ITU), a body of the UN, is the organization entrusted with harmonizing and coordinating world telecommunications. It doesn't "set" standards for phone systems and networks; rather, it "recommends" them through consultative committees that deal separately with wired and wireless communications. The International Telecommunications Regulations Treaty established the basic framework within which the ITU operates. The ITU's substantive work involves consultation among ITU staff, outside experts, and constituencies to produce its Recommendations. These are generally of a highly narrow, technical nature.

Thus far the ITU may sound quite similar to the IETF, since both operate on a voluntary, consensus-driven model. However, there are some key differences that lead to very different outcomes. The ITU's Recommendations can and do become required standards – most are adopted worldwide – whereas the IETF's Requests for Proposals (the equivalent of ITU Recommendations), often do not.

The difference involves the underlying social contracts. The ITU social contract works, first, because there is universal recognition of the need for coordinated standards in global telephony and telecommunications (which did not exist in the early part of the twentieth century). There also are well-established national systems for translating ITU Recommendations into requirements, by standard-setting agencies in various countries. The ITU's intense consensus-driven process is effective – important member countries are the source of many of the eventual Recommendations – and ITU actions are integrated into other agendas, such as international trade agreements. For instance, in 2001, when China wanted to join the World Trade Organization, its commitment to ensuring fairly priced and reliable telephone interconnection based on ITU standards was a central requirement of membership.[7]

The ITU must address different national or provider interests, and sometimes the result is a compromise. In the 1960s, for example, three different standards for colour television transmission were established in just such a compromise. But multiple standards are the exception, not the rule.

The standards that emerge from the ITU's Recommendations do two important things: they make the telephone system run worldwide, and they add new functionality. Consider, for example, many of the features that we take for granted in today's telephone systems, such as caller ID, call waiting, and electronic voicemail. None of these were possible a few decades ago. They've been enabled by new signaling protocols, whereby the signals that "manage" the workings of the telephone system travel in a separate channel from the signals that actually carry your voice. And not only do ITU Recommendations define these protocols (the current set is called "Signaling System 7"), they also establish the international public telephone numbering system (so that, for example, "44" directs the call to the United Kingdom).

To futher illustrate how Recommendations add new functionality, consider the use of 3G (third-generation) cellphones. The confidence with which telecom providers created partnerships and bid for spectrum to provide 3G services can be attributed to the ITU's creation of the International Mobile Telecommunications-2000 standard. (These standards provided a common technical framework which made it possible for different cellphone operators to work together.) More recently, an ITU Recommendation made possible the Universal International Freephone Service, whereby the called party bears the cost of a toll-free call over international networks. This service improves and simplifies customer access and gives companies greater control over their call-processing systems.

Thus, the ITU offers a model of how communication systems may be governed internationally while also allowing system operators to make choices and collaborate.

Cooperation on the Internet, however, has emerged very differently than it has within other infrastructures. When the Internet began as a small research project, it was run by a small community of researchers who trusted each other and cooperated informally as needed to make the system work. Less than thirty-five years ago, getting an Internet address involved calling one person, who maintained a list of the addresses in a simple notebook. Modifications to technical standards were accomplished by circulating proposed changes, which were then discussed in a consensual decision-making process.

Since then, some of these arrangements have become more formalized, but their essential nature has remained unchanged: Internet governance is voluntary and consensus-driven, with no legal authorities to mandate change. For instance, there is nothing to stop the development of multiple DNS systems (and in fact, several do exist). The Internet Corporation for Assigned Names and Numbers (ICANN) controls domain names through informal consensus, and not by international treaty. It has been successful simply because it represents a convenience that no one has yet had reason to disrupt.

As for the ITU, another of its advantages is that it has generally done a good job of developing Recommendations ahead of the curve. For example, the Recommendations for 3G standards allowed Japan's NTT DoCoMo, at the cutting edge of mobile telephony, to begin rolling out its strategy for 3G phone service in the early 2000s.[8] It may be a chicken-or-egg issue: perhaps the ITU stays ahead of the needs for telephony standards because those standards play such an important role in how and whether the international telephone system works. The ITU process is sometimes criticized as being slow, but in no case have important telephone functionalities been unavailable due to ITU inaction.

The same claim cannot be made for the Internet, which needs, at least for critical security protocols, to face up to the fact that it must move beyond its voluntary and undisciplined model if it is to keep up with the pace of growth and change.

An ITU-style option has, in fact, been one of the alternatives under consideration by the UN's Internet Governance Forum,[9] an outgrowth of multinational talks in the UN-led World Summit on the Internet Society. Our nations should embrace it. The "how" of achieving this goal I'll address later.

TORT LIABILITY

Holding organizations – or persons – responsible for their actions seems like such a basic and universal concept that it's hard to believe that many of the key players in network security are free of legal liability.

There are several methods of making another party legally accountable. One is through regulation: a government spells out what the party must or must not do. Another is through contract law: you and the other party sign a contract spelling out your mutual obligations, and if the other party violates the terms, you can take him/her/it to court and sue for breach of contract. Third is tort liability, for situations outside formal contracts or where those contracts do not exist. If you are harmed as a result of something the other party makes or does, you can sue to be paid for damages.

Tort liability helps to shape behaviour, and shape our lives, in some ways you may not notice. Newspapers today are generally more accurate and fair than they were in the days of yellow journalism. They usually follow their own industry's standards for verifying that a fact is true before reporting it as such, and for separating news from opinion. Newspapers are not heavily regulated in most democracies and they don't have contracts with the people they write about. They have, however, for quite a while been subject to the ongoing discipline of tort liability: they can be sued for libel.

Tort liability often works in conjunction with regulation. For example, a precedent-setting case in the U.S. was *MacPherson v. Buick*, in 1916. A wheel broke on Mr. MacPherson's Buick motor car, resulting in further damage. He sued and, despite circumstances and precedents that seemed to doom the case, he won. After that came other lawsuits over the years, along with regulations, and cars became safer and safer. Also consider the tobacco lawsuits of the late twentieth century. Repeatedly, individual and class-action suits were brought against tobacco companies, seeking compensation for lung cancer and other diseases suffered after smoking cigarettes. Repeatedly, the plaintiffs failed. Then a coalition of states sued, pointing to the costs they'd incurred for publicly provided medical care. They won. And, during the case, subpoenas for tobacco-company documents brought evidence to light that was embarrassing to the companies, and undercut their stances in situations beyond the case. Cigarette smoking has continued to decline as this changing perception of their product, combined with regulations and other actions by government, has caused people to change their behaviour.

"Government," in general, is largely immune from tort liability itself.* But other than that, our networked computer systems represent possibly the only remaining sector of society that we

---

* I am indebted to Professor Peter Shane of the Ohio State University for pointing this out.

depend on in our daily lives in which those most responsible for its safe and secure functioning are essentially immune from any legal recourse to their failings. Maybe this wouldn't be an issue if our software wasn't filled with bugs that create security holes exploited by attackers, or if network providers routinely and jointly kept up to a high standard of operating practices to remove malicious traffic from the Internet, but that isn't so.

LIABILITY FOR SOFTWARE

Today Firestone can produce a tire with a single systemic flaw and they're liable, but Microsoft can produce an operating system with multiple systemic flaws discovered per week and not be liable. This makes no sense, and it's the primary reason security is so bad today.

The quotation is from Michael D. Scott, a law professor and long-time technology attorney in the U.S. It appeared in 2008 in his article for the *Maryland Law Review* titled "Tort Liability for Vendors of Insecure Software: Has the Time Finally Come?" Among the growing number who say the answer is yes, Scott is one of the few to say so in a scholarly article thick with footnotes and citations. Our old friend Mudge, the hacker turned good guy, put it more colourfully. He said software companies keep releasing code full of vulnerabilities because "nobody's holding their feet to the fire."

And yes, it's true that you can't sue Microsoft (or any other software vendor) for insecure software. To date courts have generally refused to find software vendors liable for these defects. At least for shrink-wrapped and downloadable software, one "out" has been the fig leaf that software is not sold, it is licensed, and in the licensing agreement – the *contract* that many people do not read before clicking the "I agree" button so they can install the software – the user agrees that the producer will not be held liable.[10] I actually looked at one licensing agreement recently, for a freeware application I was considering for my PC. Printed out, it ran to twenty-eight pages. And in there was the provision that, essentially,

I hold the producer in no way responsible for anything bad that happens to me. (If this wasn't freeware, if I had had to pay real money for the software, then the vendor's liability would have been limited to the purchase cost.)

There were a few early cases in which licensees sought to have courts hold vendors liable for defective software, but these cases were unsuccessful.[11] The legal intricacies that have made insecure-software suits nigh impossible to win are arcane. A licensee might claim, for example, that the licensing agreement wasn't really an agreement because he had no choice but to agree. (In legalese, that's called an "adhesion contract.") But it isn't easy to strip the fig leaf away. Some arguments have to do with whether software is a "product" in the sense that others are and should be held to similar liability standards (or if it's a service and whether the practitioners can be held tort-liable for malpractice).

There is also a big fork in the road between suing on grounds of "negligence" or "strict liability." To argue that the producer is liable because he was negligent in making the product, you may have to show, for example, that he didn't follow reasonable standards of care – but if most other software companies are making their products with similar care, that could be difficult.

In strict liability, negligence does not have to be shown. Very roughly, the thinking behind the legal basis for it is that in situations where harm can have hugely adverse consequences, the important thing is to repair the harm. And that should be done by the party most responsible for the harm (whether negligent or not) and most able to fix the source of the harm. This is usually the producer if it can be shown that the product indeed caused the harm. Rather than focus on the behaviour of the manufacturer, strict liability claims focus on the product itself, which that party made. As one law professor told me, "The plaintiff in a strict liability suit need only show two things: I was harmed, and the defendant manufactured or sold the product that harmed me."[12]

Many experts – myself included – believe that "software is a perfect case for strict liability."[13] Defective software imposes a huge cost to users and society. Users, however, even if they use software products reasonably and only for their intended purposes, are generally unable to prevent this harm. Making users bear the risk of harm thus makes no sense. By contrast, strict liability would give the job of loss prevention to the parties most able to do that job. Liability would impose the appropriate economic incentive on software manufacturers to do the job right.

Some opponents of holding software vendors to liability argue, essentially, that software is different from other products in ways that make it impossible for society to benefit from any changes brought about by lawsuits. Products like automobiles and lawnmowers have long design life-cycles (I use a lawnmower whose design probably dates to the 1950s), so any design changes from a tort liability lawsuit are likely to be relevant even years later. Software, they say, evolves so rapidly that any legal action would be meaningless because the product would be already outdated by the time a judgment was rendered.

Also, opponents argue, most products are purchased for predictable purposes and used under somewhat predictable circumstances (as with lawnmowers), but software vendors cannot predict where their software will be installed or for what purposes it will be applied. As one commentator noted, "That same desktop application suite is, at this very instant, executing on an immense quantity of combinations of various types, versions, capacities, and complexities of computer and communications hardware and software and in the context of an immense variety of their relevant circumstances. An interaction among these variations could create a security hole of a sort that the software producer could not have anticipated. A publisher could not design, let [alone conduct a] test for more than a fraction of these possibilities."[14]

Another objection is that some industries have, in fact, suffered from product liability. There are only two manufacturers of football helmets left in the U.S.; light airplane manufacturers have similarly suffered. Furthermore, it is claimed those truly deserving of taking action will be unable to afford the legal recourse and it will be the "lawyers and experts witnesses that will profit the most."[15]

And finally, passing the cost of potential liability onto consumers might, it is argued, make some software products prohibitively expensive for many, resulting in diminished economic productivity across society as whole.

These objections are self-serving rubbish, and deserve to be treated as such. They leave software vendors exactly where they want to be: in a position of being able to produce, and foist off on the largely powerless consumer, product filled with flaws which are then "fixed" later as the flaws are discovered by the users. Unfortunately, malicious attackers discover them, too. Software is unquestionably unique, as proponents of the current system of non-accountability claim, but not for the reasons they propose. We depend on software; we know that there are ways in which software of vastly higher quality can be produced; and we suspect that some software may be more dependable than others. But we have no appeal to one of the most effective mechanisms that might actually give software producers the incentive to take the necessary steps. I regard it as one of my greatest failings during my tenure at the White House that I did not press for a finding – or at least for a process that would lead to a finding – that it was in the public interest that software producers be required to demonstrate a reasonable standard of care in making their products. And subsequent iterations of U.S. cyber-security policy have completely ignored any consideration of tort liability.

LIABILITY FOR NETWORK OPERATORS - AND USERS?

We expect that if our neighbour engages in conduct that causes us harm we should have recourse. In the case of a distributed denial-of-service attack, there is no question that the hacker who intentionally caused harm should be held responsible. However, what about the Internet service providers whose systems were used in the course of the computer attack, and who failed to take reasonable steps prior to the attack to protect against misuse of their systems?[16] Who, if anyone, should be held accountable if some ISP subscriber originates malicious Internet code, or propagates malicious code by forwarding a virus over e-mail? What about the situation where an

ISP subscriber, out of ignorance or laziness, adopts lax security precautions that in turn do not protect his computer from being co-opted by a malevolent user?[17]

Internet service providers today are largely immune from liability for their role in creating and propagating cyber attacks.[18] Yet ISPs control the gateways through which Internet attacks enter and re-enter the public networks. The technologies exist for them to filter traffic, detect unusual patterns, identify when a message is coming from a source without a valid address, and take many other actions that, especially if taken collectively, would vastly improve network security. The improvements would ensure that attack traffic could be blocked or cut off while an attack is happening. It would also be easier (though not absolutely guaranteed) that attribution of the source of cyber attacks would be possible. Cutting off the source of an attack midstream is particularly important for dealing with DDOS attacks. Security expert Paul Kurtz noted in a 2008 interview that there are at least a dozen major DDOS attacks happening at any given time.[19]

Thus, holding ISPs accountable for their role in not preventing cyber attacks seems intuitively obvious. ISPs are in a good position to reduce the number and severity of bad acts online. There are lots of steps that ISPs can take. They can prevent malicious attacks from starting, for example, by ensuring that messages that purportedly originate within their network in fact come from a valid network address. They can take actions to stop attacks (particularly DDOS attacks) that are underway from continuing, by blocking incoming traffic from suspect sites for brief periods of time. They can help in finding out where attacks originated (the attribution problem) by storing or marking message traffic. These actions would be most effective if all ISPs adopted them, but since the U.S. and Canada still account for at about 16 per cent of Internet users,[20] North American adoption would influence overall network traffic.

Cyber-security policies in almost all OECD nations recognize this, and encourage ISPs to adopt a set of good practices, but stop there. There is little evidence that ISPs have responded to these pleas. To date, no U.S. court has addressed the issue of liability for a failure to adequately secure a computer network that subsequently led to a downstream attack.[21]

Exempting ISPs from liability ignores the fact that they are in a good position to detect and deter. The concept of potential liability is to "encourage private parties to develop mechanisms and adopt organization structures that effectively allow for the control of possible bad actors."[22] Companies are always seeking ways to avoid this potential exposure – taxi companies pretend that their drivers are separate corporate entities, and certain types of nightclubs treat their entertainers as contractors and not employees. "Sadly the courts accept these sorts of excuses all too often . . . but the basic economics of indirect liability remind us that courts should instead direct a skeptical eye toward any party's self-imposed inability to detect or deter."[23]

In the U.S., courts have traditionally limited third-party liability for things like lax ISP security by excluding them for purely economic reasons (the "economic loss doctrine"), and by holding that any criminal act (in other words, the attacker's use of the ISP), breaks the "chain of causation" such that the ISP is not held responsible. (In technical terms, any breach of duty by the defendant – the ISP, i.e., the upstream party – would not be deemed the proximate cause of harm to the plaintiff, who is the downstream party.)[24] However, many courts are beginning to reject the economic loss doctrine. Similarly, if a court found that the likelihood of misconduct on networks was great enough, the fact of the "intervening criminal" act would not necessarily be sufficient to break the chain of causation.[25]

Enforcement of current law provides a partial solution in the absence of liability. Under its authority to guard against "unfair [or deceptive] acts or practices," the U.S. Federal Trade Commission has begun taking action against companies whose systems were attacked, revealing confidential data. One case involved a membership warehouse retailer on the U.S. east coast, BJ's Wholesale Club, whose failure to properly configure its computer system allegedly allowed thousands of customer records to be accessed by attackers who made millions of dollars in fraudulent purchases.[26]

In another case, Geeks.com, a large online seller of computer hardware and software, has agreed to allow federal regulators to monitor its Web site security for ten years to settle charges that it violated federal laws requiring it to adequately safeguard sensitive customer data. The agreement settles a complaint filed by the Federal Trade Commission that accused the online retailer of misleading its customers about the safety of their personal information. The company's Web site had carried a statement claiming that it employed "secure technology, privacy protection controls and restrictions on employee access in order to safeguard your personal information." During a six-month period starting in January of 2007, the site was breached repeatedly by hackers who used simple SQL injections to siphon credit-card numbers, expiration dates, and other sensitive customer data.[27]

An extension of these FTC actions would be a system of self-regulation, based on voluntary disclosures of compliance with security standards, and enforced through existing laws banning unfair and deceptive advertising.[28] For a system of this type to function effectively without public regulation, at least some major organizations would have to prominently disclose whether they comply with technical standards or industry best practices. Disclosures would be monitored for compliance by customers and competitors. In the case of deceptive advertising, in the U.S. the Federal Trade Commission could take enforcement action (though the penalties would be civil, not criminal). This strategy could spur cyber-insurance adoption, because having insurance from a reputable underwriter would signal that the organization has met the underwriter's security standards.[29] A similar approach was highly successful in addressing the Y2K problem. The U.S. Securities and Exchange Commission did not require filing organizations to take action to address the Y2K issue, merely to report publicly what, if any, action they were taking.

Here we come again to a question raised earlier. If we are to pursue action against Web site operators engaged in deceptive trade practices, what about the ISPs who allow their systems to be insecure? The case that ISPs should bear some liability for their role in facilitating attacks against other computers could equally apply to the users of home computers, but universal liability for all Internet users whose lack of security contributes to an attack is not a desirable outcome. So perhaps the best system would be to limit upstream liability to ISPs, and perhaps to include large organizations such as corporations and universities with the resources and capabilities to act more responsibly than they have in reducing their role in propagating cyber attacks. Otherwise, the logical conclusion would be for Internet users to have the equivalent of a driver's licence – neither feasible nor appealing.

CREATING LIABILITY WHERE NONE EXISTS TODAY

So how do we begin to go about establishing liability?

Liability could be established by statute. The U.S. National Academy of Science has already proposed that Congress enact legislation that "would increase the exposure of software and systems vendors and systems operators to liability for system breaches and mandate . . . reporting of security breaches that could threaten critical infrastructures."[30] A recent proposal by two European Commissioners proposed that, as part of consumer protections relating to licensing agreements, software companies could be held liable for their code. The directive would require that products, including software licensed under licensing agreements, be held to a higher standard of accountability, and that they carry a two-year guarantee.[31]

Ideally, legislated legal reform would require that strict liability apply to purely economic losses. The monetary amounts of liability could be capped – with the amount large enough to provide incentives to software vendors to improve product quality, but not so large as to damage the industry.

Alternatively, liability could emerge from developments in case law. As Michael D. Scott noted: " . . . recent developments in tort law indicate that tort law appears to be moving toward a point where at least some types of security-related software vulnerabilities will give rise to tort claims."[32]

That passage is encouraging but contains several qualifiers. Legislation – which requires political action – would be the more definitive route.

A ROBUST INSURANCE INDUSTRY

It has been said, "A trusted component or system is one that you can insure."[33] Insurance is a good thing, because it is a way of monetizing the risks we face, and allows us to shift those risks onto the insurance company. It also requires that we have some understanding of the risks and consequences of bad things happening. The availability of affordable insurance signals that the risk is manageable. We have reasonably affordable automobile insurance. After 9/11, however, it took government intervention to make terrorism risk insurance available.

Insurance against cyber attack is available – which would seem to signal that at least some computer systems are considered trustworthy enough for insurers to take on their risk – but its future is unclear. According to the trade journal *Risk Management*, "To say that the insurance market for computer-related perils is in a state of flux is putting it politely. Insuring information assets and covering risks from doing business online has never been more challenging. Policyholders are offered a dizzying array of incomplete, untested, and sometimes incomprehensible specialty insurance products supposedly designed to cover this area of risk. Worse still, they are expensive and finding the desired limits can be daunting."[34]

A vibrant cyber-security insurance market would better align private interests with society's interest in secure networks. Since insurance premiums are set according to different classes of risk, the cost of insurance encourages the company *being* insured to invest in security that will reduce the risks and consequently its fees. In the end both the investing organization and the network would generally benefit. It would now be in everyone's interests to reduce security incidents. Insurance also encourages the creation of better measuring tools for assessing security.[35] In particular, cyber-insurance premiums are a way of expressing the value of security measures in monetary terms – not a small advance in itself.[36] Because insurers have an incentive to understand and manage the risks, research on cyber-security technologies would deepen with broader coverage if there were a direct financial incentive by risk insurers to prevent incidents. The already cited research into fire protection and loss provides an example.

Cyber insurance got off to a promising start but has since been derailed. Until the late 1990s, general property and casualty policies also covered cyber attacks, making things simple for the insurance buyer. But since then exclusionary language in these policies now mean that businesses must buy stand-alone specialty policies to cover cyber risks. As one expert explains, "Computer code is deemed to be intangible . . . Property and casualty policies were never written to assess these exposures and never priced to include them."[37]

Projections made in the early 2000s that the cyber insurance market would now be on the order of over two billion dollars have not materialized.[38] Nor have the optimistic forecasts of security experts such as Bruce Schneier, who in 2002 said, "The insurance industry [is] going to move into cyber-insurance in a big way. And when they do, they're going to drive the computer-security industry . . . just like they drive the security industry in the brick-and-mortar world."[39]

Instead of a multibillion dollar market, annual gross premiums for cyber insurance policies grew from less than $100 million in 2002 to just $450 to $500 million in 2008.[40]

Part of the reason is that cyber-security risk is a relatively new phenomenon. Before the late 1990s little commercial demand existed for third-party liability insurance on property of any kind.[41] Potential liability from breaches of IT security has increased since then. However, only 34 per cent of the respondents to a recent CSI/FBI survey reported that "their organizations use external insurance to help manage cyber-security risks."[42] Cyber-security insurance remains a small, boutique market.

Cyber-security insurance faces a number of challenges, one of the biggest being the problem of *correlated risk*. This happens when an attack affects not just one or a few insured organizations, but many – as would happen if there were a serious unchecked virus spreading across the Internet, or if whole parts of the Internet were disrupted. This is the same challenge that insurers face in insuring against hurricanes or floods. A really bad hurricane (such as Katrina in 2005) or flood affects a lot of people and property at the same time. During the twentieth century, floods were the number-one natural disaster in the United States in terms of lives lost and property damage.[43] Private insurers simply don't have the reserves to handle large correlated losses, and so governments backstop private insurance (in the case of hurricanes) or replace it (in the case of floods).

Insurers like to have a good history of insured events in order to gauge what the risks are likely to be. Auto and fire insurance fit this model nicely. Cyber security does not. This doesn't stop insurers from writing cyber-security policies, just as they make insurance available for, say, rock concerts (I used to be a concert promoter in an earlier life). It does mean that cyber-security insurance may not be economically efficient. Insurers and the insured are both largely in the dark as to what the "real" risk is.

The challenge of assessing risk is compounded because insurers do not share data with each other. In contrast to auto or fire risk, where the Insurance Information Institute aggregates incident and loss information, providing a sound actuarial basis for estimating the risks of, say, an accident by a Mercedes driver of a certain age and locale, there is no equivalent mechanism for underwriters to aggregate cyber risk or loss data.[44] Indeed, some of the major providers of cyber insurance seem to regard their risk histories as a competitive advantage. The more policies are written, the greater the (proprietary) knowledge of potential risk, and the greater the competitive advantage. This is effective for the company but not for society at large. The practice ensures that the larger players are, as one insurance executive said to me, "big fish in a little pond."

Other insurance markets have grown facing similar issues. Comparing the market for insuring environmental risks to that for cyber security, one expert noted that "the initial forms and exposures were very similar in that there [were] no data to underpin the rates . . . People began by putting a very restrictive policy form with high pricing on the market; and over time, as they began to develop experience, they were able to broaden policy forms and modify the pricing significantly."[45]

Overall, the market for cyber-security insurance appears to be developing on track but very slowly compared to the magnitude of the problem.[46] The process of obtaining insurance has been stream-lined somewhat, and no longer usually requires an on-site evalua-tion by security consultants (a process analogous to having to have your car taken apart before you could get auto insurance). And pol-icy language is being standardized, although it remains complex.

But the market is still small.

We need to clarify liability law to assign liability "to the party that can do the best job of managing risk" (a famous observation by U.S. judge Learned Hand). This would increase the demand for insurance. We also need governments to require, as part of their contracts, that government contractors carry cyber liability insur-ance on projects highly dependent on IT security.[47]

In the U.S., where insurance is almost exclusively a matter of state regulation, there is a further opportunity for state-led reform, and once again fire insurance provides a model. In the early 1900s the state of New York required insurance companies to submit uniform statistics on property and casualty losses for the first time. New York's data collection requirements had far-reaching conse-quences for the entire fire insurance industry. Once a state as pop-ulous as New York mandated that insurers submit data, the imperative for a uniform classification system was born. If they had to do it for New York, they might as well do it everywhere. In 1914 the industry responded by creating what is now the National Association of Insurance Commissioners (NAIC) to establish uni-form, industry-wide classification standards. The regular collec-tion of uniform data enabled the development of modern actuarial science in the fire field.[48]

A similar state or provincial model could be applied for cyber-security insurance. The specifics of how cyber attacks and conse-quent losses are determined would have to be worked out, but the key point is that by providing a uniform set of risk data, a criti-cal foundation for a widely applicable insurance market would be created, not just in the U.S. or Canada but elsewhere in the world as well.

BETTER DATA

Good data matters. Till the mid-nineteenth century, cholera was thought to spread through "miasmic" air. But good data about the specific location of cholera deaths in London, combined with further data about water supply sources, demonstrated that in fact tainted water was the principal vector for cholera. Without the data, the skeptics would never have been convinced.[49]

Data on cyber security is a mixed bag.[50] The system of CERTs, ISACs, and other entities such as the SANS Storm Center do a pretty good job of collecting and disseminating information about systems' security vulnerabilities and new modes of attack. But data on the consequences of such attacks to companies, business sectors, and nations is still patchy. Part of the challenge is methodological: there is still no methodology to account for both the direct and indirect costs of cyber attacks. Part of the challenge is administrative: despite laws criminalizing cyber attacks, public reporting of cyber attacks remains the exception rather than the rule. As a consequence, governments and businesses are hard pressed to make informed decisions about how much to invest in cyber security and how to invest each dollar most effectively.[51]

To its credit, the U.S. government recently completed the first National Computer Security Survey (NCSS).[52] The NCSS was carefully conducted, though the response was not mandated by law, as is sometimes the case with other government surveys. It collected data on the nature and extent of computer security incidents, the monetary costs, incident details such as types of offenders and reporting to authorities, and computer security measures used by companies. Some other countries are doing similar surveys – for example, the Australian Business Assessment of Computer User Security. Statistics Canada examined the feasibility of a government survey but to date has not acted.[53] A problem with many of the more robust surveys is that they are conducted so infrequently that the data loses some value.

Other good collection and data models exist for informed decision-making. One is the public health system. Today in the developed world, the public health system comprises a wide array of governmental and nongovernmental bodies. In the U.S. this includes over three thousand county and city health departments and local boards of health, and more than 160,000 public and private laboratories, hospitals, and volunteer organizations such as the Red Cross.[54] At the core of the systems are the Public Health Agency (PHA) in Canada, and the Public Health Service, including the Centers for Disease Control and Prevention (CDC), in the U.S.

Most public health authority is regionally based in the states and provinces. The Canadian PHA and the American CDC work with the states and provinces, plus localities and other nations, to detect, investigate, and prevent disease and injury, to develop and implement prevention strategies, to monitor the effect of environmental conditions on health, and to study illness and injury in the workplace. Other federal agencies in the U.S. also have roles, from the Agriculture Department to the Food and Drug Administration to Veterans Affairs. Most of the system – particularly in reporting infectious diseases – is voluntary, and though states are not required to report to the CDC, the reporting is good. Canada has similar practices, as does the EU and the U.K.

Agencies like CDC and PHA act at a national level. Internationally, the World Health Organization acts as a global department of health. It assists and monitors public health activities around the world, and undertakes work that can be done only internationally, such as coordinating the global fight against AIDS. With partners and constituencies around the world – at every level from the national to the local, in small villages – the WHO is in the position to do and coordinate a host of things that no other entity could accomplish alone. This role includes gathering data and acting upon it.

How WHO works offers us lessons for cyber security. After an outbreak of tuberculosis in South Africa, the WHO identified a worrying strain that was resistant to the panel of drugs normally used to treat the disease. In May 2008, when a man with drug-resistant tuberculosis travelled abroad from the U.S. against the advice of the

CDC, health organizations in multiple countries worked together to track his movements and finally (in the first such action in forty-four years) place him in federal quarantine.[55] The chase and apprehension were enabled by a social contract that existed across different nations with widely varying interests, resulting in cooperation for mutual benefit.

A second model is that for reporting physical crime. The U.S. President's Crime Commission (1965–1967) noted that while crime was a growing problem, the Justice Department lacked an effective research and development program to understand the causes of, and potential solutions to, crime. As a result, what is now the Bureau of Justice Statistics was created, which funds a number of research and data collection efforts to better understand crime and criminal behaviour.[56]

Central to this are two distinct data collection methods. The Uniform Crime Reports (UCRs), now run by the FBI, collect information from police departments. However, relying only on police data may not capture the full picture, because not all crimes are reported. To capture the "dark figure of crime" the National Crime Victimization Survey (NCVS) was launched. This statistically valid sampling instrument surveys households about crimes they have experienced, including those not reported to the police. Together, the UCR and the NCVS provide an ongoing and reasonably complete picture of physical crime in the United States.

So we do have good models for collecting good data using highly distributed, heterogeneous networks. A system for gathering data on cyber incidents could be developed along similar lines.

One important reform would be to develop a systematic and accepted practice of costing out the impact of cyber insecurity. The Financial Accounting Standards Board, which does what its name implies, could and should develop recommended methodologies for organizations to use in determining the cost of cyber breaches, as well as the cost of investments made in information security.

Another key reform would be to require reporting on cyber crime. A good start has been the mandatory data breach notification laws enacted by most U.S. states (in the name of protecting personal privacy). In Canada, only Ontario has a similar disclosure requirement, and that applies only to health care data.[57] Alternatively, the Securities and Exchange Commission could, as it did with the Y2K challenge, simply require companies to report on the impact of any cyber intrusions in their financial statements. A requirement like this would not specify exactly what has to be reported, but it would encourage the investment community to work out the acceptable metrics. Furthermore, rating agencies like Moody's and Standard & Poor's could then rate companies on the extent of their information risk. No government agency can do a good job of specifying, let alone requiring, the form and nature of the information that should be reported on cyber attacks. That's a job best left to the private sector.

These reforms would vastly improve our data on cyber attacks without onerously imposing a regimen for reporting and collection. Addressing Internet security through continued reliance on anecdote and hazy analysis is a recipe for continued failure. The reforms proposed here will not result in perfect measurements of the problem, but they will move us considerably forward in our understanding.

CHAPTER 9

THE ULTIMATE PROMISE: A NEW INTERNET

The policy proposals in the last two chapters all have assumed that the Internet itself will remain fundamentally unchanged, that it will continue to run on the same basic architecture and the "packet switching" protocols now over forty years old. If these proposals are pursued, security should improve substantially: you will notice the difference.

But just as the Internet was a revolutionary network of networks, what if we started out again with a new "something" that would replace the Internet? Do we need a so-called "clean slate" network, designed from the ground up, to truly address the needs for security and other emerging challenges? In other words, is it time for some major urban renewal in the cyber city?

In fact, as you read this, groups of researchers around the world (including me) are already at work on a variety of "future Internet" projects. In the U.S., the National Science Foundation is funding research through its FIND initiative (Future Internet Design), and is building an experimental research network known as GENI, the Global Environment for Network Innovations.[1] Stanford University's Clean Slate Program – with funding from the NSF and international private firms – openly states its aim to "reinvent" the Internet.

In Europe, the FIRE initiative (Future Internet Research and Experimentation) has funding of some forty million Euros to support projects across the EU, and Germany has launched the multi-university G-Lab. AsiaFI (the Asia Future Internet Forum) draws participants from fourteen countries, including China. There are other consortia, projects, and collaborations as well, and nearly every major IT and communications firm, from NTT of Japan to Deutsche Telekom, has a hand in somewhere.

All of these research efforts are still in their early stages. At the current pace it could be fifteen years before any meaningful impact will be seen.[2] Still, the sheer scope of the activity, and the funding being committed or foreseen – GENI alone could cost $350 million – all reflect a growing consensus: replacing the Internet is an idea whose time has come.

More secure software would be a major step forward, and security-focused practices by ISPs would help. Changes in the Internet's governance would also help if administrative reforms led to network-wide adoption of more secure protocols. But if we truly want security – and a lot of other benefits as well – then we should face up to building a completely new system.

Some of the challenges to replacing the current Internet are technical, but the most critical are social and economic. We'll explore what history tells us of the issues that arose when other new networks, such as electric power, were launched. And in a few pages I will lay out a specific proposal for how to successfully build a new Internet. But first, a reasonable person might ask why a replacement for the Internet is being worked on at all.

WHY THE INTERNET SHOULD BE REPLACED

Just as a building rests on its foundation, the underlying architecture of the Internet shapes what it can and cannot do well. Is this architecture adequate for what the Internet has become, and what we want it to be? The basic design stems from that of the ARPANet, the proto-network funded decades ago by the U.S. Defense Department's Advanced Research Projects Agency. (The agency has since been renamed DARPA, with the D standing for "Defense.") And in a 2006 "Request for Ideas" memo, DARPA voiced its concern over what it had wrought:

> The Department of Defense's Global Information Grid (GIG) includes a global network currently based on Internet technology . . . It is increasingly clear that current Internet technology is an inadequate foundation for an "assurable" network, if "information assurance" comprises concerns such as confidentiality, availability, integrity, and safety, which in turn depend on authentication and accountability.[3]

Yet the first developers of the network were neither stupid nor venal. As one of the original designers said to me, "We knew, when we were first designing what became the Internet, that a lot of the choices we were making were pretty clunky and insecure. But you have to understand that our concern then was just to get the thing to work, not to worry about all the pretty details."[4]

The DARPA memorandum spells out some reasons why the Internet no longer meets the needs of key users like the military – and most of these reasons apply to everyday users as well. Top on the list, of course, are security and assurability. The Internet was designed for a trusted commune of researchers, not for a system with millions of sometimes untrustworthy or naive users. You'll never be able to be absolutely confident that a file attachment doesn't contain a virus or worm, or that the Web site you are visiting is an authentic site, and not a clever similitude created by a hacker. Spam will never completely go away.

As the memo notes, Internet operations are "based on assumptions of trust . . . that allow single inept or malicious users or administrators to create widespread chaos. Protocol 'bulkheads' do not exist to limit damage from errors or malicious users. . . . The combination of configuration complexity and human error is the largest source of vulnerability in many networks."[5]

And the systems that make the Internet run, such as its system for routing messages (DNS, the Domain Name System, and the routers themselves) are surprisingly open to attack.[6] When hackers claim that they can take down the Internet in thirty minutes, they're thinking of disabling the DNS. These vulnerabilities can't be fixed without a great deal of difficulty, and the resulting complexity may prove the solutions unworkable. For example, in theory a new protocol called DNSSec would create a highly secure way to provide the correct Internet address when you type one into your browser. But implementing DNSSec will require a whole new global hierarchy of "trust authorities" that will use cryptography to "sign" (and thereby validate) the correctness of an address. Setting up these trust authorities is an administrative nightmare requiring global cooperation, and many experts expect that this approach never will succeed.[7]

Also, unlike another common communication system, the telephone system, the Internet also lacks a good way to charge for services (since the to-from flow of packets is not well accounted for), doesn't handle mobile devices very well, and can't provide users and ISPs with desirable value-added services. And with little accountability for packet flows, it's difficult for Internet operators to monitor and correct failures and service problems.[8] Again, these shortcomings can't be fixed with the existing architecture.

Take the fact that with the Internet you do not get an exact bill for your Internet use based on where, and to whom, you sent e-mails (as with a pay-per-call telephone service). Your immediate reaction might be to say, "So what? That's good; I like it that way." But the lack of a good structure for billing and charging for services across the Internet reflects, first of all, a key security weakness: the difficulty of tracing and attributing messages to their true source. Further, it has hindered initiatives that require cooperation among ISPs, such as quality-of-service standards, multicasting, and public services such as emergency preparedness. And it affects poor countries. In international telephony, third-world nations are effectively subsidized for their connection to the global telephone system – a scheme formalized by international agreement. Such a reverse payment system would be impossible to implement with the Internet. While nations like Nigeria are believed to get a positive balance of payments from their connection to the Internet, that flow of funds comes from cyber crime, not from a system designed to benefit the global common weal.

But rather than enumerate problems, let's ask what kinds of benefits we would be looking for with a new Internet. One research paper does a good job of outlining these benefits:

> The next generation Internet should be secure. It should allow businesses to set their boundaries and enforce their policies inside their boundaries. It should allow governments to set rules that protect their citizens on the Internet the same way they protect other means of transport. It should allow people to set policies for how and where they receive information. They should have the freedom to select their names, IDs and addresses with as little centralized control as possible. The architecture should be general enough to allow different governments to have different rules . . . The next generation Internet should be designed for mobile objects . . . The naming and addressing architecture has to allow so that these objects can move and decide how and where they want to receive their Internet traffic, with full rights of privacy of their location if desired. [9]

The biggest immediate benefit would be in security. Security would be more "built in," and not so much a condition that requires extraordinary measures. Imagine a digital environment where you can store your data and retrieve it, talk with colleagues and friends, or buy something online – all with a baseline confidence that it's being done safely. Even without the advantages that greater speed would provide, the benefits of finally having a secure network would finally make real the promise of a safe cyber city. The benefits of this alone can't be overestimated. [10]

Not everyone agrees with this rosy view of the future, however.

A new network architecture isn't going to solve our problems. The question I like to ask people is, what are you going to do to the highway system to reduce crime? And when you put it that way, it sounds absolutely ridiculous, because while criminals do use the highway, no rational person is suggesting that if only we could change the transportation architecture that crime would go away.

And yet, in a certain sense, that's what people who propose that a new Internet architecture is going to solve our security problems are heard to be saying.[11]

I beg to differ with this. The comparison between the Internet and the highway system would be more apt if all cars today were anonymously black and there were no licence plates or driver's licences; if there were major obstacles to tracking movements and pursuing vehicles, and very few police. In that case, reforming the system would in fact reduce crime. And that, in analogy, is the situation on the Internet today.

Other benefits would come with a clean-slate Internet. A new network would be unbelievably fast – about two thousand times faster than what even the best-connected home users now experience. Speeds like that would require new hardware and software in your computer; right now only supercomputers have the capacity to handle them. However, with super-speeds, we could start to believe (for instance) that not only would videoconferencing cease to be the clunky joke it is today, but that virtual environments could be created with holographic projections. You could "be" in the conference room, not just seeing it on your screen.

A clean-slate Internet could also resolve some of the most pressing "political" challenges facing the current network. Today, parts of the Internet community want additional services or different levels of service. Some applications, such as streaming audio and video, demand a more sophisticated Internet that can assure a specified throughput for a data stream. These needs run counter to the "best effort delivery" system that the Internet was designed for, which makes no guarantee about the throughput that any particular application will achieve at any moment.

Today, enhanced delivery for streaming media and other advanced applications, such as VOIP (Voice Over Internet Protocol) telephone service, is both a political and competitive issue. ISPs now view enhanced data transport service as something to be provided within the bounds of a particular ISP, as a competitive differentiator – rather than as a capability to be supported, end to end, across multiple providers' networks. This raises touchy questions, for example, should those who can afford to pay have greater access to ISP-specific higher performance than others?[12]

A clean-slate Internet could resolve these conflicts through a new set of network architectures. Right now the Internet Protocol (IP) is *the* architecture. But with a clean-slate approach this need not be the case: the new network could have a foundational "substrate" on which many different network architectures could co-exist. In this world, IP would become just one of potentially many network architectures. Such a diversified network could create a range of new opportunities for users since they would now be able to choose what they wanted to use from a variety of types of networks.

A STRONG HAND IS NEEDED

If we just sit and wait for a clean-slate Internet to materialize, we're going to be disappointed. A strong hand is needed to drive the transformation. Otherwise, today's network operators could drive change in directions that are less promising. That is the point of a recent book by the Harvard academic Jonathan Zittrain, titled *The Future of the Internet – and How to Stop It*.[13] Operators could adapt the existing Internet into high- and low-performance segments, or they could create subnets that become the equivalent of gated communities.

The search for competitive advantage by Internet operators is certainly legitimate. But it raises the prospect that new needs will be met by application-specific servers and services "inside" the network, which is a departure from the "end-to-end" philosophy behind the current design. Today's Internet is (intentionally) a pretty dumb network, in that it doesn't have a lot of user functionality built in. For example, the World Wide Web technologies – which allow you, among other things, to click on links and go hopping merrily from one Web page to the next – were not part of the original Internet. They were added to it, and able to be added rather easily, thanks to an underlying network design that provides basic, uniform connectivity end to end, allowing new features and functions to be built atop it or "at the edges."

In the eyes of many this is a concept worth keeping. The simple end-to-end structure preserves flexibility, generality, and openness, permitting wide use of new applications and thus fostering innovation. But now islands of enhanced high-speed service, or trusted links, are being created by individual ISPs. The concern is that investment in such closed islands, along with content servers within each island, decreases the motivation for investment in end-to-end services. "Once started down one path of investment, the alternative may be harder to achieve."[14]

This question of whether the Internet – or its successors – will retain an end-to-end simple network structure is hardly academic. The movement to put more functions inside the network challenges the way that innovation on the Net takes place. Changes in the core design principle are taking place piecemeal. The question is whether we, as a networked community, want to go in that direction. But that's the path we seem to be on now.

And getting onto a new path, toward a new Internet redesigned from the ground up, will not be easy. Even if a new architecture can utilize much of the existing hardware, adopting it would require modifications to routers and host software (including, possibly, the software on your computer). ISPs and Network Service Providers (NSPs, the underlying Internet "backbone providers") would have to agree on the new architecture. The need for consensus is doubly damning: not only is agreement among the many providers hard to reach, it also removes any competitive advantage from architectural innovation. A number of experts have concluded that the Internet architecture, which began as a radical experiment, has now ossified into an unalterable status quo.[15]

Thus, replacing the existing Internet will take more than just developing a set of new network protocols. We need also to consider its deployment path – and here history provides us with some useful lessons. The most important lesson is that the development and adoption of a clean-slate Internet needs to be driven by a strong hand to bring it into being.

LESSONS FROM HISTORY

There have been many cases of new infrastructures replacing or supplanting the old. Railroads began to replace wagons and canal boats when George Stephenson's Rocket won a competition to become the first steam locomotive on the Liverpool–Manchester railway in 1830.[16] In the U.S. in 1869, and in Canada in 1885, the first transcontinental railroads spanned the continent. By 1900 the North American rail network as we know it was essentially complete. It was, in every sense, a new networked infrastructure.

The first freeway system was the German *Autobahn*, built in the 1930s. In North America, by the end of the '30s, the Queen Elizabeth Way connected Toronto with Hamilton, and the Pennsylvania Turnpike spanned that state. In the 1950s the U.S. Interstate Highway Act launched one of the most significant investments in public infrastructure made in that country; a comparable initiative, though on a smaller scale and provincially based, was launched in Canada.

Railroads and freeways were financed differently, but the first lesson suggested here is rather simple: new networked infrastructures begin to appear when people with resources decide to build them. Also, new infrastructures need not be universal from the start – but they must be built in fully functioning units or segments, so that users can migrate to them and have them "ready to go," and they must be built from the start for scalability and ultimate universality.

The switch from gas to electric illumination is another example of such a switch in infrastructures.[17] By the 1870s, people were familiar with electricity – it had been used since the 1840s to power the telegraph. In 1852 Boston had installed the first electric fire-alarm boxes, and the newly introduced telephone relied on electricity. But in urban areas, gas lighting was already established and had to be displaced.

We all know that Edison developed a practical light bulb in 1879. In fact, a year or two earlier, an Englishman, Joseph Swan, had already worked out most of Edison's design. Edison's real edge was that he saw the electric light bulb having value only as part of an extended and reliable electric infrastructure. He and his organization, which later became the General Electric Company (U.S.), conceived a complete system of generators, wiring, metered distribution, sockets, fuses, fixtures – and, oh yes, light bulbs. Edison's goal was to build the system as a whole – in his words, to "form one machine."[18] He recognized that he was competing against an existing infrastructure of gas lighting and intended to incorporate the best elements of the gas infrastructure while eliminating the worst.[19] In 1882, Edison's prototype system went into service. The Pearl Street Station in lower Manhattan, with a single generator, began pumping current to eighty-five customers ready to turn on their light bulbs. Facing competition, the gas industry made its first real innovation in decades – the gas mantle, which increased illuminating power fivefold. The race of competing infrastructures was on, and electricity, of course, won.

Sometimes, networked infrastructures have been changed on a large scale rapidly. In 1967, Sweden switched from driving on the left side of the road to the right in a single day. Later, Germany upgraded its telephone system with Integrated Services Digital Network capability (ISDN, allowing phone lines to carry both voice and data) nationwide; and the U.S. eliminated analogue TV broadcasting in favour of digital transmission on a single day in early 2009. But it must be noted that all of these "rapid" switches required years of planning, preparation, and negotiation. And all required the strong hand of government – as did another rapid rollout, the introduction of the Minitel communications system in France, starting in 1982. The government's monopoly over telephone service allowed it to issue, free to millions of users, home terminals with keyboards and screens. Hooked into the phone lines, these terminals could then be used for a variety of online tasks such as making travel reservations or purchases from participating stores. (Customers paid modest fees for the Minitel service by volume of use.) Minitel preceded the public Internet and persisted for many years afterwards as a competing alternative to it.

Railroads and freeways also show that the process of putting a new infrastructure in place is more than just developing a superior technology or design. The method of deployment matters, and has consequences. Railroads were built largely by private enterprise, but with substantial public support. Their financing played a large role in the development of nineteenth-century banking and investment, sometimes to the chagrin of earnest investors. With few exceptions (e.g., transcontinental railroads) there was little central public planning. With highways, on the other hand, central planning and public investment produced extensive systems in a couple of decades.

Another point: new infrastructures can be disruptive to existing social and business structures. Both railroads and highways fundamentally changed society, affecting how cities grew and where people lived. Both enabled new business models and destroyed old ones. Sears, for instance, became a retailing giant in both the U.S. and Canada by using mail order shipping – made possible by rail transport – to undercut local merchants. The railroads also made massive steel mills possible by bringing coal and iron ore together, and changed how farms could market their produce, all of this creating changes that were every bit as profound in their time as those wrought by e-commerce.

Moreover, infrastructures themselves are subject to changing needs and times. In the early years of electric power, alternating current (AC) systems won out over direct current (DC), which Edison had preferred – mainly because AC could be transmitted efficiently over long distances at high voltages, then "stepped down" to the voltages needed for use. This capability enabled the building of big centralized power plants, either coal-fired or hydro-powered like the one at Niagara Falls, which could then serve users over a wide area. But today much of the wisdom of this century-old infrastructure is being challenged. New methods of transmitting DC are actually more efficient now than those for AC; there is a growing movement toward new localized sources of power (notably solar panels, which produce direct current); and electric grids in general "need to become bigger and smarter."[20]

In developing the next-generation Internet, we would like to anticipate future needs and avoid unwanted effects or conflicts as best we can. We know that future networks of intelligent sensors, to monitor and interpret everything from the weather to conditions in factories and public buildings, will place new demands on the post-Internet architecture. So will the possibilities of end-to-end optical computing. But what about quantum computing[21] and other applications that we do not yet even contemplate? We can never foresee with perfect vision. The original designers of the Internet may be excused for not anticipating that a network meant to be a research tool would become a huge city of commerce and social interchange. But those faced with the next network design won't have that excuse.

The challenge of anticipating new needs extends to the administrative structure. We've already seen that existing Internet governance is inadequate even to force relatively modest changes, such as the adoption of IPv6 and DNSSec. A new system is needed – adequate for bringing network upgrades into place, for adopting new functionalities, and for mediating possible economic and social conflicts over network resources. For example, current management of the Domain Name System (DNS) is entangled in debate because it confounds a technical issue (giving addresses to devices connected to the Internet) with trademark issues (who owns "Hunker.com," for example). In retrospect, it would have been better to recognize that disputes over trademarks would be an area of conflict, and that trademark names were used for as little else as possible.[22] In short, both the technical architecture and the administration of any future network should be designed to accommodate the tussles over economic and social values that are inherent in the Internet as a city, as well as to continue to achieve its technical goals of scalability, reliability, and ease of evolution.

The history of one networked infrastructure replacing another suggests two other points: first, that such transformations take time, and second, that market forces alone may not be sufficient for a full shift to the new infrastructure. The full shift from telegraph to telephone as the primary means of personal communication took at least seventy years; even in the 1950s and 1960s people routinely sent telegrams, especially for long-distance communication. And while most North American cities were electrified by the turn of the century, government subsidies and other incentives were needed in the U.S., starting in the 1930s, in order to bring the electric grid to much of the low-density countryside. My father grew up using kerosene lighting.

History suggests too that at some point the development of a new infrastructure starts to take on a life of its own – that no one can really control it. A new network is a radical innovation, and like other radical innovations has some messy but important consequences. Whoever builds it, and however it is built, when the new network is built to sufficient scale those building it will have, in effect, entered into a competition for the "dominant design." Think of examples of dominant design – where one technology has become accepted. Think of the QWERTY keyboard design for typing (accepted everywhere except France). Until a dominant design emerges, it can be a mess for both consumers and providers, which is why Europeans travelling to Canada have to bring electric plug adapters. The absence of consensus on product features and capabilities introduces tremendous uncertainty for both potential providers and customers, but once consensus crystallizes around a particular design, that design can enjoy a large market share for an extended period of time. TCP/IP and the World Wide Web have been a dominant design for the last twenty years (that's between sixty and 120 in "Internet years"). But history shows that the progress of any innovation, even one starting as a simple idea, rapidly becomes a dynamic process shaped by further innovation, market forces, and the nature of the firms that emerge and compete. For example, writing from the perspective of 1994, one observer noted that

. . . even though the dust has far from settled in the personal computer industry, it is clear that the pace and direction of innovation has been heavily determined by a complex web of interrelated events taking place among integrated circuit producers, software companies, disk drive manufacturers, and others. And their progress has not been made in isolation, but has had to figure in the work habits, skills, and expectations of millions of users – many of whom formed their habits and skills in the age of the typewriter.[23]

The message for us here is that any transition to a new network may start out with "someone" deciding, but its further evolution will be shaped by complex interactions that no single entity can control. New companies may replace existing dominant firms, and new markets will certainly emerge. The relative position of nations may even change. The U.S. now more or less takes for granted its dominant role in running and shaping the Internet. Internet addresses are assigned by an organization (ICANN) indirectly controlled by the U.S. government; Internet standards are implicitly dominated by the U.S. or U.S.-linked researchers, and the U.S. is certainly well represented in the list of major hardware and software providers. All of this may change.

We need some humility in contemplating a replacement for the existing Internet. We may fix many of the problems of the existing system, while simultaneously creating new, unanticipated challenges for the future. We can plan, but we cannot control how the next network will transform our Internet city. There are many lessons we can take, both from our experience with the current Internet and from the history of telephone networks, airlines, railroads, highways, and postal services, but these lessons are only guideposts as we venture into an unknowable future.

What we do know is that the Internet city will be a very different place in a few decades. And though we have no magic wand, we should start thinking seriously and systematically about how we would like it to be.

WHAT DO WE WANT TO ACHIEVE?

Considerations of a new network raise fundamental but still unanswered questions:

Do we want a separate network that serves the special needs of some users, so that we ultimately end up with at least two separate networks – some variant of the current Internet, and a new system – or do we want to migrate from what we have now to something else that completely replaces it?

- If the latter, what elements of the current Internet should be retained?

- Should the new network be accessible by everyone, or should it be run on an invitation-only basis – at least in its early stages? (For example, much as today's Internet once did, the next could start as a network for, say, allied defence departments only, then migrate to global adoption with the current Internet being phased out as that occurs.)

- Should the new network be backward compatible with the existing Internet?

- How will existing administrative structures and economic forces react to a "clean-slate" network adoption?

- In general: How do we achieve what we want? (And who are "we"?) What R & D and implementation roadmap would lead to our goal? What cornerstone projects or experiments should be executed in the short term to best create the foundation for our ultimate goal?

To summarize, we know a great deal about the technical requirements that a new network should meet. Work is underway to develop prototypes meeting these needs. We should also be humble about what we don't know, and even more humbled by what we don't know that we don't know. Once built, a new network will be subject to the full range of economic, social, political, and technological pressures that will emerge as new markets and new applications emerge. The ability of the new network to continue to evolve is key. A great deal of work is underway on the technologies; much less is focused on issues of governance, and even less on the path of transition from the current Internet to a new network. But we do know that the gap between current Internet capabilities and the needs of major users will drive, inevitably, a new network.

We face a choice. We can manage this transition, or we can stumble toward a new network, like the French Army in the first days of World War I, under Plan D (for *débrouiller,* meaning to "make it up as we go along").[24] Transitioning to a new network will be extraordinarily difficult, for it amounts to rebuilding the Internet city while the city is still functioning, with minimal disruption. But we do need a plan for an orderly transition, even if we know that our plans will have to change, or may appear naive, in the face of future developments.

A MODEST PROPOSAL

My proposal for transitioning to a new network rests on five observations and choices.

First, we need a plan. As just noted, the gap between needed requirements and current capabilities of major users, both governments and businesses, is too great for something not to happen. We can choose to plan, or not. I say we plan.

Second, the time to act has come. Creating a new network will take many years, and if we include the move from initial incarnation to full adoption it may take decades. The long development cycle means that waiting for a catastrophe, in order to create the necessary impetus for action, is a bad idea. A catastrophe may or may not occur, and if one does, the outcome is unpredictable. (For example, it could create conditions or sentiments that drive us toward some worse version of the current Internet, not a better new version.) There is also the notion that moving quickly toward a new network – which entails making design choices – puts us in the same sort of dilemma that any potential buyer of some new consumer electronics product faces: if we just wait till next year, a better design will appear, so why not wait? This too is a bad idea. We should act and act now, understanding that part of our task is to anticipate future developments as much as possible, and to build in maximum flexibility to accommodate the unexpected.

Third, we come to the fundamental choice mentioned above. Do we want separate networks for the needs of different users – which could just involve having one or more new special-purpose sub-networks run in tandem with the current Internet – or do we plan for a network that will largely replace the Internet? Multiple communication network protocols already exist, so this is not an all or nothing choice. But it is a choice. The TCP/IP-based Internet will probably persist side by side with the new network for many years anyway, just as telephone and telegraph coexisted for over a century. I believe that we should, however, explicitly plan from the outset to rebuild the Internet city into something new.

Fourth, a new network will have to have a minimum size and scale from the start to be viable, and the required scale will be considerable. This in turn will require a single unitary authority to build out the network. The fax machine model of adoption does not appear to apply here. (Fax machines were able to spread rapidly on their own from small beginnings, because even a small network of faxes was useful within a single company, and the machines were cheap and used standard phone lines.) Someone – and that means governments – will have to take the first steps here. Later on, the private sector, individuals, and other potential users will perceive the value of the new network, and make investments to join it of their own accord. But the scale of the new network will be such that no Edison is likely to emerge to take this task on as a private-sector initiative.

Governments – I use the plural because I believe that the initial build-out of the network must be multinational – will have to be willing to make substantial, and sustained, investments. The history of the electricity infrastructure suggests that ongoing government action, including follow-up investment, subsidies, and a mix of other requirements and incentives, will be required for a complete transition. Sustained commitment to an infrastructure is nothing new;

we think little of continued government investment and involvement in other infrastructures such as roads and telephones. But a new Internet will require a commitment of a very different order than that made for the initial ARPANet. The ARPANet was a small research network attracting little outside attention at the time, and ARPA neither declared nor had any intent to see it grow into what it did. A new infrastructure explicitly meant to replace the current Internet will raise political and social issues of immensely greater magnitude.

Finally, to reiterate this point: creating a new multinational, multi-user network will require a new model of governance. The new network will quickly become the playing field for battles between different economic, social, and political interests, and its governance should be designed from the start to handle these. Governance also needs the capability to drive the implementation of technical changes, and it must recognize the needs of the economically and socially disadvantaged, in Third World nations or wherever they live.

So, here is the modest proposal:

I propose that we begin the process immediately, by having the national defence arms of the so-called Five I's – the U.S., the U.K., Canada, Australia, and New Zealand – commit to building a new network initially for their own use, and then, after a period of time, opening up access to others. Perhaps initially non-defence users could be limited to key entities with special needs, such as providers of financial services and critical infrastructure systems. But even such a phased transition should move quickly toward universal access. Accompanying the actual construction of this network would be a new administrative structure explicitly designed for transformation.

Under the aegis of the United Nations, a Working Group on Internet Governance (WGIG) was created, and led to the current Internet Governance Forum.[25] Out of this work have come alternative proposals for Internet governance, but I don't believe that they will in fact result in any meaningful change.[26] Changes in network governance will be driven by the requirements of a new network, and without it, there is little pressure for those currently "in charge" to relinquish control.

So I propose that, as the Five I's build what will initially be a defence network, a public-private organization be created that initially includes representatives of the following: the governments directly involved, the United Nations, companies that would be among the first to join the network as it is opened up to non-defence users, and non-governmental organizations or other parties that could represent the less advantaged and the public generally.

Initially, this public–private organization would have only an advisory role in shaping the defence-centric new network. But as the network is opened up to other users, its governance would shift. Eventually, oversight of the network would be transferred directly to the new governing organization. Participation, however, would be conditioned upon some basic principles:

- Technical changes accepted by the governing technical body would be backed by national commitments to adopt them.

- Explicit recognition would be made of the special needs of Third World nations and underserved populations. The concept of subsidies for universal access and a payment system that provides funding to Third World nations to support their infrastructure should be integral to the new network. These are principles well established in international telephony; they should be made equally explicit in the new network.

- To the extent possible, technical decisions should be kept separate from economic, political, and social decisions. There should be separate administrative channels to handle issues such as trademark or commercial conflicts. Countries (and individuals) should have options as to anonymity and content filtering.

- A network dispute resolution system must be created (or co-opted from existing institutions, such as the International Court of Justice in The Hague), for addressing conflicts over personal rights and liberties, inappropriate actions by governments, or other economic or political issues that might arise.

• Last but not least, *maintaining security* should be central to the governance of the network, as well as to its technical design. Participating nations must commit to coordinating their responses to cyber crime and possible acts of cyber war and terrorism.

What I've spelled out here is not easily done, but it is doable. It may, in fact, be the most feasible way of doing what needs to be done.

When we began this discussion, the building of a new network was likened to urban renewal in the cyber city. Perhaps that is the wrong analogy. Instead of urban renewal, we should think of the real task as building a new city, one so attractive that over time the old city is abandoned.

EPILOGUE

CREEPING FAILURE IS NOT INEVITABLE

The Internet is a new city – one that challenges us to deal with new and tremendous opportunities, but also with the darker sides of crime, multinational conflict, and perhaps even war. As in fast-growing cities of the past, new social, political, and technical infrastructures are needed to address the opportunities – and the problems.

The first step in confronting new problems is to recognize that the problems are different from those of the past, and therefore call for new kinds of solutions. The first part of this book has shown that the concept of the lone hacker is outdated. Organized crime is now the dominant adversary, and its actors may sometimes be motivated by political forces as well as by commercial ones. Further, the criminals' business model seems robust. It's like Prohibition out there, and the economics for continued growth of organized crime seem unlikely to change.

Existing policies – led by the U.S. and followed in form and function by Canada and the rest of the G-20 – have shown little success in the past decade. So what do we do?

The very term "Internet governance" has no commonly accepted definition. Nor does there exist a particularly coherent framework for evaluating or achieving possible future results. Indeed, there are some who would argue that "Internet governance" is an oxymoron – that the technical and social structure of the Internet inherently defies any efforts to govern it.

I'm not willing to accept that pessimistic view. One purpose of this book has been to challenge the assumption that the Internet as it is now will continue in (more or less) the same form.

The second half of the book has been built around two key points regarding the future of the Internet. First, technology is and will of course remain a critical element of the Internet, but technologies alone cannot provide all that we want and need – certainly not in the realm of security. We must also look at, and apply, "policy" solutions – which as applied to the Internet means not just governmental action, but a concerted set of responses by multiple communities. Some models for how to proceed can be gleaned from structures that already exist for managing risk in other areas of commerce and public life. However, new international frameworks – perhaps of a form different than we have seen before – need to be considered as well.

Our present Internet is already aboil with controversial issues in areas such as privacy, freedom, regulation, business competition, and international relations. Each of these issues creates possibilities for both conflict and cooperation among various constituencies. Therefore, the path forward will not be easy. In several chapters I have proposed policies that are feasible but perhaps not politically acceptable – at least not right now. In trying to move forward we will run squarely against the fundamental questions, "Can the Internet as it is currently structured be governed in any rational way, and what are the limits of governance?" These are important questions that need to be the basis of a much more considered discussion than has taken place yet.

An even more important question regards the next-generation Internet. It is clear to me (and to many others) that the current Internet structure must be replaced. In developing the next-generation Internet, we would like to anticipate future needs and avoid unwanted effects or conflicts to the best of our abilities. We know that future networks of intelligent sensors, to monitor and interpret everything from the weather to conditions in factories and public buildings, will place new demands on a new Internet architecture. But what about other applications that we do not yet even contemplate? We can never anticipate fully, only do our best. The original designers of the Internet may be excused for not anticipating that a network meant to be a research tool would become a huge city of commerce and social interaction. Those faced with implementing the next design will be held to a much higher standard of foresight.

How to go about getting a new Internet built is also a critical question, and one that has received less attention (at least in the research community) than it deserves. Unfortunately, the history of one infrastructure replacing another provides only limited guidance. In order to actually create the "future Internet" of our dreams, we will need creative approaches to problems ranging from the practical to the political.

The challenge of anticipating new needs extends to a future administrative structure. We've already seen that existing Internet governance is inadequate even to force relatively modest changes, such as the adoption of IPv6 and DNSSec. A new system of governance is needed – adequate for bringing substantial and widespread changes into place, for adopting new functionalities and for mediating possible economic and social conflicts over network resources.

I hope that you, the reader, will come away from this book persuaded of three crucial points.

- First, that the insecurity of our cyber city has changed character in the last few years, and is morphing into increasingly dangerous and costly forms.

- Second, that the actions being taken to address security in both the public and private sectors are not effective. One basic reason is simple: some security actions are costly (i.e., don't generate profit), and so long as these essential actions are voluntary, little improvement can be expected. Although the *laissez-faire* approach may have fit the prevailing view when the problems of cyber security were first being recognized it is no longer a model that fits. There is a role for government; there has to be.

• Finally, that the Internet as designed was never meant to be a basis for secure economic and social transactions.

It's time, therefore, to build a completely new network; not one driven by the design parameters of the 1960s, but one that will (to the best of our ability) anticipate what the world now demands of its electronic city.

All of these points – along with specific policy solutions that I've proposed – have been explored, discussed, and debated for several years among security professionals and researchers. My intent has been to illuminate the debate while bringing it to the attention of a wider audience, including the general public and the public's representatives. For meaningful change to happen, there have to be many of us who see cyber security as a *priority* issue and who are unwilling to settle for the current pattern of creeping failure.

History has shown that creeping failure is not inevitable. It can be turned around, turned into success, by members of an informed populace who follow a simple rule: look for practical solutions that can work, and then work to get them implemented. Citizens of early industrial-age London and members of the public health movement worldwide have achieved great things by following this rule. Radical change can be wrought in the cyber city, too – indeed, in every area of public life now afflicted by creeping failure. With you on board, the future already looks brighter.

NOTES

CHAPTER 1

1. Although the US-CERT, based in Washington, is now officially the central response-coordinating organization, much of its real work is done by the CERT/CC at Carnegie Mellon.

2. According to the US-CERT Web site: "Worldwide, there are more than 250 organizations that use the name 'CERT' or a similar name and deal with cyber security response. US-CERT is independent of these groups, though we may coordinate with them on security incidents. The first of these types of organizations is the CERT® Coordination Center (CERT/CC), established at Carnegie Mellon University in 1988. When the Department of Homeland Security (DHS) created US-CERT, it called upon the CERT/CC to contribute expertise for protecting the nation's information infrastructure by coordinating defense against and response to cyber attacks. Through US-CERT, DHS and the CERT/CC work jointly on these activities. US-CERT is the operational arm of the National Cyber Security Division (NCSD) at the Department of Homeland Security (DHS)." (www.us-cert.gov)

3. "Results of the Distributed-Systems Intruder Tools Workshop, Pittsburgh, PA, USA, November 2–4, 1999." Pittsburgh, PA: CERT Coordination Center, Software Engineering Institute, Carnegie Mellon University, 7 December 1999.

4. Ibid.

5. CERT Advisory CA-2000-01, "Denial-of-Service Developments," original release date January 3, 2000, www.cert.org/advisories/CA-2000-01.html.

6. Remarks by the President in photo opportunity with leaders of high-tech industry and experts in computer security, 15 February 2000.

7. "Cybercrime," International Crime and Terrorism Web page, Foreign Affairs and International Trade Canada, http://www.dfait-maeci.gc.ca/foreign _policy/internationalcrime-old/cybercrime-en.asp.

8. "Fight Against Cyber Crime: Cyber Patrols and Internet Investigation Teams to Reinforce the EU Strategy," Press release, Reference IP/08/1827, Brussels: Council of Ministers of the European Union, 27 November 2008.

9. One paper in 2006 noted that "we discovered evidence of botnet infections in 11% of the 800,000 DNS domains" investigated; another found botnet infections at the rate of 25% in China, 14% in the EU, and 8% in the USA. No figures for Canada were provided. See Moheeb Abu Rajab, Jay Zarfoss, Fabian Monrose, and Andreas Terzis, "A Multifaceted Approach to Understanding the Botnet Phenomenon," in Proceedings of the 6th ACM SIGCOMM conference, 2006, pp. 41–52; and Rick Wesson, "Botnets and the Global Infection Rate: Anticipating Security Failures," EE Department Systems Colloquium, Stanford University, 6 June 2007. For a more recent comment on the ranges of bot estimates see Brian Krebs, "Oprah, KFC and the Great PC Cleanup?," *Washington Post*, 11 May 2009, at http://voices.washingtonpost.com/ securityfix/2009/05/oprah_kfc_and_the_great_pc_cle.html.

10. John Markoff, "Thieves Winning Online War, Maybe in Your PC," *The New York Times*, 6 December 2008.

11. Dan Tynan, "The 15 Biggest Tech Disappointments of 2007," *PC World*, 17 December 2007.

12. Arbor Networks, *Worldwide Infrastructure Security Report*, October 2008, p. 28.

13. Michael S. Mimoso, "IT Security Risks Dismissed by Boards, Survey Finds," SearchSecurity.com, 4 December 2008. The report itself: Jody R. Westby and Richard Power, *Governance of Enterprise Security Survey: CyLab 2008 Report*, Carnegie Mellon CyLab, 1 December 2008.

14. "Largest US Power Company Is a Network Security Black Hole," Layer 8 by Michael Cooney, 21 May 2008, NetworkWorld Blogs & Columns, http://www.networkworld.com/community/node/28031.

15. The results of the Institute for Information Infrastructure Protection's research on SCADA are available on their Web site, http://www.thei3p.org/.

16. James Niccolai, "IPv6 Adoption Sluggish: Study; Vendor-sponsored Survey Shows Slow Migration Rate," Computerworld, Fairfax [NZ] Media Group, 25 August 2008, http://computerworld.co.nz/news.nsf/tech/ 8CF2F74925C98009CC2574AC00750583.

17. James A. Lewis et al., "Securing Cyberspace for the 44th Presidency," Center for Strategic and International Studies, Washington, D.C., December 2008.

18. The stories of false sites related to Obama's campaign and election are from news reports and public Web postings, such as Ed Dickson, "Fake Obama Site Is a Malware Booby Trap," blogspot.com, 19 January 2009, http:// fraudwar.blogspot.com/2009/01/fake-obama-site-is-malware-booby-trap.html, and many similar. "Patch Tuesday": Dan Goodin, "Microsoft Issues Emergency IE Patch as Attacks Escalate," *The Register*, 17 December 2008, http:// www.theregister.co.uk/2008/12/17/emergency_microsoft_patch/; John Leyden, "Bumper MS Patch Batch Spells Client-side Misery / IE Still Vulnerable after Bombardment," *The Register*, 10 December 2008, http://www.theregister .co.uk/2008/12/10/ms_patch_tuesday_december/. Heartland breach: Brian Krebs, "Payment Processor Breach May Be Largest Ever," Security Fix blog, washingtonpost.com, 20 January 2009, http://voices.washingtonpost.com/ securityfix/2009/01/payment_processor_breach_may_b.html. Helicopter security breach: Angela Moscsaritolo, "Blueprints of Obama's Marine Helicopter Leaked on P2P," *Secure Computing Magazine*, 3 March 2009, http://www .securecomputing.net.au/News/138741,blueprints-of-obamas-marine-one -helicopter-leaked-on-p2p.aspx, and many similar.

CHAPTER 2

1. Angela Chang, "Q&A: William Gibson," *PC Magazine*, 1 October 2007, p. 19.

2. The full story of these hackers' exploits and the FBI sting was told years later in Art Jahnke, "Alexey Ivanov and Vasiliy Gorshkov: Russian Hacker Roulette," CSO Online, 1 January 2005. http://www.csoonline.com/ article/219964/Alexey_Ivanov_and_Vasiliy_Gorshkov_Russian_Hacker _Roulette?page=1.

3. Portions of this are based on conversations with Mudge in August 2007.

4. For an interesting survey of hacker attitudes and motivations during this period, see Dorothy Denning, *Information Warfare and Security* (Reading, MA: Addison-Wesley, 1998), pp. 45–47.

5. Critical Foundations: Protecting America's Infrastructures; The Report of the President's Commission on Critical Infrastructure Protection, Robert T. Marsh, Chairman (Washington, D.C.: The Commission, October 1997). Available at http://www.fas.org/sgp/library/pccip.pdf.

6. 18 USC 1030.

7. Scott Berinato and Renee Boucher Ferguson, "Hack Alert: Where's the Outrage," *eWeek*, 16 September 2000, http://dailynews.yahoo.com/h/zd/20000916/tc/hack_alert_where_s_the_outrage_1.html.

8. A paper from Berkeley calculates that spam costs $80 per million messages, while direct mail costs $250,000 per million. See Chris Kanich, Christian Kreibich, Kirill Levchenko, et al., *Spamalytics: An Empirical Analysis of Spam Marketing Conversion*, http://www.icsi.berkeley.edu/pubs/networking/2008-ccs-spamalytics.pdf.

9. Gregg Keizer, "Can-Spam Law 'Big Disappointment,'" *Information Week*, 28 December 2006, www.informationweek.com/shared/printable ArticleSrc.jhtml?articleID=196702438.

10. "ID Theft Nets £85,000 a Head: Study," *The Register*, 19 January 2007, http://www.theregister.co.uk/2007/01/19/id_theft_nets_85000_a_head/.

11. Denise Pappalardo and Ellen Messmer, "Extortion via DDOS on the Rise," Computerworld.com, 16 May 2005, www.computerworld.com/networkingtopics/networking/story/0,10801,101761,00.html.

12. James Middleton, "Zero-day Excel Hacker Takes on eBay," Vunet.com, 10 December 2005, http://www.v3.co.uk/vnunet/news/2147412/zero-day-excel-hacker-fights.

13. Jim Giles, "Listening in to the Cyber-Underworld," *New Scientist*, 23 May 2009, pp. 36–39.

14. Marc D. Goodman and Susan W. Brenner, "The Emerging Consensus on Criminal Conduct in Cyberspace," *International Journal of Law and Information Technology* 10 (Summer 2002): 139.

15. 419 scams use spam e-mail to find a victim for traditional fraud. Though the response rates are low, successful attacks can earn on the order of $100,000. As cited by Klaus Kursawe and Stefan Katzenbeisser, "Computing Under

Occupation," New Security Paradigms Workshop, North Conway, NH, 18–21 September 2007.

16. Individuals personally interviewed by the author.

17. Kursawe and Katzenbeisser, "Computing Under Occupation."

18. *2008 CSI Computer Crime and Security Survey,* Computer Security Institute, San Francisco, available through links at http://www.gocsi.com/.

19. See, for example, Jeffrey Hunker and Carla Bulford, *Federal Prosecution of Insider Threats Demonstrates Need for Reform,* Pittsburgh, PA: Jeffrey Hunker Associates, performed under RAND subcontract 9920080013, February 2009.

20. Dan Goodin, "Botmaster Owns Up to 250,000 Zombie PCs: He's a Security Consultant; Jail Beckons," *The Register,* 9 September 2007, http://www.theregister.co.uk/2007/11/09/botmaster_to_plea_guilty/.

CHAPTER 3

1. Gregory C. Wilshusen and David A. Powner, *Information Security: Persistent Weaknesses Highlight Need for Further Improvement,* U.S. Government Accountability Office, GAO-07-751T, 19 April 2007.

2. Lance Whitney, "Report: Spam Now 90 Percent of All E-mail," CNET News, 26 May 2009, http://news.cnet.com/8301-1009_3-10249172-83.html.

3. Byron Acohido, "Hackers Breach Heartland Payment Credit Card System," USA Today.com, 23 January 2009, http://www.usatoday.com/money/perfi/credit/2009-01-20-heartland-credit-card-security-breach_N.htm.

4. The Commission Communication "Towards a General Policy on the Fight Against Cyber Crime," Brussels, European Commission, 22 May 2007, http://europa.eu/rapid/pressReleasesAction.do?reference=MEMO/07/199.

5. "Hacker Holding Health Records Hostage Demands Ransom," Channel Wire blog, Channel Web.com, 6 May 2009, http://www.crn.com/security/217300538;jsessionid=4C5UN0R2TQDSBQE1GHPSKHWATMY32JVN.

6. Lucian Constantin, "The Personal Details of Millions of American Patients Stolen by Hackers," Softpedia.com, 7 November 2008, http://news.softpedia.com/news/The-Personal-Details-of-Millions-of-American-Patients-Stolen-by-Hackers-97437.shtml.

7. Brian Krebs, "Payment Processor Breach May Be Largest Ever," Security Fix blog, washingtonpost.com, 20 January 2009, http://voices.washingtonpost

.com/securityfix/2009/01/payment_processor_breach_may_b.html.

8. Brad Stone, "3 Indicted in Theft of 130 Million Card Numbers," *The New York Times*, 18 August 2009, http://www.nytimes.com/2009/08/18/technology/18card.html.

9. Dan Goodin, "TJX Employee Fired for Exposing Shoddy Security," Security Focus, *The Register*, 25 May 2008, http://www.securityfocus.com/news/11520.

10. Jim Finkle, "Monster.com Took 5 Days to Disclose Data Theft," Boston, Reuters, 24 August 2007, http://www.reuters.com/article/internetNews/idUSWNAS278320070824.

11. Telephone interview with ex-hacker who declined to be identified here; 22 October 2008.

12. The story of the Morris Worm has been oft told; see, for instance, John Markoff, "Computer Intruder Is Put on Probation and Fined $10,000," *The New York Times*, 5 May 1990, http://www.nytimes.com/1990/05/05/us/computer-intruder-is-put-on-probation-and-fined-10000.html?scp=2&sq=robert+tappan+morris&st=nyt.

13. See http://setiathome.ssl.berkeley.edu/.

14. Interview with security expert who declined to be identified.

15. Paul Kurtz, Good Harbor Consulting, in a speech at the IFACS Conference, Arlington, VA, 18–19 March 2008.

16. Bruce Schneier, *Secrets and Lies: Digital Security in a Networked World*, Second Edition (Indianapolis, IN: Wiley Publishing, 2004), p. 184.

17. Robert Vamosi, "Study: DDOS Attacks Threaten ISP Infrastructure," ZDNet, 12 November 2008, www.zdnetasia.com/news/security/0,39044215,62048177,00.htm.

18. Dan Ilett, "Expert: Online Extortion Growing More Common," ZDNet, 11 October 2004, http://www.zdnetasia.com/news/security/0,39044215,39197040,00.htm.

19. "Eight Times More Malicious Email Attachments Spammed Out in Q3 2008, Sophos Reports," Sophos, 27 October 2008, www.sophos.com/pressoffice/news/articles/2008/10/spamreport.html.

20. See Spamcop.net for total spam report volume graph, www.spamcop.net/spamgraph.shtml?spamyear2009.

21. "Don't Fall in Love with the Storm Trojan Horse, Advises Sophos," 18 January 2008, www.sophos.com/pressoffice/news/articles/2008/01/love-storm.html.

22. "Visa Europe Statement: Phishing Incident in Sweden," News release 28 May 2008, http://www.visaeurope.com/pressandmedia/newsreleases/press360_pressreleases.jsp.

23. Jim Carr, "'Rock Phish' Gang Adds Malware Download to Attacks," *SC (Secure Computing) Magazine of Australia*, 23 April 2008, http://www.securecomputing.net.au/News/109044,rock-phish-gang-adds-malware-download-to-attacks.aspx.

24. Finkle, "Monster.com Took 5 Days to Disclose Data Theft."

25. Once it infects the victim's PC, the Trojan can steal personal data such as usernames, passwords, and Social Security numbers the victim transmitted while interacting with other Web sites.

26. Carr, "'Rock Phish' Gang Adds Malware Download to Attacks."

27. Computer Crime and Security surveys for 2007 and 2008, Computer Security Institute, San Francisco, available through links at http://www.gocsi.com/.

28. Ben Fenton, "FBI Spy Who Sold Out to Russia Did 'Megaton Damage,'" *The Telegraph*, 21 February 2001, http://www.telegraph.co.uk/news/main.jhtml?xml=/news/2001/02/21/wspy21.xml.

29. Joel Predd, Shari Lawrence Pfleeger, Jeffrey Hunker, and Carla Bulford, "Insiders Behaving Badly," *IEEE Security and Privacy* 6, no. 4 (July 2008): 66–70.

30. Jeffrey Hunker and Carla Bulford, *Federal Prosecution of Insider Threats Demonstrates Need for Reform*, Pittsburgh, PA: Jeffrey Hunker Associates, performed under RAND subcontract 9920080013, February 2009.

31. Arabaci, Case 1:97mj02280 Southern District of New York. Complaint filed 27 July 1998.

32. Lockwood, Case 2:06cr20331, Eastern District of Michigan. Complaint filed 31 January 2005.

33. Cummings, Case 1:03cr00109, Southern District of New York. Complaint filed 23 January 2003.

CHAPTER 4

1. This conclusion is impossible to prove definitively, given poor or absent data gathering. However, more records were breached in 2008 than in the previous four years combined, based on the cases investigated by Verizon Business. See Wade H. Baker, Alex Hutton, C. David Hylender, Christopher Novak, Christopher Porter, Bryan Sartin, Peter Tippett, and J. Andrew

Valentine, *2009 Data Breach Investigations Report: A Study Conducted by the Verizon Business RISK Team* (Verizon Business, 2009), p. 32, http://www.verizonbusiness.com/resources/security/reports/2009_databreach_rp.pdf.

2. "Data breach affects 10000 at Behrend," *The Erie Times-News,* 10 April 2009, p.1.

3. Kevin D. Mitnick and William L. Simon, *The Art of Deception: Controlling the Human Element of Security,* Wiley, 2002. Mitnick is a well-known former hacker who was, among other things, adept at "social engineering."

4. Hassan Osman, student research project for Cyber Security Policy and Implementation Course, Carnegie Mellon University, 2004.

5. Brian Krebs, "European Cyber-Gangs Target Small U.S. Firms, Group Says," *Washington Post,* 25 August 2009, http://www.washingtonpost.com/wp-dyn/content/article/2009/08/24/AR2009082402272.html.

6. "Boom Time for CyberCrime," 2009 annual State of the Net report, Consumer Reports, June 2009, http://www.consumerreports.org/cro/magazine-archive/june-2009/electronics-computers/state-of-the-net/state-of-the-net-2009/state-of-the-net-2009.htm.

7. mi2g, *2004: Digital Attacks Report – SIPS Monthly Intelligence Description.* See table: "Yearly Economic Damage Report – All Attacks (from 1995)." Available through links at www.mi2g.com/cgi/mi2g/.

8. U.S. Government Accountability Office, *Cybercrime: Public and Private Entities Face Challenges in Addressing Cyber Threats,* GAO-07-705, June 2007.

9. John P. Mello Jr., "Cybercrime Costs US Economy at Least $117B Each Year," TechNewsWorld, 26 June 2007, http://www.technewsworld.com/story/58517.html.

10. McAfee, *Unsecured Economies: Protecting Vital Information,* as reported by CNET, 28 January 2009. The report was released at the World Economic Forum annual meeting in Davos, Switzerland.

11. Y2K computer fix, electric blackout, and major natural disasters from Bureau of Economic Analysis, U.S. Department of Commerce, cited in Congressional Research Service reports; all crime (U.S.) from David A. Anderson, "The Aggregate Burden of Crime," *Journal of Law and Economics* 42, no. 2 (1999): 611–42.

12. Discussions with personal colleague and friend who wishes to remain anonymous, "so as not to further irritate the wireless monitoring thought police in my organization," March 2009.

13. Steve Ragan, "Microsoft Pushes Massive Fixes in Monthly Patch Release," Techherald.com, 15 April 2009, http://www.thetechherald.com/article.php/200916/3461/Microsoft-pushes-massive-fixes-in-monthly-patch-release.

14. Ellen Messmer, "Security Will Eat IT Budgets in 2009, Says Survey," Techworld, 6 January 2009, http://news.techworld.com/security/109069/security-will-eat-it-budgets-in-2009-says-survey/. The full survey report, available from Forrester Research but expensive, is *The State of Enterprise IT Security: 2008 to 2009.*

15. Computer Economics, Inc., *IT Spending & Staffing Benchmarks 2009/2010,* 2009, pp. 1–10. The Executive Summary (which includes this page) is available free through links at www.computereconomics.com/.

16. See, for instance, the $79 billion figure cited by John Markoff, "Do We Need a New Internet?" *The New York Times,* 15 February 2009.

17. See, for example, *Live Free or Die Hard,* Twentieth-Century Fox, 2007, in which Bruce Willis as NYPD detective lieutenant John McClane takes on an Internet-based terrorist organization that is systematically shutting down the U.S.

18. Steven Johnson, *The Ghost Map: The Story of London's Most Terrifying Epidemic and How It Changed Science, Cities, and the Modern World* (New York: Riverhead Books, 2006), pp. 90–93.

19. Alan Paller, SANS Institute, presentation at Carnegie Mellon University, Spring 2005.

20. Dennis Fisher, "Hackers Get Free Reign to Develop Techniques Says Microsoft Chief," SearchSecurity.com, 18 April 2007, http://searchsecurity.techtarget.com/news/article/0,289142,sid14_gci1252018,00.html?track=sy160.

21. Charles Perrow, *Normal Accidents: Living with High-Risk Technologies* (New York: Basic Books, 1984), pp. 3–4.

22. Ibid.

CHAPTER 5

1. Mark Landler and John Markoff, "Digital Fears Emerge After Data Siege in Estonia," Reuters, 29 May 2007. See http://www.nytimes.com/2007/05/29/technology/29estonia.html.

2. Statesmen's Forum: Jaak Aaviksoo, Minister of Defense, Republic of Estonia, Center for Strategic & International Studies, 28 November 2007, http://csis .org/event/statesmens-forum-jaak-aaviksoo-minister-defense-republic -estonia.

3. Jill R. Aitoro, "National Cyber Security Initiative Will Have a Dozen Parts," Nextgov, 1 August 2008, http://www.nextgov.com/nextgov/ng_20080801 _9053.php.

4. "War," *The Encyclopaedia Britannica*, 11th Edition, 1912.

5. Barbara Tuchman, *The Guns of August* (New York, Macmillan, 1962).

6. *Tracking GhostNet: Investigating a Cyber Espionage Network.* Information Warfare Monitor, 29 March 2009, Munk Centre for International Studies, JR02-220, University of Toronto, http://www.citizenlab.org/modules.php?op= modload&name=News&file=article&sid=1815.

7. As per many news reports, such as John Markoff, "Vast Spy System Loots Computers in 103 Countries," *The New York Times*, 28 March 2009, http://www.nytimes.com/2009/03/29/technology/29spy.html.

8. Michael Kirk, director. *Frontline: Cyber War!* Public Broadcasting Service, WGBH Educational Foundation, Washington, D.C., 23 April 2003, http:// www.pbs.org/wgbh/pages/frontline/shows/cyberwar/warnings/.

9. Richard A. Clarke, as quoted in "The Net's Mid-Life Crisis," in On the Media, WYNC Radio Web site, 13 March 2009, www.onthemedia.org.

10. Ibid.

11. Shane Harris, "Hacking the Hill – How the Chinese – or Someone – Hacked into House of Representatives Computers in 2006, and What It Will Take to Keep Out the Next Electronic Invader," *National Journal Magazine*, 20 December 2008, http://www.nationaljournal.com/njmagazine/print_friendly .php?ID=cs_20081220_6787.

12. This and following material comes from news stories on the Titan Rain attacks, notably Nathan Thornburgh, "The Invasion of the Chinese Cyberspies (And the Man Who Tried to Stop Them)," *Time*, 29 August 2005, http://www .time.com/time/magazine/article/0,9171,1098961,00.html.

13. Scott Sandlin, "Analyst, Sandia Settle Suit," *Albuquerque Journal*, 14 October 2007.

14. "Reported Internet Spy Network Just Tip of Iceberg: Researcher; Hackers Targeted Governments and Other Organizations in 103 Countries," CBC

News, 30 March 2009, http://www.cbc.ca/technology/story/2009/03/30/
tech-090330-cyberspy-china.html.

15. David A.Wheeler and Gregory N. Larsen, *Techniques for Cyber Attack Attribution*, Institute for Defense Analysis, IDA Paper P-3792, October 2003, p. 1.

16. Jeffrey Hunker, Bob Hutchinson, and Jonathan Margulies, *Roles and Challenges for Sufficient Cyber-Attack Attribution*, Institute for Information Infrastructure Protection, Dartmouth College, January 2008, http://www.thei3p.org/docs/publications/whitepaper-attribution.pdf.

17. Howard F. Lipson, *Tracking and Tracing Cyber-Attacks: Technical Challenges and Global Policy Issues*, Carnegie Mellon University Software Engineering Institute, Special Report CMU/SEI-2002-SR-009, November 2002, p. 53.

18. U.S. Joint Chiefs of Staff, *Department of Defense Dictionary of Military and Associated Terms, Joint Publication 1-02* (Washington, D.C.: 22 March 2007), p. 138.

19. Andrew F. Krepinevich, *The Pentagon's Wasting Assets*, Foreign Affairs, Council on Foreign Relations, July–August 2009, p. 25.

20. CSIS, *Securing Cyberspace for the 44th Presidency: A Report of the CSIS Commission* (Washington, D.C.: Center for Strategic and International Studies, December 2008), p. 13, http://csis.org/files/media/csis/pubs/081208_securingcyberspace_44.pdf.

21. USCC, *2008 Report to Congress of the U.S. – China Economic and Security Review Commission* (Washington, D.C.: Government Printing Office, November 2008), pp. 163, 167, http://www.uscc.gov/annual_report/2008/annual_report_full_08.pdf.

22. "Hackers Attack U.S. Government Web Sites in Protest of Chinese Embassy Bombing," CNN.net, 10 May 1999, http://www.cnn.com/TECH/computing/9905/10/hack.attack/.

23. Mark Landler and John Markoff, "Digital Fears Emerge After Data Siege in Estonia," Reuters, 29 May 2007.

24. Article 5 of the Washington (North Atlantic) Treaty says: "The Parties agree that an armed attack against one or more of them in Europe or North America shall be considered an attack against them all and consequently they agree that, if such an armed attack occurs, each of them, in exercise of the right of individual or collective self-defense recognized by Article 51 of the Charter of the

United Nations, will assist the Party or Parties so attacked by taking forthwith, individually and in concert with the other Parties, such action as it deems necessary, including the use of armed force, to restore and maintain the security of the North Atlantic area." Available: www.nato.int/terrorism/five.htm.

25. John Markoff, "Before the Gunfire, Cyberattacks," *The New York Times*, 12 August 2008.

26. Ibid.

27. Ibid.

28. "Perspectives on Security: An Interview with John Gilligan," *Engineering Enterprise*, Fall 2003, pp. 10–15.

29. John A. Serabian, Jr., Information Operations Issue Manager, Central Intelligence Agency, testimony before the Joint Economic Committee on Cyber Threats and the U.S. Economy (Washington, D.C.; U.S. Congress, 23 February 2000), http://www.cia.gov/cia/public_affairs/speeches/2000/cyberthreats_022300.html.

30. A few of the many sources on cyber warfare and China are: Charles Billo, "Cyber Warfare: An Analysis of the Means and Motivations of Selected Nation States," Institute for Security Technology Studies at Dartmouth College, Dartmouth University, December 2004, pp. 7–8; Dai Qingmin, "On Integrating Network Warfare and Electronic Warfare," *Zhongguo Junshi Kexue [China Military Science]* 15, no. 2 (February 2002): 112–17, translated and downloaded onto the Foreign Broadcasting Information Service (FBIS) Web site, https://www.opensource.gov; William C. Triplett III, "Potential Applications of PLA Information Warfare Capabilities to Critical Infrastructures," in *People's Liberation Army After Next*, edited by Susan M. Puska, U.S. Army War College Strategic Studies Institute, 2000, p. 90; and U.S. Office of the Secretary of Defense, "Military Power of the People's Republic of China 2006," in *Annual Report to Congress*, May 2006, p. 36.

31. Qingmin, "On Integrating Network Warfare and Electronic Warfare"; Billo, "Cyber Warfare," p. 7.

32. Triplett, "Potential Applications of PLA Information Warfare Capabilities to Critical Infrastructures."

33. Billo, "Cyber Warfare," p. 8.

34. Office of the Secretary of Defense, "Military Power of the People's Republic of China 2006."

35. Christopher Casteilli, "DOD and Thailand Run Classified 'Eligible Receiver' Info-War Exercise," *Defense Information and Electronics Report* 77, no. 44 (2002).

36. Clay Wilson, *Computer Attack and Cyberterrorism: Vulnerabilities and Policy Issues for Congress*, Washington, D.C., Congressional Research Service, RL 32114, 1 April 2005, p. 12.

37. Ibid, p. 8.

38. The White House, "To Develop Guidelines for Offensive Cyber-Warfare," *National Security Presidential Directive 16 (NSPD-16)* (Washington, D.C.: July 2002), http://www.fas.org/irp/offdocs/nspd/.

39. Kevin Wright, *Cyber-Warfare: The Doctrinal Disparity*, report prepared for the U.S. Army War College, Carlisle, PA, May 2008, p. 5.

40. Noah Schachtman, "U.S. Cyber Command: 404 Error, Mission Not (Yet) Found," wired.com, 26 June 2009, http://www.wired.com/dangerroom/2009/06/foggy-future-for-militarys-new-cyber-command/.

41. Andrew F. Krepinevich Jr., "The Pentagon's Wasting Assets," *Foreign Affairs*, July/August 2009, pp. 30–31.

42. Jeff Schogal, "Official: No Options 'Off the Table' for Response to Cyber Attacks," *Stars and Stripes*, Mideast Edition, 8 May 2009.

43. John Markoff and Andrew E. Kramer, "U.S. and Russia Differ on a Treaty for Cyberspace," *The New York Times*, 28 June 2009.

44. Seymour E. Goodman, Jessica C. Kirk, and Megan H. Kirk, "Cyberspace as a Medium for Terrorists," *Technological Forecasting and Social Change* 74, no. 2 (February 2007): 193–210.

45. Jason Fritz, *Hacking Nuclear Command and Control*, Executive summary, research paper commissioned by the International Commission on Nuclear Non-Proliferation and Disarmament, n.d.

46. T. K. Kelly, *The Just Conduct of War against Radical Islamic Terror and Insurgencies* (Pittsburgh, PA: The Rand Corporation, 2007).

47. Key provisions are as follows: Article 2(4), prohibiting the threat or use of force against the territorial integrity or political independence of any state, with the following exceptions: Article 51, which recognizes each state's inherent right to self-defence against armed attack; Article 39, which permits the Security Council to identify and label an event as a "threat to peace, breach of peace, or act of aggression"; Article 42, stating that "should measures [such

as economic sanctions or diplomatic actions] be inadequate or have proved to be inadequate, it [the United Nations] may take such action by air, sea or land forces as may be necessary to maintain or restore international peace and security."

48. Article 5 in part says that "the Parties agree that an armed attack against one or more of them in Europe or North America shall be considered an attack against them all and consequently they agree that, if such an armed attack occurs, each of them, in exercise of the right of individual or collective self-defence recognised by Article 51 of the Charter of the United Nations, will assist the Party or Parties so attacked by taking forthwith, individually and in concert with the other Parties, such action as it deems necessary, including the use of armed force, to restore and maintain the security of the North Atlantic area."

49. Rick Aldrich, *Computer Network Defense Attribution: A Legal Perspective*, prepared for the Defense-wide Information Assurance Program, 5 July 2002, p. 6.

50. Brian Keirn, "Large Hadron Collider's Hacker Infiltration Highlights Vulnerabilities," *Wired Science*, 14 September 2008, http://www.wired.com/wiredscience/2008/09/hackers-infiltr/.

51. Shane Harris, "China's Cyber-Militia: Chinese Hackers Pose a Clear and Present Danger to U.S. Government and Private-sector Computer Networks and May Be Responsible for Two Major U.S. Power Blackouts," *National Journal*, 31 May 2008.

52. The Canadian Cyber Incident Response Centre (CCIRC) is part of Public Safety Canada; see responsibilities at http://www.publicsafety.gc.ca/prg/em/ccirc/index-eng.aspx.

53. U.S. Department of Homeland Security, *The National Strategy to Secure Cyberspace*, February 2003, p. 8.

54. "Fighting the Worms of Mass Destruction," *The Economist*, 27 November 2003.

55. Wright, *Cyber-Warfare: Doctrinal Disparity*, p. 5.

56. Michael Hanlon, "Attack of the Cyber Terrorists," Mail Online, 24 May 2007, http://www.dailymail.co.uk/sciencetech/article-457504/Attack-cyber-terrorists.html.

57. See, for example, the Online Etymology Dictionary at http://www.etymonline.com/index.php?term=terrorism.

58. Section 4 of the *Anti-terrorism Act*, RSC 2001, c. 41, inserted a new definition of "terrorist activity" into the federal *Criminal Code*, RSC 1985, c. 46. Section 83.01 of the Canadian *Criminal Code*.

59. 22 USC 2656f(d).

60. Eben Kaplan, *Terrorists and the Internet* (New York: Council on Foreign Relations, 8 January 2009).

61. Ibid, p. 9. See also George Butters, "Expect Terrorist Attacks on Global Financial System," *The Register*, 7 October 2003, http://www.theregister.co.uk/content/55/33269.html.

62. Nuclear Regulatory Commission, *Fact Sheet on the Three Mile Island Accident*, http:www.nrc.gov/reading-rm/doc-collections/fact-sheets/3mile-isle.html.

63. "Northeast Blackout of 2003," Wikipedia.

64. Peter Behr and David Vise, "Stock Market Suffers Largest Loss in History as Dow Industrial Average Drops 508 Points," *Washington Post*, 20 October 1987.

65. John Markoff and Thom Shanker, "Halted '03 Iraq Plan Illustrates U.S. Fear of Cyberwar Risk," *The New York Times*, 1 August 2009, http://www.nytimes.com/2009/08/02/us/politics/02cyber.html?_r=1.

66. CSIS, *Securing Cyberspace for the 44th Presidency*.

CHAPTER 6

1. James Niccolai, "IPv6 Adoption Sluggish: Study; Vendor-sponsored Survey Shows Slow Migration Rate," Computerworld, Fairfax [NZ] Media Group, 25 August 2008, http://computerworld.co.nz/news.nsf/tech/8CF2F74925C98009CC2574AC00750583.

2. W. Parsons, *Public Policy: An Introduction to the Theory and Practice of Policy Analysis* (Brookfield, VT: Edward Elgar, 1995), p. 14.

3. President William J. Clinton and Vice President Albert Gore, Jr. *A Framework for Global Electronic Commerce* (Washington, D.C.: The White House, 1 July 1997), pp. 1–2.

4. Stephen D. Crocker, "How the Internet Got Its Rules," *The New York Times*, 6 April 2009, http://www.nytimes.com/2009/04/07/opinion/07crocker.html.

5. Adam Smith, *An Inquiry into the Nature and Causes of the Wealth of Nations*, 1776, Book 4, Chapter 9.

6. Paul Krugman, "The Perfect, the Good, the Planet," *The New York Times*, 18 May 2009, http://www.nytimes.com/2009/05/18/opinion/18krugman.html.

7. 18 USC 1030, *Fraud and Related Activity in Connection with Computers*. The statute criminalizes both access to a "protected computer without authorization" and access that exceeds authorization.

8. The Commission Communication "Towards a General Policy on the Fight Against Cyber Crime," Brussels, European Commission, 22 May 2007, http://europa.eu/rapid/pressReleasesAction.do?reference=MEMO/07/199.

9. Canada, Public Policy Forum/Forum des politiques publiques, Cyber Security: Developing a Canadian Strategy, conference, Ottawa, 27 March 2008.

10. Public Safety Canada, "Government of Canada Announces Cyber Security Initiatives," news release, Ottawa, 2 February 2005.

11. See U.K. sites referenced in 2008: www.mi5.gov.uk/output/page76 .html; www.getsafeonline.org/media/GSO_Cyber_Report_2006,pdf; www .cabinetoffice.gov.uk/csia/ia_governance; www.cpni.gov.uk; www.warp .gov.uk.

12. Chris Pounder, "Cyber Crime: The Backdrop to the Council of Europe Convention," *Computers & Security* 20, no. 4 (31 July 2001): 311–15.

13. Committee on Critical Information Infrastructure Protection and the Law, *Critical Information Infrastructure Protection and the Law: An Overview of Key Issues*, Stewart D. Personick and Cynthia A. Patterson, eds. (Washington, D.C.: National Academies Press, 2002), p. 42.

14. Kristen Archick, *Cybercrime: The Council of Europe Convention; CRS Report for Congress*. Congressional Research Service, Report RS21208, 28 September 2008, p. 6.

15. See Council of Europe, "Convention on Cybercrime CETS No.: 185, Treaty open for signature by the member States and the non-member States which have participated in its elaboration . . . ," http://conventions.coe.int/Treaty/ Commun/ChercheSig.asp?NT=185&CM=1&CL=ENG.

16. *National Strategy for the Physical Protection of Critical Infrastructures and Key Assets*, The White House, February 2003, http://www.dhs.gov/xlibrary/ assets/Physical_Strategy.pdf.

17. *Strategy for Homeland Defense and Civil Support* (Washington, D.C: Department of Defense, 2005).

18. *National Infrastructure Protection Plan* (Washington, D.C.: U.S. Department

of Homeland Security, 2006).

19. See for example Ryan Singel, "U.S. Has Launched a Cyber Security 'Manhattan Project,' Homeland Security Chief Claims," *Wired*, 8 April 2008, http://www.wired.com/threatlevel/2008/04/feds-cyber-cent/.

20. Sinead Carew and Christopher Doering, "Cybersecurity Chief Beckstrom Resigns," *The New York Times*, 6 March 2009.

21. Commission of the European Communities, *Green Paper on a European Programme for Critical Infrastructure Protection*, COM (2005) 576 final (Brussels: The Commission, 17 November 2005).

22. "Fight Against Cyber Crime: Cyber Patrols and Internet Investigation Teams to Reinforce the EU Strategy," Press release, Reference IP/08/1827, Brussels: Council of Ministers of the European Union, 27 November 2008.

23. Brian Krebs, "ICANN De-Accredits EstDomains for CEO's Fraud Convictions," *The Washington Post*, 29 October 2008, http://voices.washingtonpost.com/securityfix/2008/10/icann_de-accredits_estdomains.html.

24. United States Computer Emergency Readiness Team (US-CERT), http://www.us-cert.gov/.

25. It was noted earlier that at least one federal agency had over 800 incidents reported internally that were not reported to the US-CERT. See U.S. General Accountability Office (GAO), *Critical Infrastructure Protection: Department of Homeland Security Faces Challenges in Fulfilling Cybersecurity Responsibilities*, Report GAO-05-434 (Washington, D.C.: GAO, May 2005).

26. Financial Services Information Sharing and Analysis Center, http://www.fsisac.com/.

27. The electric power industry has created a decentralized ISAC through the North American Electricity Reliability Council (NERC), which already monitors and coordinates responses to disruptions in the national electric grid. The government and industry work together in the NERC to ensure the resiliency of the electricity infrastructure. For Information and Telecommunications there are two ISACs. For telecommunications, through the NCC (National Coordinating Center), each member firm monitors and analyzes its own networks, and a decision is made as to whether to report an incident to the government. The IT-ISAC includes major hardware, software, and e-commerce firms, including Cisco Systems, Microsoft, Intel, Computer Associates, and the like. Other ISACs cover the Chemical Industry and

Hazardous Materials, Emergency Services, Food and Agriculture, Surface Transportation, and Water sectors.

28. GAO, *Critical Infrastructure Protection*, p. 12.

29. James Risen and Eric Lichtblau, "Control of Cybersecurity Becomes Divisive Issue," *The New York Times*, 17 April 2009.

30. The Toxic Release Inventory, which, under the Emergency Planning and Community Right-to-Know Act of 1986, requires many industrial facilities to report release of toxic chemicals annually.

31. Steve Ranger, "Data Breach Laws 'Make Companies Serious About Security,'" Silicon.com, 3 September 2007, http://management.silicon.com/itdirector/0,39024673,39168303,00.htm?r=1.

CHAPTER 7

1. "Software," Webopedia definition, 10 May 2009, http://www.webopedia.com/terms/software.html.

2. U.S. President's Information Technology Advisory Committee, "Investing in Our Future," 24 February 1999, www.nitrd.gov/pitac/report/index.html.

3. Anick Jesdanun, "GE Energy Acknowledges Blackout Bug," Associated Press, 12 February 2004.

4. Interview with "Mudge" (Peiter Zako), BBN Technologies, 20 April 2009.

5. See for example Stephen Manes, "Dim Vista," Forbes.com, 26 February 2007, http://www.forbes.com/forbes/2007/0226/050.html.

6. William R. Nichols, Senior Member of the Technical Staff, Software Engineering Process Management Program, Software Engineering Institute, "Deploying TSP to a Nation: Early Results from Mexico," 4th Annual TSP Symposium, New Orleans, LA, 21–24 September, 2009.

7. Watts S. Humphrey, "What's New: Defective Software Works," News@sei, No.1, 2004, p. 3, and subsequent conversations with Watts Humphrey, November 2008.

8. Personal communication with Rich Pethia, CERT, Software Engineering Institute, Carnegie Mellon University, May 2008.

9. David Rice, *Geekonomics: The Real Cost of Insecure Software* (Upper Saddle River, NJ: Addison-Wesley, 2008), p. 121.

10. See "List of fixes included in Windows XP Service Pack 2 [Last review 19 June

2008]," Microsoft Help and Support page, http://support.microsoft.com/kb/811113.

11. Randall Stross, "They Criticized Vista and They Should Know," *The New York Times*, 9 March 2008.

12. Bruce Schneier, *Secrets and Lies: Digital Security in a Networked World*, Second Edition (Indianapolis, IN: Wiley Publishing, 2004), pp. 202–203.

13. Quote from "Computer Failure Puzzling In Peruvian Crash," CNN World News, 3 October 1996; examples cited from Scott Rosenberg, *Dreaming in Code: Two Dozen Programmers, Three Years, 4,732 Bugs, and One Quest for Transcendent Software* (New York: Crown Publishers, 2007), p. 20.

14. General Accounting Office, *Patriot Missile Defense – Software Problem Led to System Failure at Dhahran, Saudi Arabia*, Report B-247094, 4 February 1992, http://www.fas.org/spp/starwars/gao/im92026.htm.

15. Meeting with William Nichols, Software Engineering Institute, Carnegie Mellon University, 13 May 2009.

16. "Prius Hybrids Dogged by Software," *CNN/Money*, 16 May 2005, http://money.cnn.com/2005/05/16/Autos/prius_computer/.

17. David Becker, "Microsoft Issues Patch for Word Crash Bug," silicon.com, 28 January 2004, http://software.silicon.com/applications/0,39024653,39118016,00.htm.

18. Specifically, instead of "$2Applications/iTunes.app" the program read $2Applications/iTunes.app – without the quotation marks. See Farhad Manjoo, "Glitch in iTunes Deletes Drives," *Wired*, 11 May 2001, http://wired.com/science/discoveries/news/2001/11/48149.

19. Mobile geek posting on BlackBerry forums, "Blackberry 8830's Crashes and Burns," BlackBerry Forums.com, 13 November 2007, http://www.blackberryforums.com/general-8800-series-discussion/99831-verizons-blackberry-8830-crashes-bugs.html.

20. Personal communication, William Nichols, 16 May 2009.

21. John Markoff, "iPhone Users Plagued by Software Problems," *The New York Times*, 12 July 2008.

22. Bruce Schneier, "Software Problems with a Breath Alcohol Detector," Schneier on Security – A blog covering security and security technology, 13 May 2009, http://www.schneier.com/blog/archives/2009/05/software_proble.html.

23. Chuck Crow, "RTA HealthLine Ticket Machines Still Not Working Because

of Software Problems," *The Cleveland Plain-Dealer*, 17 January 2009, http://blog.cleveland.com/metro/2009/01/rta_healthline_ticket_machines/print.html.

24. Gregg Keizer, "Microsoft Patches 'Insane' Number of Bugs," *Computer World*, 14 April 2009, http://www.networkworld.com/news/2009/041409-microsoft-patches-insane-number-of.html.

25. "New Standish Group Report Shows More Projects Failing and Less Successful Projects," The Standish Group, 23 April 2009, http://www.standishgroup.com/newsroom/chaos_2009.php.

26. Edward Cone, "The Ugly History of Tool Development at the FAA," *Baseline*, 9 April 2002, http://www.baselinemag.com/c/a/Projects-Processes/The-Ugly-History-of-Tool-Development-at-the-FAA/.

27. Fred Brookes, *The Mythical Man-Month* (Reading, MA: Addison-Wesley, 1982).

28. Capers Jones, *Applied Software Measurement: Assuring Productivity and Quality* (New York: McGraw-Hill, 1991), p. 307.

29. Personal interview with Rich Pethia, Software Engineering Institute, Carnegie Mellon University, May 2008.

30. Mark Raby, "Woman Scammed QVC for $400,000+ in Internet Glitch," *Trendwatch*, 30 October 2007.

31. Clay Wilson, *Computer Attack and Cyberterrorism: Vulnerabilities and Policy Issues for Congress*, Washington, D.C., Congressional Research Service, RL 32114, 1 April 2005.

32. There are two good sources on these observations: Watts S. Humphrey, "Security Changes Everything," News@sei, No. 2, 2004, p. 2; Watts S. Humphrey, "Defective Software Works," Software Engineering Institute: News@SEI, No. 1, 2004, p. 4. Also see *SANS Top 20 2007 Security Risks*, available at http://www.sans.org/top20/.

33. There are several fine and detailed discussions of buffer overflows – see Schneier, *Secrets and Lies,* pp. 207–210; or Charles P. Pfleeger and Shari Lawrence Pfleeger, *Security in Computing*, 3rd edition, Prentice Hall, 2002, pp. 104–106.

34. Pfleeger and Pfleeger, *Security in Computing*, p. 3.

35. See for example Danny McPherson, "Morris Worm to MS08-067 – 20 Years of Evolution," Arbor Networks, 29 October 2008, http://asert.arbornetworks.com/2008/10/morris-worm-to-ms08-067-20-years-of-evolution/.

36. See "Malware FAQ: Code Red – ISS Buffer Overflow," SANS Institute (no

date posted), http://www.sans.org/resources/malwarefaq/code-red.php.

37. Jason Rafail, *Cross-Site Scripting Vulnerabilites*, CERT Coordination Center, 2001. www.cert.org/archive/pdf/cross_site_scripting.pdf.

38. Steve Christey and Robert A. Martin, "Vulnerability Type Distributions in CVE (version 1.1)," MITRE Corporation, 22 May 2007, http://cwe.mitre .org/documents/vuln-trends/index.html.

39. Scott Berinato, "Software Vulnerability Disclosure: The Chilling Effect," CSO (CXO Media, 1 January 2007), p. 7, http://www.csoonline.com/ article/221113.

40. Pfleeger and Pfleeger, *Security in Computing*, pp. 108–109.

41. A list of information security exposures and vulnerabilities sponsored by US-CERT and maintained by the MITRE Corporation. The CVE can be searched online using the National Vulnerability Database (NVD) at http:// nvd.nist.gov or downloaded in several formats from MITRE Corporation at www.cve.mitre.org/cve.

42. See CERT Statistics (Historical), www.cert.org/stats/.

43. Sharon Gaudin, "Public in the Dark About 95% of Software Bugs, IBM Says," *Information Week*, 5 June 2007, http://www.informationweek.com/story/ show/Article.jhtml?articleID=199901292.

44. Shari Lawrence Pfleeger, Les Hatton, and Charles Howell, *Solid Software* (Upper Saddle River, NJ: Prentice Hall, 2001), p. 3.

45. "Managing Complexity," *The Economist (US)*, 27 November 2004, p. 71.

46. Ibid., pp. 72–73.

47. Personal communication with Peiter "Mudge" Zatko, BBN Technologies, 17 April 2009.

48. Personal communication, Robert Seacord, Software Engineering Institute, Carnegie Mellon University, June 2008.

49. William Nichols and Rafael Salazar, *Deploying TSP on a National Scale: An Experience Report from Pilot Projects in Mexico*, Software Engineering Institute, Carnegie Mellon University, CMU/SEI-2009-TR-01, April 2009, p. 15.

50. Personal conversation with Rich Pethia, Software Engineering Institute, Carnegie Mellon University, May 2008.

51. Nichols and Salazar, *Deploying TSP on a National Scale*, May 2009; figure confirmed in private communications with other expert sources, also during May 2009.

52. See for example Pfleeger and Pfleeger, *Security in Computing*, p. 171.

53. Matthew Fisher, "When Writing Software, Security Counts," The Industry Insiders blog on TechNet, 20 May 2005, http://blogs.technet.com/industry _insiders/articles/405182.aspx.

54. Barry Boehm and Victor R. Basli, "Software Defect Reduction Top 10 List," *IEEE Computer* 34, no. 1 (January 1991), p. 91.

55. Keizer, "Microsoft Patches 'Insane' Number of Bugs."

56. Fisher, "When Writing Software, Security Counts."

57. Jeffrey Seifert, *Computer Software and Open Source Issues: A Primer*, Congressional Research Service, Report RL31627, 17 December 2003.

58. Interview with Robert Seacord, author of *Secure Coding in C and C++*, CERT, November 2005, www.cert.org/books/secure-coding/LWM%203-11%20 (Haddad).pdf.

59. For example, personal communication with Dave Farber, University of Pennsylvania and Carnegie Mellon University, 10 May 2009.

60. Scott Ambler, *Disciplined Agile Software Development: Definition*, AgileModeling.com, 2009, http://www.agilemodeling.com/essays/agile SoftwareDevelopment.htm.

61. Thomas McGibben, Daniel Ferens, and Robert L. Vienneau, "A Business Case for Software Process Improvement (2007 Update)," DACS Report Number 347616, Data & Analysis Center for Software, 30 September 2007.

62. Noopur Davis and Julia Mullaney, *The Team Software Process (TSP) in Practice: A Summary of Recent Results*, CMU/SEI-2003-TR-014, ADA 418430, Software Engineering Institute, Carnegie Mellon University, 2003, http://www.sei.cmu.edu/publications/documents/03.reports/03tr014.html.

63. Personal communication, Bill Nichols, Software Engineering Institute, 16 May 2009.

64. Various personal communications with Noopur Davis, Robert Seacord, Bill Nichols, Software Engineering Institute, July 2008 through May 2009.

65. Personal communication, Bill Nichols, 13 July 2009.

66. See for example "The Art of Innovation" on Kawasaki's "How to Change the World" blog, 10 January 2006, http://blog.guykawasaki.com/2006/01/the _art_of_inno.html.

67. Schneier, *Secrets and Lies*, p. 366.

68. Personal communication, Robert Seacord, Software Engineering Institute,

Carnegie Mellon University, June 2008.

69. Personal communication with Dave Farber, 10 January 2009.

70. See *Escola v. Coca Cola Bottling Co. of Fresno*, 24 Cal. 2d 453. 462; 150 P.2d 436, 440: 1944 Cal. LEXIS 248, (Cal. 1944), as cited in Daniel J. Ryan, p. 71, "Two Views on Security Software Liability: Let the Legal System Decide," *IEEE Security and Privacy* 1, no. 1 (January–February 2003): 70–72.

71. Ryan, "Two Views on Security Software Liability."

72. Joel Predd, Shari Lawrence Pfleeger, Jeffrey Hunker, and Carla Bulford, "Insiders Behaving Badly," *IEEE Security and Privacy* 6, no. 4 (July 2008): 66–70.

73. The damage done to the U.S. by one notorious insider spying for the Russians, FBI agent Robert Hanssen, is incalculable. See Ben Fenton, "FBI Spy Who Sold Out to Russia Did 'Megaton Damage,'" *The Telegraph*, 21 February 2001, http://www.telegraph.co.uk/news/main.jhtml?xml=/news/2001/02/21/wspy21.xml.

74. This example is taken from the matter of *Binney v. Banner Therapy Products*, 631 S.E. 2d 848 (2006), 850 (North Carolina Court of Appeals). Some of the material quoted is taken from the dissent to the majority decision.

75. There is some ambiguity about the details, so press accounts differ. Some report that he used the "reply" function and that the problem was the server settings established by a government contractor; others mention the "reply all" function. Eric Lipton, "Security Bulletin Problem Creates Message Flood," *The New York Times*, 4 October 2007 (National Section), http://www.nytimes.com/2007/10/04/us/04bsecure.html?ref=us. *The New York Times* also published the text of a number of the chain of responses with the addresses redacted, in "An E-Mail Chain Reaction," 4 October 2007 (National Section), http://www.nytimes.com/2007/10/04/us/04bsecure.html?ref=us.

76. A Homeland Security spokesman told the *The New York Times* that a human error resulted in a change to the server settings for the unclassified bulletin, which allowed the recipients to send it to all subscribers.

77. Del Quentin Wilber, "Tax Scam Leader Gets More Than 17 Years," *Washington Post*, 1 July 2009.

78. Dan Keating, "Tax Suspects Guidance on Software Left D.C. at Risk," *Washington Post*, 10 June 2008, p. A01.

79. Ibid.

80. Ibid.

81. An example of this is the "masquerader attack" in which a user leaves her computer on while, say, going for lunch. If another person uses this computer while the legitimate user is away, he appears, according to all computer logs at least, to be the legitimate user. For a discussion of this and other issues of U.S. law, see Jeffrey Hunker and Carla Bulford, *Federal Prosecution of Insider Threats Demonstrates Need for Reform,* Pittsburgh, PA: Jeffrey Hunker Associates, performed under RAND subcontract 9920080013, February 2009.

82. Personal communication with Dave Farber, Carnegie Mellon University and University of Pennsylvania, 16 April 2009.

83. Brian Krebs, "European Cyber-Gangs Target Small U.S. Firms, Group Says," *Washington Post,* 25 August 2009, http://www.washingtonpost.com/wp-dyn/content/article/2009/08/24/AR2009082402272.html.

84. Personal communication, Dave Farber, Carnegie Mellon University. 21 June 2009.

85. David Bank, "Spear Phishing Tests Educate People about Online Scams," *The Wall Street Journal,* 17 August 2005, http://online.wsj.com/public/article/0,,SB112424042313615131-z_8jLB2WkfcVtgdAWf6LRh733sg_20060817,00.html.

86. Ibid.

87. Pieter Zatko (also known as "Mudge," a former hacker). Personal conversation, 2 July 2009.

88. Brian Krebs, "Tighter Security Urged for Business Banking On-line," Security Fix blog, washingtonpost.com, 24 August 2009, http://voices.washington post.com/securityfix/2009/08/tigher_security_measures_urge.html.

CHAPTER 8

1. For the events in the section on "Fire" there is a vast amount of historical literature, including much available on the Web. I have drawn from more than fifty sources, many for purposes of background and cross-checking, and thus will mention only a few representative sources here: the London Fire Brigade Web site, http://www.london-fire.gov.uk/; for the Great Fire of London, excerpts on various sites from the diaries of John Evelyn and Samuel Pepys, and from books such as Adrian Tinniswood, *By Permission of Heaven: The Story of the Great Fire of London* (London: Jonathan Cape, 2003); for

later events, profiles of James Braidwood, e.g, at http://www.glosfire.gov.uk /sections/schools/school_rc_modern.html; and the Underwriters Laboratories site at http://www.ul.com/global/eng/pages/corporate/aboutul /history/.

2. As with the history of fire protection, material on the history of public health has been drawn from many historical sources and I will cite only a few representative ones here: James H. Cassedy, "Hygeia: A Mid-Victorian Dream of a City of Health," *Journal of the History of Medicine and Allied Sciences* 17 (April 1962): 217–228, doi:10.1093/jhmas/XVII.2.217; articles about and profiles of Edwin Chadwick, such as at http://www.victorianweb.org/history/ chad1.html; in general, Stephen Halliday, *The Great Stink of London: Sir Joseph Bazalgette and the Cleansing of the Victorian Metropolis* (Stroud, UK: The History Press, 2001); Steven Johnson, *The Ghost Map: The Story of London's Most Terrifying Epidemic and How It Changed Science, Cities, and the Modern World* (New York: Riverhead Books, 2006); history portals such as http://www.victorianlondon.org/, and organizations' Web sites such as that of the World Health Organization, http://www.who.int.

3. Johnson, *The Ghost Map*, p. 113.

4. "London," *Encyclopaedia Britannica,* 11th edition, 1912, Vol. XVI, p. 951.

5. "One in Four DNS Servers Still Unpatched for The Kaminsky Vulnerability, Says a New Worldwide Study," *Network World*, 10 November 2008, http://www.circleid.com/posts/20081110_one_in_four_dns_servers_still_un patched/html.

6. Carolyn Duffy Marsan, "U.S. Plots Major Upgrade to Internet Router Security," Network World, 19 January 2009, http://www.networkworld .com/news/2009/011509-bgp.html.

7. M. Bushehri, *Interconnectivity in China's Telecoms Market*, Asia Case Research Centre, The University of Hong Kong, 2006.

8. Ali Farhoomand and Vincent Mak, *NTT DoCoMo: Establishing Global 3G Standards*, Centre for Asian Business Cases, The University of Hong Kong, 15 January 2003, http://harvardbusiness.org/product/ntt-docomo-establishing -global-3g-standards/an/HKU241-PDF-ENG?N=4294958507+4294960657.

9. With the support of the International Telecommunications Union (ITU), a UN-sponsored body overseeing the telecommunications system, there has been ongoing since the early 2000s a set of discussions about Internet governance

called the World Summit[s] on the Information Society: http://www.itu.int /wsis/index.html.

10. Ryan, "Two Views on Security Software Liability," p. 70.

11. Michael D. Scott, "Tort Liability for Vendors of Insecure Software: Has the Time Finally Come?" *Maryland Law Review* 2008, 67 Md. L. Rev. 425, p. 426. This article cites *Chartlos Sys. Inc. v. Nat'l Cash Register Corp.*, 479 F. Supp. 738, 740–741 & n.1 (D.N.J. 1979).

12. Personal communication with Professor Peter Shane, Ohio State University, 22 May 2009.

13. Ibid.

14. Carey Heckman, "Two Views on Security Software Liability: Using the Right Legal Tools," *IEEE Security and Privacy* 1, no. 1 (January–Februrary 2003), 73–75; p. 73.

15. Ibid, p. 74.

16. *Critical Information Infrastructure Protection and the Law*, p. 45.

17. Doug Lichtman and Eric P. Posner, "Holding Internet Service Providers Accountable," in *The Law and Economics of Cyber Security,* Mark F. Grady and Francesco Parisi, eds. (Cambridge University Press, 2006), pp. 221–58.

18. Ibid., p. 221.

19. Personal communication with Paul Kurtz, now of Good Harbor Consulting, March 2008.

20. *Internet Usage Statistics: The Internet Big Picture*, Internet Coaching Library, 30 September 2009, http://www.internetworldstats.com/stats.htm.

21. Erin E. Kenneally, "The Byte Stops Here: Duty and Liability for Negligent Internet Security," *Computer Security Journal* 16, no. 2 (2000). Though dated, subsequent research by the author still makes this statement true.

22. Lichtman and Posner, "Holding Internet Service Providers Accountable," p. 232.

23. Ibid.

24. *Critical Information Infrastructure Protection and the Law,* pp. 49–50; also Sarah Faulkner, "Invasion of the Information Snatchers: Creating Liability for Corporations with Vulnerable Computer Networks," *Journal of Computer and Information Law* 18 (2000): 1019–47.

25. *Critical Information Infrastructure Protection and the Law*, p. 50.

26. Scott, "Tort Liability for Vendors of Insecure Software," p. 481, citing *In re*

BJ's Wholesale Club, Inc., No.C-4148 (FTC September 20, 2005), www.ftc
.gov/os/caselist/0423160/092305comp0423160.pdf.

27. Dan Goodin, "Geeks.com Settles Charges Claiming Its Security Was Crap,"
The Register, 6 February 2009, http://www.theregister.co.uk/2009/02/06
/geeks_etailer_settles_ftc_suit/.

28. J. Winn, *Should Vulnerability be Actionable? Improving Critical Infrastructure
Computer Security with Trade Practices Law,* George Mason University Critical
Infrastructure Protection Project Papers, Vol. II, 2004, available through
links at http://www.law.washington.edu/Faculty/Winn/Publications/Should
_Vulnerability.pdf.

29. Walter S. Baer and Andrew Parkinson, "Cyber-insurance in IT Management,"
IEEE Security and Privacy 5, no. 3 (May–June 2007): 55.

30. National Research Council, *Cybersecurity Today and Tomorrow: Pay Now or Pay
Later,* (Washington, D.C.: National Academies Press, 2002), p. 14.

31. Michael Decicco, "EU Consumer Protection Reform: Liability for Software
Code," IP Osgoode, 22 May 2009, http://www.iposgoode.ca/2009/05/
eu-consumer-protection-reform-liability-for-software-code/.

32. Scott, "Tort Liability for Vendors of Insecure Software," p. 481.

33. Ross J. Anderson, "Liability and Computer Security: Nine Principles," in
Dieter Gollman, ed., *Proceedings of the Third European Symposium on
Research in Computer Security,* 7–9 November 1994. London: Springer-
Verlag, pp. 231–45.

34. Joshua Gold, "Cyber Insurance in Disarray," *Risk Management Magazine,* July
2008, www.rmmagazine.com/Magazine/PrintTemplate.cfm?AID=3711.

35. Baer and Parkinson, "Cyber-insurance in IT Management," p. 51.

36. Rainer Bohme, *Cyber-Insurance Revisited,* Workshop on the Economics of
Information Security (WEIS) 2005.

37. Daintry Duffy, "Cybersecurity Insurance: Safety at a Premium," CSO, 9
December 2002, http://www.csoonline.com/article/217739/Cybersecurity
_Insurance_Safety_at_a_Premium.

38. Dimitry Elias Leger, "Virus Protection? Why Internet Insurance Isn't the Best
Policy," *Fortune,* 10 July 2000, p. 260.

39. Bruce Schneier, "2002 Computer Security: It's the Economics, Stupid,"
Economics and Information Security Workshop, Berkeley, California, 16 May
2002, http://www.ljean.com/classes/05_06/525/I590_06reading.html.

40. Geoffrey Allen, "Cyber: Cyber Risk Goes Mainstream," Willis HRH Executive Risks Practices, 2009, http://www.willis.com/Documents/Publications/Services/ Executive_Risks/2009/Marketplace_Realities_Spring_update_Cyber.pdf.

41. The insurance industry refers to policies covering the insured's property losses as "first-party" coverage, and those covering liability as "third-party" coverage.

42. The quotation is from Lawrence A. Gordon, Martin P. Loeb, William Lucyshyn, and Robert Richardson, *2005 CSI/FBI Computer Crime and Security Survey,* Computer Security Institute, 2005, http://www.cpppe.umd .edu/Bookstore/Documents/2005CSISurvey.pdf. Another good (and more recent) source is Robert Richardson, 2008 CSI/FBI Computer Crime and Security Survey, Computer Security Institute, San Francisco, 2008, http://i.cmpnet.com/v2.gocsi.com/pdf/CSIsurvey2008.pdf.

43. U.S. Geological Survey, *Significant Floods in the US in the 20th Century,* USGS, May 2009, http://ks.water.usgs.gov/pubs/fact-sheets/fs.024-00.html.

44. Insurance companies are active members of the FS/ISAC (Financial Services Information Sharing and Analysis Center); see http://www.FS/ISAC.com. However, involvement in the FS/ISAC or any other recommendations from the National Strategy to Secure Cyberspace do not appear to have had much effect on cyber insurance industry practices. See also Baer and Parkinson, "Cyber-insurance in IT Management," p. 55.

45. Harrison Oellrich, Guy Carpenter & Co., as quoted in Duffy, "Cybersecurity Insurance: Safety at a Premium," http://www.csoonline.com/article/217739/ Cybersecurity_Insurance_Safety_at_a_Premium.

46. Allen, "Cyber: Cyber Risk Goes Mainstream."

47. Baer and Parkinson, "Cyber-insurance in IT Management," p. 55.

48. Dalit Baranoff, "Fire Insurance in the United States," EH.Net Encyclopedia, Robert Wahaples, ed., 16 March 2008, http://eh.net/encyclopedia/article/ Baranoff.Fire.final.

49. Johnson, *The Ghost Map.*

50. The best known sources for data on the number and costs of cyber security incidents include cyber security consulting firms, Mi2g (www.mi2g.com/cgi/mi2g/), Computer Economics, Inc. (www.computereconomics.com), and ICSA Labs (www.icsalabs.com). Public sources include the annual Australian Computer Crime and Security Survey (www.auscert.org.au/render.html?it=2001), the Information and Security Breaches Survey periodically conducted by the U.K.

Department of Trade and Industry (www.infosec.co.uk/files/DTI_Survey _Report.pdf), and the annual CSI/FBI Computer Crime and Security Survey (www.usdoj.gov/criminarl/cybercrime). In addition there are global surveys in particular sectors; the Deloitte-Touche Global Security Survey focuses on financial services (www.deloitte.pt/dtt/research). The CVE (Common Vulnerabilities and Exposures) was developed by MITRE in 2000, and provides a useful framework for categorizing vulnerabilities. See cve.mitre.org.

51. Shari Lawrence Pfleeger, Rachel Rue, Jay Horowitz, and Aruna Balakrishnan, "Investing in Cyber Security: The Path to Good Practice," *Cutter IT Journal* 19, no. 1 (January 2006): 11.

52. Bureau of Justice Statistics, U.S. Department of Justice, *Cybercrime Against Businesses, 2005*, 2009, http://www.ojp.usdoj.gov/bjs/abstract/cb05.htm.

53. Statistics Canada, The Canadian Center for Justice Statistics, *Cyber-crime: Issues, Data Sources and Feasibility of Colleting Police Reported Statistics*, 2002.

54. Sarah A. Lister, *An Overview of the U.S. Public Health System in the Context of Emergency Preparedness*, CRS Report for Congress, updated 17 March 2005, CRS RL 31719, p. 3.

55. John Donnelly, "CDC Quarantines Man Who Has Lethal TB Strain," *Boston Globe*, 30 May 2007, http://www.boston.com/news/nation/articles/2007/05/30/cdc_quarantines_man_who_has_lethal_tb_strain/.

56. Personal communication, Professor Alfred Blumstein, Carnegie Mellon University, November 2007.

57. Personal communication, Michelle Chibba, Office of the Information and Privacy Commissioner of Ontario, August 2009.

CHAPTER 9

1. www.GENI.net

2. Personal communication, Professor Dave Farber, Carnegie Mellon University, June 2008.

3. Defense Advanced Research Projects Agency (DARPA), *Request for Information – Assurable Global Networking*, DARPA, 2006, p.1.

4. Personal communication, Dave Farber, August 2009.

5. DARPA, *Assurable Global Networking*, pp. 2–3.

6. Steven Bellovin, David Clark, Adrian Perrig, and Dawn Song, *A Clean-Slate*

Design for the Next Generation Secure Internet, GENI NSF Workshop Report GDD-05-05, July 2005, p. 2.

7. Matt Bishop, Carrie Gates, and Jeffrey Hunker, *The Sisterhood of the Travelling Packets,* New Security Paradigms Workshop, Oxford, U.K., 9–11 September 2009.

8. DARPA, *Assurable Global Networking,* p. 107.

9. Raj Jain, *Internet 3.0: Ten Problems with Current Internet Architecture and Solutions for the Next Generation,* paper presented at the Military Communications Conference (MILCOM 2006), Washington, D.C., 23–25 October 2006.

10. Personal communication with Professor Dave Farber, University of Pennsylvania and Carnegie Mellon University, May 2009.

11. Stephan Savage, quoted in *On the Media,* National Public Radio, 3 April 2009.

12. Marjory S. Blumenthal and David D. Clark, "Rethinking the Design of the Internet: The End-to-End Arguments vs. the Brave New World," *ACM Transactions on Internet Technology.* Vol. 1, no.1 (August 2001): 70–109, http://portal.acm.org/citation.cfm?id=383037.

13. Jonathan Zittrain, *The Future of the Internet – and How to Stop It* (New Haven, CT: Yale University Press, 2008).

14. Blumenthal and Clark, *Rethinking the Design of the Internet: The End-to-End Arguments vs. the Brave New World,* unpublished draft, 10 August 2000.

15. L. Peterson, S. Shenker, and J.Turner, *Overcoming the Impasse Through Virtualization,* Proceedings of ACM Hotnets-III, November 2004. Also Thomas Anderson, Larry Peterson, Scott Shenker, and Jonathan Turner, *Overcoming Barriers to Disruptive Innovation in Networking,* GENI: Global Environment for Network Innovations NSF Workshop Report GDD-05-02, January 2005, p. 6.

16. Mary Bellis, Outline of Railroad History, http://inventors.about.com/library/inventors/blrailroad.htm.

17. This example is drawn from James Utterback, *Mastering the Dynamics of Innovation* (Boston: Harvard Business School Press, 1994).

18. Ibid.

19. Ibid.

20. "A Special Report on the Future of Energy; Trade Winds," *The Economist,* 21 June 2008, Special Section, p. 8.

21. Quantum computing is a completely different way of doing computing.

Rather than relying on a "zero or one" or "on or off" basis for doing calculations, as digital computers do, quantum computing would rely on the quantum-mechanical properties of subatomic particles. A practical quantum computer is decades away. A good introduction at a non-technical level to this truly revolutionary approach to computing is in Scott Aaronson, "The Limits of Quantum Computers," *Scientific American,* February 2008.

22. David Clarke, Karen Sollins, John Wrockawski, and Robert Braden, "Tussle in Cyberspace: Defining Tomorrow's Internet," SIGCOMM'02, 19–23 August 2002, Pittsburgh, PA, ACM, pp. 2–3.

23. Utterback, *Mastering the Dynamics of Innovation.*

24. Barbara W. Tuchman, *The Guns of August* (New York, Macmillan, 1962; Bantam edition 1976). See p. 394 for reference to *se débrouiller* – to muddle through somehow.

25. See http://www.intgovforum.org/cms/.

26. For those interested, four main alternatives are (1) to create a Global Internet Council, consisting of members from governments, with appropriate representation from each region and with involvement from other stakeholders, which would essentially take on the responsibilities for running the Internet; (2) no specific oversight organization (i.e., stay with the existing structures), but with perhaps an enhanced role for governments in ICANN; (3) a "middle of the road" option to replace the U.S. Government's oversight of ICANN with an International Internet Council whose functions would include any public policy issues not covered by any existing intergovernmental organizations, and (4) to create a series of UN-sponsored organizations: the Global Internet Policy Council, contributing public policy perspectives to Internet-related technical standards; the World Internet Corporation for Assigned Names and Numbers (WICANN), a private sector–led body made up of a reformed and internationalized ICANN linked to the United Nations; and the Global Internet Governance Forum, responsible for facilitating coordination and discussion of Internet-related public policy issues.

ACKNOWLEDGMENTS

I would acknowledge first the contributions of Mike Vargo, of Pittsburgh, who has served not just as an editor but also as an essential contributor to my thinking as expressed in this book. Without him the book would not have been possible. Also, Charles and Shari Lawrence Pfleeger provided important reviews of earlier drafts, and to them I am eternally thankful.

Alan Paller, several years ago, suggested a book on the overall topic; I have not forgotten his (perhaps off-the-cuff) spark of inspiration.

Tom Smart first introduced me to McClelland & Stewart, the publishers. Thank you, Tom. And thank you, of course, McClelland & Stewart, in particular Susan Renouf, who skillfully guided the manuscript into its final form.

Monica van Huystee has provided important intellectual and moral support in this project. It is more than fitting that this book is dedicated to her.

Andrian Schwartz Feit and Kate Feit provided important research and moral support. Thank you both.

Dr. Afeworki Paulos, the Social Sciences Librarian at Carnegie Mellon University and an adjunct faculty member, was essential in supporting my research. His insight and enthusiasm were critical; I owe him greater thanks than can be expressed here.

Many of my professional colleagues provided important contributions. I will no doubt offend most by not including their names, but Dave Farber, Matt Bishop, and Christian Probst stand out.

If there are others I have inadvertently neglected to mention, it is only because of my imperfect memory. Thank you all.

Jeffrey Hunker, November 2009

INDEX